# *Raising a Temple*

## A Mother's Guide to Training Godly Kids

Lori Jane Hensley

Copyright © 2016 by Lori Jane Hensley

All rights reserved. No part of this book may be reproduced, stored in a retrieval system, or transmitted in any form or by any means–electronic, mechanical, photocopying, recording, or otherwise–without the prior written permission of the publisher and the copyright owner. The only exception is brief quotations in printed reviews.

7710-T Cherry Park Dr, Ste 224
Houston, TX 77095
713-766-4271

The views expressed in this book are those of the author, and do not necessarily reflect those of the publisher.

Scripture quotations, unless otherwise noted, are from The Holy Bible, New International Version.

Cover design: Rebekah Harrison.
**Malerapaso** Stock photo ID:12180791 Type font (Cinzel regular and decorative) by Natanael Gama.

Published in the United States of America.

eBook: 978-3-9602-8727-8
Paperback: 978-0692737620
Hardcover: 978-1-68411-028-5

# What Others Are Saying

"This is a really helpful resource that will benefit any parent. As I read it, I found myself wishing it had been available when my kids were younger. So don't wait to read it! In addition, if your kids are older, it's never too late to start applying these godly principles. *Raising a Temple* is based on solid, biblical teaching, and it is very, very, practical. I guarantee the benefits from reading this book will start immediately."
—Jon Walker, author, *Breakfast with Bonhoeffer*, and Managing Editor, Rick Warren's *Daily Hope Devotionals*.
http://gracecreates.com

"Matthew 6:8 says your Father knows your need before you ask Him. That is truly what I experienced with Lori thirty years ago when He sent us Carol Kohl to mentor us in raising godly children. God knew that we needed a scriptural foundation to train our children to love the Lord with all their hearts. I am so thrilled that Lori is sharing this book to help mothers with the hardest but most rewarding job of a lifetime!"
—Kay Rew, 1st grade teacher and co-founder of *Camp Icthus* for elementary ages, in its 28th year of seeing God change lives.
http://camp-icthus.org

"Lori's book is full of practical advice that was gained through experience. I am grateful she took the time to share her wisdom and her love for God's instructions to mothers. Any mother will gain much from her book."
—Leighann McCoy, mother of three and author, *Spiritual Warfare for Your Family*, Prayer and Next Generations Minister at *Thompson Station Church*, Thompson Station, Tennessee.
http://leighannmccoy.com

"The instruction in Lori's book needs to be broadly taught to every Christian mother — the sooner the better."
—Eddie Smith, author and conference speaker, President of the *U.S. Prayer Center* and proud father of four.
http://usprayercenter.org

"This book is an essential teaching tool for every mother, especially new mothers. It is truly a gift from God and a road map for raising temples for the Lord, packed with wisdom as well as hands-on instructions. I pray it gets placed in the hands of every mother."
—Rev. Kathleen Bailey, Associate Pastor, *Hillcrest Worship Center*, Auburn, Massachusetts

"Struggling to raise godly children? Wishing there was a practical guide or an instructor's manual? If so, this book is "a must read"! Lori Hensley masterfully provides practical tools, all based in Scripture, for every stage of your child's life. Through decades of leading children's ministries across the United States and Mexico, she brings real world experience and does so with humor, humility, and with the love of the Lord."
—Joanne Masters, *Masters and Masters, LLC*, co-founder, *Royal Link Women's Ministry*

"Lori Hensley walks the talk. She is the real 'in the trenches' deal. Her ministry and family life shines with the godly applied wisdom held between these pages. Parents often say, 'I wish my child came with a manual.' Well, here it is. You will find Bible-based child-raising principles that will make your life a joy and your child's foundation solid."
—Trish Publico, mother of three adult children, co-founder, *Royal Link Women's Ministry*, former Children Ministries Director, *North Coast Presbyterian Church*, Encinitas, California

"What a wonderful collection of wisdom for moms desiring to raise godly kids! In this book, Lori gives Holy Spirit-inspired and biblical principles that work in a real world. With the challenges facing parents today, we need clear and effective tools to help us raise children who love God and know their identity and calling. Who better to teach them these valuable principles than their own mothers? This book will inspire and guide moms in raising a temple for God."
—Dr. Timothy and Rodica Lambert, Pastors, *Christian Embassy International Church*, Chesapeake, Virginia. http://ceicva.org

"I attended one of Lori's parenting classes many years ago and encouraged her to put the class into writing. She has done an amazing job of putting into written form a way to help raise your children in a godly home. If you want a "manual" of how to ignite the passion and love of Jesus Christ into the hearts of your children, this is a must read."
—Melissa McCrea, mother of two, special education teacher, Encinitas, California

"Lori Hensley is the real deal! We had the honor of witnessing Lori and her husband in action as they raised their three godly children. These principles are a tried and true model of successful parenting based on biblical values and morals."
—Pastor Tim and Kim Broihier, *Liberty Worship Center*, Edwardsville, Illinois. lwcedw.org

"We had the privilege of learning the principles of *Raising a Temple* from Lori when I was pregnant with our first child. Eager to raise godly children, but unequipped with a strategy or any real life experience, my husband and I soaked up her teachings like a sponge. Lori's teaching inspired us to believe for children who would not only know God but also glorify Him, and Lori gave us real life examples and practical applications on how to cultivate that. Now 13 years and four children later, these biblical principles have been effective through every stage of development and have remained a part of our everyday parenting strategies. And though we are imperfect parents raising imperfect kids, we are, by the grace of God and the implementation of these principles, bringing up kids who love God with their whole hearts and desire to serve Him."

—Jamie and Kimber Smith, Teaching and Youth Pastor, *Liberty Christian Fellowship*, Outer Banks, North Carolina.
http://libertyobx.com/about-us/leadership

# *Dedication*

*"You then, my son [and daughters], be strong in the grace that is in Christ Jesus. And the things you have heard me say ... entrust to reliable people who will also be qualified to teach others."*
(2 Timothy 2:1-2)

I dedicate this book to my Lord Jesus Christ,
my supportive husband*
to my beautiful daughter and her family,*
to my two awesome sons and their families,*
and to Carol Kohl, because this teaching would not be possible if she had not come into my life 32 years ago to teach me the principles of raising godly kids.

I dedicate this to the next generation, women who strongly desire to raise temples of the Holy Spirit,
and to Melissa McCrea, Beth Newman, and Kimber Smith, who have organized classes and represent the many.
Within my "knower,"[1] I *know* that I will hear from these women in 15 or 20 years and learn about their "temples" as well as the classes they will be teaching to the next generation!

*The names of my family and people in other stories have been changed for their protection.

# A Blessing

Father, I ask that You would bless and anoint this book and the time young moms take to read it. I thank You that the eyes, ears, and hearts of these women are already open and ready for Your word. Let it multiply, Lord. Bless the work of their hands, hear the cry of their mother's hearts, and grant them the desire of their heart — to raise godly kids, temples for You to dwell in. Thank You for Your presence as they seek You through the study of raising godly kids. Give them creative ideas that they need to bring Your Word alive in the hearts of their children. Let this book simply be a springboard for many more ideas, principles, and truths to come forth!

Lord, may their children be pure in heart, mind, and body. May they be mighty in spirit, and may the enemy be bound in their lives. I pray this in the precious name of Jesus Christ. Amen.

# Thank You!

Many thanks to so many people, who have encouraged me, read my stories, proofread, and pushed me along to finish this work. My husband has been my biggest encourager to complete this work. My kids have cheered me along as I have talked about and worked on it.

My brother, Jon Walker, has been right by my side, encouraging me and giving me his professional help. Heidi Short, I could have never published this book, many articles, and blogs without you! Allison Dolbeer to the rescue! Your editing helps and formatting are a godsend, and I am grateful! Some people, like Patti Wiggins, have the gift of helps and I appreciate your labor of love. Ryan and Rebekah Harrison for your invaluable encouragement and behind the scenes help with prioritizing and creating the cover. Thanks to Sherry Walker for her invaluable input on design. I am grateful to many who have pushed me along and helped with reading: Trish Publico, Joanne Masters, Oona Noon, Kimber Smith, Linda Salzman, Melody Green, Victoria Phelps, Erica Aust, Carol McGlothlin, Kindra French, Anne Manning, Lauren Dowler, Amber Hallowell, Tanya Aviles, Nila Whelan, Sherry Johnson, and Hope Lopez.

# Table of Contents

Dedication .................................................................................... 7
A Blessing .................................................................................... 8
Thank You! ................................................................................... 9
Foreword Becky Fischer ................................................................ 12
Foreword Carol Kohl .................................................................... 16
Introduction ................................................................................ 19
**Part 1: The Five Cs of Commitment** ........................................... 24
   Chapter 1 Call and Commitment of a Mother ......................... 25
   Chapter 2 Count the Cost of Commitment .............................. 31
   Chapter 3 Clear the Land: It's a Heart Issue ............................. 41
   Chapter 4 Cultivate the Soil: Going Deeper into the Heart of Things .................................................................................. 51
   Chapter 5 Commit to the Destiny of Children .......................... 57
   Chapter 6 Loving Your Husband .............................................. 67
**Part 2: All Aboard the Training of a Temple** ............................... 80
   Chapter 7 What Does It Mean to Train? ................................... 85
   Chapter 8 Why Train? What's the Big Deal? ........................... 103
   Chapter 9 When to Start Training ........................................... 113
   Chapter 10 How to Train Jesus' Way ....................................... 121
   Chapter 11 Who Is This Kid? ................................................... 131
   Chapter 12 Where to Train ...................................................... 153
**Part 3: What to Train** ................................................................ 160
   Chapter 13 Wisdom and Godliness ......................................... 161
   Chapter 14 Worship and Love God .......................................... 169
   Chapter 15 Honor Your Father and Mother ............................. 175
   Chapter 16 Breaking Family Curses ......................................... 183

Chapter 17 Hearing the Voice of God ..................................... 191
Chapter 18 Words Are Powerful ............................................... 205
Chapter 19 Generosity and Blessing Enemies ........................ 217
Chapter 20 Friends and Fools .................................................. 227
Chapter 21 Eternal Thoughts .................................................... 235
Chapter 22 Purity ....................................................................... 239
Chapter 23 Holidays and Summers ......................................... 247
Chapter 24 Times Are Changing: Raising Generals for the Kingdom of God ........................................................................ 257

**Part 4: Bits and Pieces That Add Value to Your Training .......... 268**
Chapter 25 Prompts and Ideas for Family Talks .................... 269
Chapter 26 Choices: the Bottom Line ...................................... 277
Chapter 27 Weaving the Gospel into Discipline .................... 283
Chapter 28 Prodigal, Come Home! .......................................... 291
Chapter 29 Grown Kids ............................................................ 297
Chapter 30 Loving Final Thoughts for You, Mom ................. 301

**Appendix A: Yearly Goals (three-month segments) .................. 305**
**Appendix B: Proverbs Categories ................................................ 307**
**Appendix C: Inquire of the Lord .................................................. 321**
**Appendix D: Lessons from Shadowland .................................... 325**
**Footnotes ........................................................................................ 330**

# Foreword

I met Lori "gradually." That may sound odd, but it has been over time she has come to my attention and I have gotten to know her. I first noticed Lori when she began to frequent our annual leadership meetings with Kids in Ministry International here in North Dakota, eventually staying in my house several times. She became a certified graduate of our School of Supernatural Children's Ministry, and later we ordained Lori, and then asked her to be the director of a branch of KIMI in Tennessee, her home state. I was not surprised to discover that she had close to thirty years of experience in children's ministry in local churches, because she was clearly not a novice in ministry to children.

More recently, I have gotten to know her on a personal level, as she has become a travel assistant for me when I do conferences in Tennessee. I can say I have learned to love, respect, and appreciate her as a coworker and friend. I know her to be soft spoken, generous, anointed, capable, gifted, and a committed servant of God, family, and KIMI.

I found out just in the last couple of years that Lori was also a writer and had this book burning in her heart. The more she talked about how it was lying in a back closet due to the demands of life; I began to encourage her to get it done. This was because she would give us glimpses of what she planned to put in the book. We even had her speak on the topic at one of our annual conferences. Because our focus in KIMI has turned increasingly to the importance of helping parents disciple their children, I knew it was a book that we would want to make available in our store. It was our DNA. Now here it is, and it is everything I hoped it would be.

There have been more than 75,000 parenting books published in the last twenty years. That is a lot of books on parenting! You can imagine that only a fraction of them come from a Christian perspective, and even though I have not read a lot of them, I have read enough to know that what Lori has to say is both fresh and refreshing. It truly comes from the perspective of parenting to raise children who grow up to be temples of the Holy Spirit — spirit, soul, and body. In fact, this is a recurring theme in the book. She gives you, the reader, many ideas of how to parent your child's spirit, soul, and body, which is completely in line with how Scripture says we are made in the image of God. All three areas of your child's life have to be parented to line up with Scripture.

Another of the repeated themes I have never heard anyone else talk about at length is remembering you are not just raising one child, but in your parenting you are scripturally raising up to four generations by what you put into the one. This comes from the Old Testament concepts of parenting. Our God is a generational God. He's the God of Abraham, Isaac, and Jacob. Abraham was surrounded by pagan cults and raised by a father who worshipped idols. But God chose him to be the father of the Jewish nation specifically because He knew he would raise his son to be a follower of the Most High God, Creator of Heaven and Earth. He was going against the culture of his time and had never seen anyone else model how to raise a child to follow God. But God recognized he'd be a purposeful parent in spiritual matters. Our heavenly father cares about how we parent our children.

The perspective Lori brings to the table of Kingdom parenting has to become the new wineskin of the Church, along with the new wineskin of children's ministry. Someone once said that the Church fails the children when she doesn't teach the parents how to disciple them. I was stunned when reading the book by George Barna titled *Transforming Children into Spiritual Champions*. He wrote that even though 85 percent of Christian parents believe they have the number 1 responsibility to disciple their children spiritually, they had no strategy to do so other than take their children to church every Sunday morning. His research found only one in ten parents ever read their Bibles regularly with their children or ever prayed with their children other than at mealtime. He continued that only one in twenty ever had a worship experience with their children at home. Today I meet parents everywhere, in our country and others, who are broken-hearted because they thought they were doing the right thing by simply taking their children to church. However, their adult children ultimately walked away from their faith. It wasn't enough.

One of the things I love about Lori's book is the dozens of real life stories of how she raised her three children through the precarious stages of life. It's impressive how she did not compartmentalize her faith on one side and their daily life on the other. Lori truly had a vision for weaving their Christian walk into the fabric of their everyday lives. That's how Deuteronomy 6:7 dictates it should be done: *"when you sit at home and when you walk along the road, when you lie down and when you get up."* Daily at every juncture of life she spoke the Word of God into them creatively, relevantly, and purposefully. All I can say is "Wow!" to the chapter on purity! What a right-now word from the Lord on this topic!

We need a new wineskin of Kingdom parenting. In addition, you will find keys in the following pages. I hear all the time from children's pastors who know the importance of parental involvement in the spiritual development of their kids. They are discouraged and frustrated at how difficult it is, not just to get parents to come to services where they can give them aid and help on the topic, but how many parent's eyes simply glaze over when the subject is even brought up. It's as though there is a cultural blindness over their minds that home is home, and spiritual things belong at church. Dr. James Dobson once said, "The greatest delusion is to suppose our children will be devout Christians simply because their parents have been."

As you begin to devour and glean from Lori's experiences, I leave you with a question: What are you willing to sacrifice to raise children that follow hard after Christ?

As Barna says, you can do everything right, and there is no guarantee your children will walk with God. But to do little or nothing almost guarantees they will not. Take the advice in this book to heart. Whatever ages your children are at the moment, begin now to raise them to be temples for the Holy Spirit to dwell in.

Your fellow servant,
Becky Fischer
Founder/Director of *Kids in Ministry International*

# *Foreword*

I wanted to say a word about my dear friend Lori Henley. Years ago, our mutual friend Kay Rew called me and asked if she and another friend, Lori, could come over and talk to me about how to raise children in the principles of God. I agreed for several reasons. My children were older and they could learn from my mistakes, but more than that I was passionate about teaching them what God's Word had to say on this topic of raising children. These young ladies were hungry for more and wanted to share it with other moms. I remember Lori saying, "You can't keep this to yourself!" Kay encouraged me to start a Bible study. After much prayer and Bible study, I felt God had given me the message for this class. It was called *Building a Temple* using God's Word as the blue print, and the idea was to build on a strong foundation of God's Word in the lives of their little ones. The Bible says to teach our children, *"for he established a testimony in Jacob, and appointed a law in Israel, which he commanded our fathers, that they should make them known to their children; that the generation to come might know them, the children who would be born that they may arise and declare them to their children. That they may set their hope in God and not forget the works of God, but keep his commandments"* (Psalm 78:5-7 KJV). God commanded Israel to teach their children. This is a truth from God's Word that Lori has shared in her book.

I remember the first time I met Lori, I felt a kindred spirit. She was a thirsty young mom who had a passion and determination to raise her children in the way they should go. She needed the tools to accomplish this and I knew that God's Word had everything she needed to be successful. Lori learned the principles of God's Word and applied them to raising her little ones, and now thirty years later that same passion of God's Word is burning in her heart for other moms who are hungry to know how to raise godly children who will stand for Christ in this ungodly generation. The principles she learned years ago are written in her book.

*A word to the wise*: There is one thing to keep in mind when it comes to raising children. We have to take a look at God as the perfect parent raising His children in a perfect place. You know the story. God didn't make them robots, but He gave them a free will and sometimes we parents can apply every principle of God's Word and our children can choose to go their own way. Nevertheless, if you know your child, *"Be sure you know the condition of your flocks"* (Proverbs 27:23) and your child has been taught the truths of God's Word, they have truly repented of their sins and have received Christ as their Savior, and they are growing in their faith, they will have a strong spiritual foundation that will never crumble. They can return and repent, like the Prodigal. He said, *"I will arise and go to my father, and will say unto him, Father, I have sinned against heaven, and before thee"* (Luke 15:18 KJV). That is what every parent desires for their children.

The youth of today have no spiritual foundation, and, as a result, they spend their lives on foolishness and never come to the knowledge of Christ. You have no guarantee that your children will never stray in this ungodly world, but if they have a spiritual foundation, they will come home. Proverbs 22:6 says, *"Train up a child in the way he should go: and when he is old,* **he will not depart from it**" (KJV, emphasis mine).

Thank you, Lori, for the flame of your passion that God ignited years ago that burns brightly for another generation of moms to have a book with tools they can use every day in the training of their children.

Carol Kohl, Director of *Child Evangelism Fellowship* of Gwinnett County, Georgia

# Author Note

This book is based on principles that Carol Kohl, who was my mentor, taught me when my children were very young. These principles reflect the heart of a proven godly mother, and Carol generously planted these principles in my heart as well as the hearts of many other mothers. In many places, what I present in this book is taken directly from the notes I took as a young mom. How does one footnote the exchange given, heart-to-heart? She is an amazing example of the mentorship of young women spoken of in Titus 2:3-5. Carol has given me permission to write these principles in this book so that other young moms can receive her godly counsel. May the Lord richly bless her and her influence.

# *Introduction*

*"Train a child in the way he should go, and even when he is old, he will not turn from it."*
*(Proverbs 22:6)*

*"Do you not know that your bodies are temples of the Holy Spirit?"*
*(1 Corinthians 6:19a)*

My spirit raced. I began to intercede quietly for the prayer requests I was hearing. Mentally, I worked at holding back the passion I felt as my spirit began to storm the heavens on behalf of my friends and their children. I was among some of my closest and most precious prayer partners, and my spirit couldn't wait for the appointed prayer time, so I let loose in prayer. These were moms who love the Lord and intercede with devotion for others. Their prayer requests were on behalf of their children, all who had chosen rebellious lifestyles with drugs, alcohol, and sex. I kept my own prayer requests to myself. They seemed light in comparison. My daughter, Ann, was planning a Christ-focused wedding and marrying a godly young man. They wanted their wedding to be a witness to others. My son Pete was attending Bible college and seeking wisdom for a life career of serving the Lord. My youngest son, Mark, had just left for China to serve as a summer missionary. Yes, all of our children needed prayer — prayer for God's glory and wisdom in their individual endeavors.

Later that day, I cried out to the Lord, "Why in our group were we praying for You to lift these kids out of the miry pit instead of praying them from glory to glory? Wouldn't that be a better place to be? Surely this would be the desire of each of the moms in my prayer group!" I realized how blessed I was to have three kids who, in their young adulthood, desired to serve the Lord. I knew in my heart - and am still convinced beyond any shadow of a doubt - that this was through God's grace. He has walked with us every step of the way, through good times and bad. I also knew that it was the bottom line desire of each one of my dedicated friends.

The story is played out thousands of times per day. I noticed when I started on the introduction for this piece for the *fifteenth time* that I had a trail of introductions all motivated from prayer appointments. Over the years, I have spent much time in prayer with distressed mothers who had broken hearts over their kids' wrong choices, from teens taking drugs to unwed pregnant daughters. The details may vary, but the story is always the same: parents everywhere crying out to God for changes in the lives and lifestyles of their teens and adult children.

My prayer group often receives calls from distraught mothers over their prodigal sons and daughters. We don't have to go far to find teenagers and young adults who have left the church and are experimenting with a secular lifestyle. In fact, Barna Research claims that 59 percent of youth who have been raised in the church disconnect from the church after age 15.[1]

A desperate parental cry goes out to God: "*Help!* I don't understand. I thought You promised that if I trained my child in Your ways that he would not turn from it when he's older" (see Proverbs 22:6). Good parents who have dutifully raised their children in the church are perplexed. This story is not new. The father of the prodigal son in the biblical story faced the same problems. Can you relate? Do you wish your child came with a "how to" manual? I often hear that cry.

My plea for parental wisdom began thirty-four years ago, while pregnant with my first child. I saw so many in my generation departing from the church that I began to ask the same questions. What is happening? Why doesn't this verse work? If we are to believe that the Bible is without error and full of promises, then what is going wrong? I concluded that either God's Word was wrong or we, as parents, don't understand the word "train." My faith told me that the problem was the latter. I didn't want to find out when Ann was 5 years old what I *should* have been doing at age 2! I longed to know, *with an unquenchable desire*, how to "train" my kids from the beginning. I remember pressing in at the altar of prayer and telling God that I would *wrestle and not let go until I knew I had heard from Him*.[2]

With another young mother, Kay Rew, I began a search for the answers on training. We found an awesome woman of God, Carol Kohl, who had raised two godly teenagers. We spent a hot Atlanta summer afternoon at her feet, listening and asking questions for hours. She taught us some very practical tips on how to train our children and instill godly principles. This eye-opening afternoon grew into mentoring classes for other young women. The principles have proven the test of time and parenting for several families.

I was only able to stay under Carol's mentorship for one year, but the biblical principles she taught me have influenced the training of my children in every stage and age my family has walked through. After teaching these principles with my own illustrations over the years, women have asked that these treasures be compiled into a book so that other parents could have a biblical manual for raising their children.

This book will be your beginner's manual for raising godly children, *temples for the Holy Spirit to dwell in.* Your creativity will be unleashed so that your own Holy Spirit-directed intuitions become your advanced manual. You will learn the process of "teach, train, and then trust." Character qualities reflecting Christ don't just happen; they must be purposefully cultivated in the lives of our children. I have developed techniques on how to see what character qualities need to be developed and how to instill them in the children through training so that they can be ultimately trusted with the characteristic.

This book includes information on how to:
- Effectively discipline and even sow the Gospel seed during the disciplining process.
- Develop your relationship with the Lord, your husband, and your children.
- Train your kids in correctly choosing friends and knowing the "five fools."
- Develop a desire for purity in body, mind, and spirit in this perverse generation.
- Break generational or family curses.
- Pray over your family using the Word of God.
- And much, much more!

As you read and apply the principles in this book, you will become encouraged in your ability as a parent with renewed hope — not only for the next generation but for the next *four* generations. *Yes*, that is right — dysfunction stops here and now! God's blessings are promised even to the next four generations, even to a thousand generations to those who love Him and keep His law (Exodus 20:4-6).

> *Dysfunction stops here and now!*

Oh, dear parent, I am thrilled as I write this. You will be blessed as your hope is renewed, not only for your children but your heritage as well. I am so energized to be able to tell you that I believe God's Word and that I have not only claimed my children to be godly for Him, but I have also claimed my entire seed for thousands of generations to come.

Now *that* is world change!

# PART 1:
## The Five Cs of Commitment

# Chapter 1
# *Call and Commitment of a Mother*

*"By wisdom a house is built, and
through understanding it is established;
through knowledge its rooms are filled with rare
and beautiful treasures."*
*(Proverbs 24:3-4)*

**Structure of the House**

Moms, this chapter, is dedicated to you! It is all about *you* and *your* commitment. Being a mom is one of your most important priorities. Worshipping God and being a partner to your husband are the only two things that trump "being mom." It is your ministry, even in the midst of workplace responsibilities (if you work outside of the home), mopping the floor, cleaning, washing dishes, changing diapers, washing clothes, wiping noses, carpooling, and doing all the thankless things that all mothers do. And, if you are like me, there is also the juggling of office work, church work, and other interests. Through all of this, we need to get our focus on *our calling as a mom*.

Colossians 3:23 says, *"Whatever you do, work at it with all your heart, as working for the Lord, not for human masters."*

Being a mom is the most important thing; in fact, it is the greatest ministry ever given to a woman. You need to make a decision: Are you willing to do whatever it takes to raise godly kids, to *raise temples* for the Holy Spirit to dwell in? Are you willing to discover what training *really* means and stay committed to the process?

The church and the world are full of good kids, but you picked up this book because you want practical, creative advice on how to raise *godly* kids. Your calling is to be a mom; your goal is to *raise godly kids, temples for the Holy Spirit.*

> *God was content for years in a tabernacle or a tent, but He was glorified in the temple.*

Let me explain further. God was content for years in a tabernacle or a tent, but He was glorified in the temple. The Israelites set up a temporary tent in the desert (the tabernacle), and God dwelt there (Exodus 25:8-9). Solomon built a temple in Jerusalem as a central place of worship, and that was the ultimate dwelling. God was glorified in the temple (2 Chronicles 7:2-3).

Our bodies are *temples of the Holy Spirit*, and of course, we want our children to not only say "yes" to Jesus but to glorify Him (1 Corinthians 3:16). The goal is godly kids, not just good kids. Do you see the difference? In raising your kids, do you want to raise a tent or a temple for the Holy Spirit?

Yes, each child and adult have been given freedom of choice, but you are going to make a commitment to do everything you know to do to create a thirst in your child's heart for seeking first the Kingdom of God and His righteousness (Matthew 6:33). Do you see the difference between this and behavior modification? The goal is to create an atmosphere for your child's heart to want to cultivate a relationship with the Holy Spirit, not be forced to change a behavior. Again, you need to make a decision: Are you willing to do whatever it takes to raise godly kids?

Your decision may be made in a second, but working through it takes a lifetime of focus and choices, a lifetime of working through the joys and the heartaches, a lifetime of re-evaluating priorities to make sure they line up with the calling, a lifetime of keeping your eyes on the goal in spite of what the world presents as reality.

This is not to say that you have to give up all of your interests and work. But you do need to make a conscious decision to be empowered by the Holy Spirit. And as you seek the Lord for direction, God will order your steps (Psalm 37:23). There will be times when you can juggle more in your schedule than other times. Only God knows. The key is to be continually sensitive to His leading.

**I Knew It in My Knower**

There was a time when I was director of women's ministry, taught a Bible study, taught Sunday School, hosted a home group with my husband, and wrote a monthly newsletter, all while trying to juggle the schedules of three elementary kids. For that season of time, I literally felt like my ability was supernatural, and I was riding on the wings of the Holy Spirit. There came a time when I knew in my knower[1] that I needed to make changes and focus more on home and my kids' activities. Although I gave plenty of notice, as I began to step down from some of these responsibilities, some people disagreed with my decision and challenged my choice. The process was difficult because I did love what I was doing, but my focus and bottom line were to go in the direction I believed God was leading me during that season of my life and which was best for my family.

My oldest son, Pete, was playing more and more baseball, and there is nothing more delightful on a summer night than to be under the stars and lights with a ballpark hot dog, cheering our son on to victory.

My youngest son, Mark, was coming to the age where he needed more assistance with his homework. The Holy Spirit knew.

My family needs were changing, and I needed to change and adapt to them.

Years later, I can reflect back with gratitude that I stuck with my Holy Spirit-led intuitions. My family benefited greatly. My daughter, Ann, was beginning the "tween–age" years, and I came to understand that "availability" for emotional needs is so important. Children don't always want to talk at convenient times. I could be available after school and even try to engage in conversation but get nothing. Then about midnight, when the lights were out, and I was drifting off to sleep, I might hear, "Mom, can we talk?"

My reaction? I rolled over in my slumber and patted the bed next to me. "Yes. What's up?" Make yourself available to tweens and teens, and take it when you can.

My point is, there are different seasons while raising your kids, and the Holy Spirit knows what season you are in and which one you are about to enter. Stay tuned to Him, and He will order your steps. You may face tough decisions that result in giving up activities you enjoy, but know this: The bottom line is, what is best for the family? Are you willing to do what it takes to be the mom that God called you to be and raise temples for the Holy Spirit? Are you ready to make a difference for the next four generations?

## *Prayer Corner*

**Reality check:** If you have kids, then you already have your calling. If you picked up this book, then you already have the desire to raise a temple for the Holy Spirit. We are taking time now to accept and seal the calling in prayer.

**Prayer:** Dear Heavenly Father, I accept my calling of being the mom You have destined me to be. I choose this day to raise godly kids, not just good kids. I will diligently do what it takes all of my years to reach that goal. I will know Your Word, Your character, and Your ways - in order to impart them to my kids. I will work through personal struggles in order to uphold my commitment. I know You will be by my side, giving me wisdom, courage, and insight. With unbreakable determination, I pray this commitment in the name of Jesus. Amen.

# Chapter 2
# *Count the Cost of Commitment*

*"Suppose one of you wants to build a tower. Won't you first sit down and estimate the cost to see if you have enough money to complete it? For if you lay the foundation and are not able to finish it, everyone who sees it will ridicule you, saying, 'this person began to build and wasn't able to finish.'"*
*(Luke 14:28-30)*

*"Don't you know that you yourselves are God's temple and that God's Spirit dwells in your midst?"*
*(1 Corinthians 3:16)*

Solomon had "building" on his mind as he constructed the temple and wrote Proverbs: *"Put your outdoor work in order and get your fields ready; after that, build your house"* (Proverbs 24:27).

There is much for us to learn on how to build a temple from Solomon's writing in Proverbs. You are preparing a temple, your child's heart, to be ready and sensitive to the Holy Spirit. Mom, you will be building, and there is a cost involved. The person referenced in Luke began to build and couldn't finish because he didn't count the cost. You have made your decision; now count the cost. This is a lifetime cost and commitment.

> *You are preparing a temple, your child's heart, to be ready and sensitive to the Holy Spirit.*

This part of the book is all about *"putting your outdoor work in order and getting your fields ready"* (Proverbs 24:27). It is about preparing your heart to be ready for the work of building your house. We are counting the cost, clearing the land, and cultivating our hearts. This means getting ready to make a difference in the lives of the next four generations and up to 1,000 generations (Exodus 20:4-6).

**Lots of Time in Prayer**

There is a prayer that Carol Kohl taught me years ago to pray every day for my kids. It is simple, yet so profound in its effectiveness. I remember it best by seeing it in outline form, so I am going to provide it that way for you. I have added to it over the years. Earnestly and diligently:

A. Pray that Satan will be bound in the heart of your child (Matthew 12:29; Matthew 16:19).

He wants to destroy the child (John 10:10) because:

1) He or she is made in God's image (Genesis 1:27).

2) He or she is a *temple of the Holy Spirit* (1 Corinthians 3:16).

3) He or she is a weapon of righteousness (2 Corinthians 6:7).

B. Pray for your children:

1) To be pure in heart (spirit)

2) To be pure in body

3) To be pure in mind

4) To be mighty in spirit

5) That the enemy will be bound and powerless in their lives.

C. Pray that the Lord will prepare your child's heart: *"I will give them an undivided heart and put a new spirit in them; I will remove from them their heart of stone and give them a heart of flesh"* (Ezekiel 11:19).

D. Pray for godly friends. Be specific in what you are praying for. For example, pray for friends who love the Lord and make healthy choices. Ask the Holy Spirit how to pray for specific friends for your kids that will complement them in interests and gifts. The list will change over time with endless possibilities.

E. Pray that the Lord will raise godly spouses for your children.

F. Pray that the Lord will speak to your children in their dreams.

G. Pray daily for discernment and for your children to see things as they really are.

**Illustrations on the Fruit of Prayer**

I prayed diligently that my kids would be pure in heart, body, mind, and spirit and that the enemy would be bound in their lives. You can imagine my surprise one day when Ann was about 6 years old, and I started detecting suspicious activity between her and a neighborhood boy. The two of them would run to the side of the house, stay a few minutes, and come back giggling. I think it was the nudge of the Holy Spirit that told me that something was up. I called Ann into the house and asked her what they were doing. She didn't say anything, and I observed a little fear in her eyes, so I knew I needed to get to the bottom of this.

We sat down on the living room floor, and I looked her in the eye and said, "Ann, I will grant you immunity if you tell me the truth of what you and Alex are doing." (Where that offer came from I don't know — I had never used it before or since then!) She said that they were going behind the house, and he wanted her to raise her shirt. I was *floored* and *shocked* but tried to keep my composure. Inwardly, I cried out, "Lord, *help*!"

I don't remember my exact words, but I began explaining to Ann the importance of purity and doing things that please God. I told her that when God was looking for someone to be the mother of His Son, He looked down and found Mary, a young lady who was pure and had a heart to please God. I reasoned with her: "Don't you want to be like Mary, so that God can choose you for something special?"

Another surprise: My daughter looked at me quite seriously and said, "Mary didn't have the temptations that I face!" *Oh, my.* So at the tender age of 6, I walked Ann through a little Bible study on how to fight temptation.

Once this encounter was over and I was alone in my thoughts and prayers, I cried out to God, "I have been praying for purity all these years, and my prayers didn't work. I feel so discouraged." I heard His still small voice say, "I exposed this because of your prayers. We are nipping it in the bud!"

Moms, something I have learned over and over again as I look back on my life as "Mom" is that each incident seemed like a world changer or a failure. But, in light of all eternity, or even the eighteen or twenty-one years that you have your kids at home (which may seem at times like eternity!), these little hiccups are simply opportunities to stay on task and continue to love, guide, and nudge them toward Kingdom living. As mothers, we are skilled at overreacting, but no single incident is the end of the world!

Just as God has provided a way of escape for temptations, He has also provided a way of redemption and restoration for every circumstance known to man (1 Corinthians 10:13, Psalm 51:12, Psalm 80, Jeremiah 15:19, 1 Peter 5:6).

**Pray for God to Speak to Your Kids in Their Dreams**

I want to share an illustration of the value of asking God to speak to your kids in their dreams (Job 33:14-15). I often begin this teaching by asking my listeners, "What was Solomon doing when he had a conversation with God and was asking for wisdom?" No one seems to know. I get some interesting guesses ranging from "He was having a discussion at a place equivalent to the Oval Office" to "He was having morning devotions in the temple." They are surprised when I reveal to them that this famous conversation took place while Solomon was asleep! Check it out in 1 Kings 3:5-15. The story starts with, "At Gibeon the Lord appeared to Solomon during the night in a dream..." and concludes with "Then Solomon awoke — and he realized it had been a dream."

Isn't that interesting? Are you having an "Aha!" moment? This revelation puts a whole new perspective on the importance of covering your child's sleeping time in prayer. Why do you think God chose sleep as the time to ask Solomon what he wanted? My guess is that the Lord wanted to get to Solomon's bottom line. When all distractions were out of the way, what was the bottom line response in Solomon's heart?

Isn't God good? He knows that sometimes we react or answer things based on circumstances or what our eyes and ears are seeing and hearing. What would Solomon's answer have been if he were in the middle of a cabinet meeting? Or reading his financial reports? Or receiving security information? Would he have requested more riches for better chariots? Or more glory to impress people? Or a greater army to protect his borders?

God's graciousness brings me great comfort. I also find it remarkable that it was during this time that God imparted wisdom. Solomon was not in the midst of striving to hear and receive from God. He was not in a powerful praise and worship service. He was not in a service hearing wisdom from a mighty prophet or evangelist. Solomon was sleeping!

I did not understand this while my kids were growing up to the extent that I do now. Therefore, the testimony I am about to share is an experience I had praying for my husband, Gene's, dreams. The same application can work for your kids.

Here's the backstory: Gene's uncle and aunt are lifelong missionaries to the Ilongot people in the Philippines. Ilongots were a headhunting tribe that changed their lifestyle with their conversion to Christianity. The missionaries were not only instrumental in bringing Christ to this people group, but they also converted their native language to writing and then translated the Bible into the Ilongot language. Over time, with outside civilization influencing the tribe more and more, it became necessary to publish a new Bible paralleling the Ilongot language with Tagalog (the Philippine language). I longed to be able to help with the financial aspect of the endeavor and began sending them a little extra each month, knowing that this amount was but a drop in the bucket to meet the need.

About the same time, we put our house up for sale. An offer came in that Gene was willing to accept. I felt like we could get more. As we discussed it, I asked him that if he was satisfied with this amount, could I have anything over and above that amount. He knew what I wanted it for and said "yes."

We had 24 hours to respond, so I suggested that we "sleep on it" and ask God for wisdom. I stayed awake most of that night praying that God would give Gene wise counsel while he slept. I prayed fervently for his dreams, for wisdom, for the price of the house to be perfect.

The next morning, the first thing Gene said to me was, "I woke up with this great idea…" What followed was amazing. We got the price I wanted for the house, and we were able to send the New Tribe missionaries the money for the publication of the parallel Bible. I rejoice in the Lord every time I think of God's provision and goodness and how His Word works! We need to work His Word in prayer and as we do, watch it work! His Word says that He speaks to us in dreams. Ask Him to reveal Himself to you and your family, not only while awake but also while sleeping.

The Lord always encourages us to approach Him in prayer with the desires of our heart, and the closer we draw to God, the closer our hearts align with His. As we invest our time in prayer, we unlock doors and change history and our world. It is well worth the cost of time!

**Corporate Prayer Times**[2]

In addition to the time you spend in your personal prayer closet, it is also beneficial to join or create a prayer group. There were times when a group of my friends would regularly come together for the purpose of praying for our families. There were other years when I joined *Moms in Touch*[3] and added this hour into my routine. There are many benefits of practicing corporate prayer. The discipline of gathering regularly once a week gives unspoken accountability to your personal habits. It adds creativity, fresh ideas, and experiences in prayer as well as prayer warriors, to call on when a backup is required.

Let me explain it this way: When I take a painting class, I often find myself working on the craft outside of the class. When I take an evangelism class, I am thinking about evangelism during the week and practicing it more. The same applies to belonging to a prayer group. Let's face it: We all know we are supposed to pray, and we do. But if our prayer life is enhanced by experiencing it corporately at least once a week, then it is a valuable hour invested.

**Keep Priorities**

Another cost to count in our commitment to raising godly children is the time and effort and determination it takes to maintain priorities. The list below looks simple, but you know how life is — schedules get busy, urgent things overtake the important, and before you know it, the priority list is upside down! It costs the discipline of taking the time to continually adjust and work on priorities. We need to prepare our schedules in prayer as we cultivate the following relationships:

#1: Relationship with the Lord

#2: Relationship with spouse

#3: Relationship with children

#4: Relationship with church, work, hobbies, etc.

Before teaching Sunday school or attending more meetings at church or volunteering at the school, we must meet the needs of God, husband, and children first because we are training the next generation! We are *raising temples.*

In the last chapter, I mentioned a time when I found myself with a long list of leadership activities at church. For a season it was meant to be, and I enjoyed it. Then there came a time for re-evaluation and adjusting my schedule to meet current family needs. When activities bring pleasure, it is often hard to take a good, hard look at prioritizing. The process is not easy. It might even feel offensive. Listen to the direction of your heavenly Father. He will give you strategy on how to re-work your schedule.

We all want to be the Superwoman of Proverbs 31, juggling everything, doing it well, and having everyone singing our praises at the end of the day. As a young woman, I would read that chapter, and if I wasn't performing at Superwoman status, I would begin to feel like I was not measuring up. A very wise woman told me years ago that the Proverbs 31 woman didn't accomplish it all at one time. There are many seasons of life, and her accomplishments were over time. Now that I am an "older and wiser" woman, I completely concur with that. I look back over the years, and I have done all I have wanted to do — just not all at one time.

> *There are many seasons of life. I have done all I have wanted to do — just not all at one time.*

In other chapters, we will talk about the priority of building relationships with your husband and children. Paul exhorts Titus to encourage the younger women to *"love their husbands and children"* (Titus 2:4), because there are times it is hard to love them. Husbands don't always treat you graciously and lovingly. Kids don't always obey, and they can be rebellious, loud, and time consuming. So, you need to learn to love in all situations and seasons, even though it is often a thankless job.

But it is worth it! Remember: We are training the next four generations. We are raising temples.

Part of the cost may be making some heart changes in order to be in for the long haul. We are preparing and training for a marathon — not a sprint. So we need to take a good look at ourselves and the conditions of our hearts. We will do this in the next chapter.

## *Prayer Corner*

**Reality check:** Take an honest look at how you spend your time. Do you have enough time to pray as you are led? Do you have sufficient time to listen? Are your husband's needs being met? Do you feel pulled? Do you often feel rushed because "time is running out"? Are you living outside of the margin (so to speak)?

**Prayer:** Father God, You are the King of Kings and the Master of this universe! You hold all things in Your hands. I am willing for You to show me any area of my time that needs adjusting. I am ready to count the cost of "preparing a temple," and that is most important to me. Right now, making changes seems impossible. Give me Your wisdom for strategy. I put my time and my energy into Your hands for Your guidance. In the name of Jesus. Amen.

# Chapter 3
# *Clear the Land: It's a Heart Issue*

*"The wise woman builds her house, but with her own hands the foolish one tears hers down."*
*(Proverbs 14:1)*

In the past, my husband and I have had the fun task of picking out a vacant lot and choosing a builder for a new house. Often the land is full of woods, rocks, and garbage. The builder spends considerable time clearing the land.

Imagine your heart like the unprepared land. Allow the Lord to walk with you through the chambers of your heart and clear the land to prepare your heart for the building to come.

Before we get started, I hear you asking, "Why do I need to do this? I don't have any issues! Or what few I have, I can handle. And what does this have to do with training kids? All I want to do is learn the quick tricks of the trade for successful training."

**News flash:** Children are mirror images of you. They copy everything you do. One of my favorite memories is five-year-old Pete wearing little green plastic glasses. He created them from sunglasses that he popped the lens out of so he could have them on all the time. Why? Because his daddy wore glasses, and he wanted to be just like him. We all have images of our little girls sporting our high heels, with lipstick everywhere except on their lips. I am sure you are grinning right now as you think of your kids imitating you.

In the spiritual realm, your attitudes and "issues" are transferred to your kids. This doesn't always seem so obvious, but if you train yourself to look, you will see it. When you see a rebellious spirit or a jealous spirit in your child, first pick them up (figuratively speaking) as if looking into a mirror, and ask the Lord if there is anything in you that needs to be dealt with. Sometimes the answer is "yes." Rebellion can be as mild as not purposefully following through on a request from your husband or boss. If you deal with your rebellion, repent, and get it under the blood of Jesus,[4] you will often see the behavior in the child diminish. Don't be fooled by the manifestation. The root cause could be rebellion, but it presents itself in a different way with a child.

Another example is when a parent is addicted to prescription drugs and sees it manifested in a child with an addiction to alcohol or drugs. In a recent class I taught, one of the attendees responded to my last teaching on parental relationships by praying for the forgiveness of the offenses she experienced from her parents. She then called them to meet for dinner at a restaurant. It was difficult, but she restored her relationship with her parents. For her, the unexpected fruit was a difference in her relationship with her daughter. She said that she did not mention anything to her teenage daughter, but there was suddenly a change in her daughter's behavior. Rebelliousness was gone. She spoke kindly. She listened to instructions. This surprising list of healthy behaviors went on and on, and she was ecstatic over the changes.

I explained to her that though she was cooperating with Jesus in practicing forgiveness, another principle came into play as well. The other underlying spiritual law is that our kids are subconsciously mirror images of our attitudes. She got a "twofer" on that one act of obedience. She

> *You need to teach your kids by example. Don't expect them to do what you don't do!*

saw a restored relationship with her parents and changed behavior in her daughter. Her daughter did not even know what was going on in the background, such as the release through forgiveness, the restoration of relationship, and the fresh walk in handling offenses to maintain the relationship. Mom, you need to teach your kids by example. Don't expect them to do what you don't do!

**The Umbrella of Protection**

I heard a good explanation of how this works at a conference where the transference of sin was illustrated by using an umbrella. As parents, we are the protective covering over our children, much like an umbrella protects us from the rain. If we have sin in our life, then there is a hole in our umbrella, giving the enemy permission to influence our kids. Many times, I have fought temptation from the sheer conviction that I did not want any holes in my umbrella, which could expose my kids to the schemes of the devil (Ephesians 6:11, 1 Peter 5:8).

Another benefit to teaching your kids the "umbrella of protection" principle is that as your kids grow, they can pray for you and any perceived "holes in the umbrella" as they detect it from their temptations.

**Clear the Land**

"Clearing the land" is an ongoing process. We always want to keep our hearts clean and holy before the Lord. Let's take some time and go through the process. If I were speaking to you in person, I would ask you to shut your eyes and be in an attitude of prayer. I would ask you to let your mind and spirit take a walk with the Lord. One of the first things you want to pick up and toss out are the hard rocks of rebellion. What is rebellion? The Bible says that rebellion is like the sin of witchcraft (1 Samuel 15:23). Rebellion and witchcraft are closely related because they both expose us to needless temptations. Both keep us out of God's realm of authority and put us under the authority of the evil one, giving an open door for the enemy of our souls to work. First, think through who is in authority over you — in the home, at work, at school, in any organization. Reject the thought that you are too old to be under authority. The Bible says differently: *"Likewise you younger people, submit yourselves to your elders. Yes, all of you be submissive to one another, and be clothed with humility, for 'God resists the proud, but gives grace to the humble'"* (1 Peter 5:5 NKJV).

Now that you have identified who it is you answer to, prayerfully consider if there is any place where you are causing division either through word or action. How is your attitude? Pray it through, repent, and put it under the blood. Say a prayer of blessing over your authority.

Take a deep breath, because we still have work to do! The *rocks of rebellion* have cleared the land, and now we need to dig out the *stumps of stubbornness*. We can cut down trees, but they always leave *stumps* that need to be excavated, roots and all. I saw a demonstration of sheer stubbornness in the veterinarian's office when a huge dog did not want to come in. He sat his big rear end down and dug in all four paws and would not budge. He was heavy, and the owner could not pull him or coax him into obedience. Ask the Lord to reveal places in your heart where you have dug in your feet and emphatically refused to do something that you are supposed to do. Make a plan of action to become more flexible.

I always kid my husband that the stubbornness in our kids comes from his side of the family. Later we will talk about how to break through prayer the undesirable family traits that we all have.

**Weeds of Discontent**

As we continue to *clear the land*, we run across lots of *weeds of discontent*. Are there situations where you are dissatisfied and unhappy? Do you have a restless desire for something better? Are you envious of another? Ask the Lord to help you work through the process to contentment. Job 36:11 says, *"If they obey and serve Him, they will spend the rest of their days in prosperity and their years in contentment."* Job is not the only one promising great gain with an attitude of contentment. Timothy also says, *"Godliness with contentment is great gain"* (1 Timothy 6:6).

Think of the times when your kids are ungracious and complaining because they are not satisfied. How does it make you feel? The Lord feels the same. Don't forget: If you see ungratefulness or discontentment in your kids, you need to look in the mirror. Sometimes we need to deal with ourselves first. Is your discontentment rooted in selfishness? Have you made a choice to be a homemaker, but you are feeling deprived because you are not pursuing your career? Remember your call and commitment and that this is part of the cost of raising godly kids.

**Big Black Trash Bags**

Now we need to go get the big black trash bags, because we need to clear the land of garbage from our secret habits and thoughts. Believe me, when I tell you that nothing is secret to your kids. You live your day minute-by-minute in front of them, and they know your little habits. You know what these habits are, and so does Jesus. The Lord showed Ezekiel the secret sins of the priests. Nothing is hidden (Luke 8:17). Ask God to cleanse you of all unrighteousness (1 John 1:9). He will gladly do it in a second and give you a plan for victory. *There is no condemnation in Christ Jesus, and He always gives us a plan of escape* (Romans 8:1, 1 Corinthians 10:13).

| Clear Your Land ||
|---|---|
| Rocks of Rebellion | |
| Stumps of Stubbornness | |
| Weeds of Discontentment | |
| Secret Habits and Thoughts | |

Whew! That was a lot of work, but we are not done yet. Let's look at what Hebrews 12:1 says about weights: *"Therefore we also, since we are surrounded by so great a cloud of witnesses, let us lay aside every weight, and the sin which so easily ensnares us, and let us run with endurance the race that is set before us"* (NKJV).

> *SIMPLICITY TIP:*
> *Only keep one-third of toys out at a time. Change them every couple of months. Then they will be fresh and fun for the kids, and it will help maintain order in the house.*

Let's work through what could be some weights. Preparing and maintaining a peaceful atmosphere creates a place for the Holy Spirit to speak to you and your kids in a still, small voice. A few ideas are listed below; you add some more.

| What are some weights? | Plan of action to throw off the weight |
|---|---|
| Is your house organized? A cluttered house brews confusion and is a weight. | |
| Do you personally have too much to do? Do you burn your candle at both ends? | |
| Are your family meal times unplanned and unorganized? | |
| Is your family involved in way too many activities, with little time to relate? | |
| Is the TV or other distracting noise constantly on? | |
| Is there a spirit of discord, with constant arguing? | |

Through it all, refuse to fear or worry! Fear allows Satan the freedom to fulfill your fear (Job 3:25). Fear and worry are the opposite of faith. For every fear or worry, God has a promise. Find a verse with the promise, declare it, and believe it. Ask the Lord to increase your faith level and remove all fear. Peter says that the enemy, the devil, "prowls around like a roaring lion looking for someone to devour" (1 Peter 5:8).

Who gave you the fear (2 Timothy 1:7)?
_____

Remember: You hold the next four to 1,000 generations: "... punishing the children for the sin of the parents to the third and fourth generation of those who hate me, but showing love to a thousand generations of those who love me and keep my commandments" (Exodus 20:5-6).

**TIP for simplifying the house:** Only keep one-third of the toys out at a time. Change them every couple of months. They will be fresh and fun for the kids and it will help maintain order in the house.

## *Prayer Corner*

**Reality check:** Prayerfully consider the chart above, and let His light expose and correct anything that is out of order. What are some things you are fearful of? If fear did not come from God, why are you hanging on to it?

**Prayer:** Father, I want to clear the land. Create in me a clean heart, ready for service to You. This very day, I ask You to help me to get rid of the rocks of rebellion, the stumps of stubbornness, the weeds of discontentment and selfishness, and the garbage of secret habits. And Lord, I also ask You to help me get rid of every weight that would hinder me from accomplishing my goal of being a great mom and raising godly kids. There are times that I feel fearful and I worry about _____, but I choose to trust You and Your promise, and I declare it here: _____. Lord, I trust in You! In Jesus' name. Amen.

# Chapter 4
# *Cultivate the Soil: Going Deeper into the Heart of Things*

*"But the seed on good soil stands for those with a noble and good heart, who hear the word, retain it, and by persevering produce a crop."*
*(Luke 8:15)*

You may be thinking, "Hey, I'm a mom! I love my kids, so isn't my heart already prepared to raise them, just by being a mom?"

Yes, but when the going gets tough, when you have been tried and pushed to your limit, you will need to be able to dig down a little deeper to keep your commitment. There is a reason why Timothy exhorts the older women to admonish the younger women to love their husbands and their children (Titus 2:4). Quite frankly, sometimes we simply don't feel like loving them because they are acting very unlovable. Examining the heart is the beginning of the process for passing the love test.

**Parable of the Sower**

Let's take a look at the Parable of the Sower to see a reflection of heart conditions. It is told in Matthew 13:3-23, Mark 4:2-20, and Luke 8:4-15. Jesus spoke in parables because the people's hearts, ears, and eyes had become spiritually closed. Telling stories created a curiosity and created a thirst for more. Take some time to read this parable and examine your heart, and allow the passage to be an indication of things you need to do. Prepare your heart, and then you will be able to prepare the hearts of your children. Allow the Lord to do the work through you.

Are you tempted to skip this step and move on? Don't. Taking care of *you* first is a principle that even the world knows. When we travel by air, we tend to tune out the pre-flight instructions. Next time, pay attention. If you are traveling with a small child, you are told to put the oxygen mask on yourself first and then on the child. Why? Because you can't help the child if you have passed out from lack of oxygen, since you didn't put your mask on first. Likewise, we need to tend to the conditions of our own hearts before we can help prepare the hearts of our children.

You, however, do not have a closed heart, eyes, or ears. I declare over you the words from Matthew 13:16: *"Blessed are your eyes because they see, and your ears because they hear."*

In this parable, the seed is the Word, and the soil where it is sown represents the heart. Jesus wants to expose the heart condition of people.

| Symbol in Parable | Symbol Represents | Result | This space is for you. Where do you see yourself? What changes can you make to ensure that you are "good ground"? |
|---|---|---|---|
| Received seed by the wayside. | Hears Word and doesn't understand it. | Seed is snatched by the enemy. | When you hear the Word and don't understand it, what can you do to prevent the enemy from snatching the truth before it is understood? |

| Symbol in Parable | Symbol Represents | Result | This space is for you. Where do you see yourself? What changes can you make to ensure that you are "good ground"? |
| --- | --- | --- | --- |
| Received seed on stony places (rocks), had no depth or moisture. | Hears the Word and immediately receives it with joy; sun scorched and no root, so it withers away. | Plant is starved. Heart stumbles when tribulation and persecution comes. | Can you think of an activity that will give root to the words you hear? What will water and deepen the Word? |
| Received seed among the thorns and thorns choked it. | Hears the Word, but the cares of this world and the deceitfulness of riches choke the Word. | Fruit is smothered with worldliness; becomes unfruitful. | Is there anything in your life that smothers the Word of God? Can you identify any cares of this world that would prevent your spiritual growth?<br><br>The only way to detect deceitfulness of the heart is to take time and allow the Holy Spirit to show you (Psalm 139:23-24). |

| Symbol in Parable | Symbol Represents | Result | This space is for you. Where do you see yourself? What changes can you make to ensure that you are "good ground"? |
|---|---|---|---|
| Receives seed on good ground. | Hears the Word with noble and good heart and understands it. | Bears fruit with endurance; 30, 60, or 100 percent return. | Read John 15 slowly. Meditate on verses 4 and 16. Write your reflections and your plan for change so you can go for 100 percent. |

**A little side note:** Pay attention to one of Jesus' techniques for training. He uses object lessons, something familiar to explain something unfamiliar. This creates a thirst or a curiosity.

Luke references "hearing" nine times in the Parable of the Sower. We build our faith by hearing the Word of God. One of my favorite Bible teachers, Warren Wiersbe, explains the parable this way: "The Word is like seed because it has life in it and produces fruit when it is planted (received and understood). The human heart is like soil and must be prepared if the Word is to be planted and fruitful… It takes patience to cultivate the seed and produce a harvest and we must not give up. It is important that we sow the seed in our own heart as well as in the hearts of others."[5] (see 1 Corinthians 3:16).

**Seeds for the Heart:**

God's Word is living and powerful (Hebrews 4:12).

Do not be discouraged (Galatians 6:9, Psalm 126:5-6).

## *Prayer Corner*

**Reality check:** Work through the above chart that reflects the soil of your heart and the soil that you are preparing. Do you feel discouraged in any area? Take it to the Lord in prayer.

*"Do not lose heart.... our light and momentary troubles are achieving for us an eternal glory that far outweighs them all. So we fix our eyes not on what is seen, but on what is unseen, since what is seen is temporary, but what is unseen is eternal"* (2 Corinthians 4:16-18).

**Prayer:** Dear Jesus, I invite You to help me cultivate my heart and prepare it for receiving Your Word and understanding it. I will prayerfully consider Your Word so it will be deeply rooted in my heart. In fact, Lord, I invite You to write Your Word on my heart. Show me any areas of worldliness or where the riches of this world may deceive me. I know You will never leave me or forsake me, and with You by my side, I know I can have endurance for the long haul. I expect to be the recipient of 100 percent fruit from my labor as I continue to keep my heart ready for Your Word.

Father, help me to keep my eyes on the unseen, the eternal things. I confess that I sometimes get discouraged because my eyes are on the seen, or the temporal things of life. In Jesus' name. Amen.

**You are making a difference.**

**Your legacy is impacting the next 1,000 years!**

# Chapter 5
# *Commit to the Destiny of Children*

*"'For I know the plans I have for you,' declares the* LORD, *'plans to prosper you and not to harm you, plans to give you hope and a future.'"*
(Jeremiah 29:11)

Now that you clearly understand your calling, have counted the cost, and have cleared and cultivated the land, you need to commit to the destiny of your children.

This step is important, because *"where there is no revelation, people cast off restraint"* (Proverbs 29:18). Taking time to "see" what you are choosing will help establish imperishable determination. Take some time and choose. This is not about a particular career or talent destiny; this is about character and righteousness.

> *We need to base our theology on the Word of God and not on our perceived experiences.*

This is a good place to address a couple of concerns that I often hear about the validity or the hope of being able to raise a godly child. I want to help eliminate any doubts so that faith can grow freely. The first concern raised is that Proverbs 22:6, *"Start children off on the way they should go, and even when they are old they will not turn from it,"* is not a promise but a proverb. I hear things like, "There is no guarantee because proverbs are just nice things to live by, not truth." I think people believe this because it helps justify the fact that we all know wonderful Christian families whose kids have gone astray. We need to base our theology on the Word of God and not on our perceived experiences.

**The Concept of Training**

Thirty years ago, I read this verse as a promise, and I clung to it and decided that the key was discovering how to train. I find nothing in the Word of God that suggests we eliminate Proverbs or not take it seriously. We have misunderstood the word "train" and have simply applied it to mean taking the kids to church and maintaining an image of a Christian home. Or we have only trained in behavior modification and not in spiritual application and molding the heart of the child.

This book is full of ideas on how to train and all that is involved in training. Many are from my years of raising three kids and always being on a search for new and fresh ideas on how to impart godly principles. Other insights come from researching the Jewish lifestyle, the faith that Jesus was raised in, and how His parents possibly imparted godly truths and principles. I also took a peek at how terrorists train their kids to grow up and be so passionate about their faith that they are willing to go on suicide missions. We can learn from the best and worst; we just can't stay lackadaisical.

Praise God, the training in this book is for life and so that we can help our children learn to live the abundant life (John 10:10). As moms, we need to get a grip and choose this day to believe the Word of God and cling to all of its promises. Most promises do have conditions, and it is important to understand and fulfill the stipulations.

**Free Will**

The second concern that I hear is that we are all given free will, and we can't force our kids to choose the right path. After all, God was the perfect parent, and yet His first two kids sinned. Yes, that is true, and there is by no means any condemnation to anyone who has done all they know to do and whose kids still make a wrong lifestyle choice (Romans 8:1). God gave us the first example of practicing tough love when He sent His kids out of the Garden of Eden (see Genesis 3:23-24). But God wanted fellowship with His kids so much that He gave His only Son and did all that He could do to provide redemption and restore relationship.

We too as parents may be faced with laying down our pride and dreams, giving a little more, making tough choices, and even giving tough love, just like God did with Adam and Eve. But we are also given lots of opportunities to provide a repentant and redemptive atmosphere so that every prodigal can have a chance to run home and be restored. My hope is in a loving God who will always reveal to a parent a way to help show a child, even an adult child, the redemptive opportunity to restore the relationship. I believe that as long as there is breath, there is hope.

This book is targeted at young mothers of babies and preschoolers, but the hope and the principles work for all ages.

**Discouraged? Doubtful?**

Discouraged or doubtful moms, ask for an increased faith level, knowing God will provide for you all the wisdom and love that you need to accomplish the call and reach the goals of being a number one mom and raising a temple in which the Holy Spirit can reside and be glorified.

Are you discouraged because you have "blown it"? Hey, from time to time we all do! This book is not for perfect moms. It is for human moms. As my kids were growing up, there were so many times that I would cry out, "Oh, I blew it! I've damaged them by reacting emotionally! Oh, my! Oh, me!" Thankfully, this diminished as I matured in Christ, as it will for you, too.

I am here to tell you, discouraged mom, that one incident is but a fleeting moment in all of eternity, and it can be quickly remedied with this "secret weapon": forgiveness. It is the key to the redemptive process.

When necessary, I would go to my kids and say: "Mommy over-reacted when you did _____. I had an angry attitude. I should not have done those things. Will you forgive me?"

**Here's a tip in asking for forgiveness:** Don't overdo it. When you ask for forgiveness, state the attitude problem rather than recounting the bad behavior. Your purpose is to clear the air and receive forgiveness.

> *One incident is but a fleeting moment in all of eternity, and it can be quickly remedied with this "secret weapon": forgiveness.*

Stating the bad behavior does nothing but recreates the scenario and bring up the emotion. Keep it simple for the best fruit.

The restoration process will begin the instant that the forgiveness process is put into motion. It is a humble expression, and the success of it is not dependent upon another's response. There is a verse in Joel that I have often claimed throughout my life, and I encourage you to do the same. Turn this verse into a prayer for yourself: *"I will restore to you the years that the swarming locust has eaten"* (Joel 2:25a).

I hear someone reading this and saying, "But my family mess can't be fixed, because it was my fault. Why would God restore what the locusts have eaten away when some of this is my fault or my spouse's fault?"

**God Restores Chaotic Situations**

I hear in that an attitude of condemnation and discouragement. It is true that some of you may need to do a little spirit/soul examination and surgery and see why the locusts came and ate. God will give you wisdom. Let me give you an encouraging word. God is able to take a chaotic situation, even one you feel responsible for, and restore it. At the beginning of time, God spoke light into a dark and chaotic world, and it was good. You see, dear mother, God is looking into the chaos of your life, and He is saying, "Let there be light." Scripture has many stories of God's restorative power, but one I especially relate to is about Peter. He walked with Jesus, yet blew it big time when he denied Jesus in His most dire need (John 18:25). Peter's restoration plan came from Jesus and was right around the corner (John 21:17). He is ready and waiting to do the same for you. Though you go through the fire, He will bring you out to fulfillment (Acts 10:34, Psalm 66:12). Now, let Him turn the ashes into beauty and mourning to joy as you commit to making the right choices from this moment forward (Genesis 1:3, Isaiah 61:3, Psalm 51:12).

Another benefit of the parent asking the child for forgiveness is the opportunity to model the process humbly. The benefits so outweigh the consequences that it is a wonder why we don't automatically do this. Chances are, if you are like me, you didn't see it modeled so it just didn't occur to you and you didn't know how to do it.

Another reason why we might neglect seeking forgiveness from our kids is that there could be a concern that the child will feel like he or she is off the hook because we are admitting that we have done something wrong. That can be remedied by adding something like this: "Mommy was wrong in her response, but that doesn't make what you did right, and you still need to receive the discipline."

Now let's roll up our sleeves and get to work. As you walk through these steps, read them prayerfully, and write down your answers.

Commit your heritage! Make some decisions on what you want. Do you want:

- Godly kids or simply good kids?
- Temples or tent dwellers?
- Blessings or judgment?
- Roses or weeds (weeds don't need training)?
- Lasting joy or temporary happiness?
- Peace or confusion?
- A life full of grace or criticism?
- Discernment and forgiveness or judgmentalism?
- Godly wisdom or worldly wisdom?
- Oak trees or shrubs?
- _____

*"Seek first his kingdom and his righteousness, and all these things will be given to you as well"* (Matthew 6:33, see also Psalm 37:4).

**Raising a Temple: Building the Structure**

Plan for it. Pray for it. Below is a list of what your goals might look like during the growing up years. They will progress and look different at different stages of life. In fact, as your kids grow, I would suggest you set aside time every year for recommitment and to write out fresh goals. I believe creativity breeds creativity, and throughout this book, you will have space to write in your ideas.

When the anointing flows, so do the ideas and wisdom, so take the time to make this your book and your message.

Our goals:
- Kids who know that Jesus loves them and protects them.
- Kids who eagerly look forward to reading the Bible and prayer time.
- Kids who want to be "helpers" just like Jesus.
- Kids who are seeking the Lord and take time for personal devotions.
- Kids who understand that, through Jesus, they have a capacity beyond their own abilities.
- Kids who desire to have a ministry.
- Kids who seek the Lord in all their choices.
- Kids who desire to have a godly boyfriend/girlfriend.
- Kids who choose to be drug and alcohol free.
- Kids who choose to have pure relationships and give their mate the gift of purity.
- Kids who (you fill in the next few)
- _____
- _____
- _____
- _____

> ### *Prayer Corner*
>
> **Reality check:** The person referenced in Luke 14 began to build and couldn't finish because he didn't count the cost. Make a decision about what you want, and record what it will cost you. Is there anything you need to give up to make it happen?
>
> **Prayer:** Dear heavenly Father, I choose this day to raise godly kids. I want my kids to be a temple for the Holy Spirit in which You will be glorified. I know that You have given them free choice, but I am committed to doing all that I can to create a righteous thirst in them and to nourish them in Your character. As I dedicate my kids to You, I do so in the precious name of Jesus. Amen.

Mom, now that you have read this far, are you scratching your head and wondering if you even have a relationship with Jesus to impart this kind of training to your kids? Perhaps you have been in church all of your life, but you've never understood how to have a personal relationship with Jesus. A personal relationship with Jesus is more than a religious activity. If you believe He is who He says He is, then He calls you friend. As a friend, you can call upon Him not only in times of trouble but also for everyday wisdom. He enjoys talking with you.

Peace to you! I have Good News. The process is simple, yet profound and life changing. First, you simply admit you are not perfect. Next, you believe that Jesus was perfect, died on the cross for your imperfections (sins), and rose again on the third day, conquering death so that you can live with Him for eternity. The

Bible says, "*Believe in the Lord Jesus, and you will be saved*" (Acts 16:31a).

I suggest you seal your belief with a prayer of simply telling Jesus that you believe Him. Using your words, pray something like this:

*"Jesus, I believe that You died on the cross for my sins. I want to commit my life to You. I want to call upon You for godly wisdom and direction in my life."*

**Mark this date.** You need not ever doubt again! The Holy Spirit has quickened your spirit and resides in you from this moment forward. He will never leave you or forsake you (Hebrews 13:5).

For some basic help, go to gotquestions.org/new-christian.html. Also, look for a Bible based church where you can worship.

# Chapter 6
# *Loving Your Husband*

*"Then they can urge the younger women to love their husbands and children, to be self-controlled and pure, to be busy at home, to be kind, and to be subject to their husbands, so that no one will malign the word of God."*
*(Titus 2:4-5)*

We can't leave this part of the book without addressing the importance of maintaining a godly and loving relationship with your husband. Yes, in the midst of changing diapers, wiping noses, cooking meals, mopping floors, and teaching godly principles, your priority is your husband!

> *Find balance by thinking of it this way: Our kids are our number one ministry, but our husbands are our number one priority.*

Mom, I know you did not buy this book for this chapter. You bought this book to get creative ideas and encouragement on raising godly kids. However, it would be wrong not to include it. Knowing this is not your purpose for reading this book, I am going to write this in an outline, that will enable you to do a quick read and take to heart the principles.

So how does this work? If being a mom is the number one ministry and with all the time that it takes to raise kids, where does this fit in? Just think, "pre-baby" you would not have wondered! Loving your husband as a number one priority doesn't equate to time given. Obviously, it takes more time to juggle all the activities of children and a home. But Mr. Right needs to be your focus. God is our first priority and focus, and then your hubby comes next.

**Focus looks like this:**

1. Love God.
2. Love your husband.
3. Love your children.
4. Be sensible, busy workers at home (and many juggle this with work outside the home).

> *The Holy Spirit's job is to always point to Jesus. Likewise, the mother should direct the kids to their father.*

Time might look a lot different from one mom to the next. So let's commit our time to the Lord. We can have an abundant life with husband and children. Ask the Lord to help you with time management. Sometimes being loving doesn't take extra time; it's more about attitude adjustments.

A way to honor and give your husband respect, just in the course of routine activity, would be to point your children to him for answers to their questions. For example, if you and your children are in a discussion about anything, be alert for a moment when you can say, "Let's go ask Dad and see what he says" or "I bet Dad has a good idea about this; let's ask him." The family can often reflect the roles that the Godhead has. Often the father is a picture of Christ, and the mother is a picture of the Holy Spirit. The Holy Spirit's job is always to point to Jesus. Likewise, the mother should direct the kids to their father.

**Four Things to Know and Abide By in Marriage**
1. **Commit to your man.**
    - Commit 100 percent to your husband.

- The word "divorce" must be taken out of your vocabulary. Do not use it, even in a joking matter. My Uncle Bob, who married us, gave us this advice, and it has served us well.
- Do not walk out of a room and shut the door in anger. If you do it, each time it will become easier to walk out the front door and shut it.
- Make him your king, and he will make you his queen!
- Respect and honor your husband.
- Live together until you die.
- Attitude makes a difference.
- Commit to being a helpmate, to support and encourage him, and to build him up.
- Work toward a spiritual and physical oneness.
- Pray for him openly and daily.
- Make your home his refuge; if it's not, then he won't want to come home.

2. **Communicate.**
   - Show him kindness through words, action, and deeds.
   - Don't be verbally abusive, unforgiving, or bitter.
   - Have a willing, quiet, and submitting spirit.*
   - Submit by praying together.
   - Communicate without arguing, which is a sign of rebellion.

*I would like to clarify what is meant by a meek or gentle and quiet spirit, described in 1 Peter 3:4. Having a sanguine personality that is usually loud and dramatic, these words would haunt me! This verse is referring to the inner spirit, the attitude of a person, not the personality. A definition of meek is "strength or power under control." Meekness means that one is not reacting to challenging circumstances with outbursts of anger. There is nothing wrong with discussing different points of view and letting your opinion be known in a kind and loving manner.

### 3. Cultivate the relationship.

Isn't it interesting that Paul gave the instruction that older women should encourage younger women to love their husbands (Titus 2:4)? He knew there are sometimes days when love is not based on what we feel. We need to understand that love is an action word. Therefore, we need to work actively and intentionally on the relationship.

- Cultivate the relationship, and you will grow together. If you don't cultivate, you will grow apart.

- List all of the reasons you fell in love with your husband to remind yourself on the days you don't feel "in love."

- The Bible says, *"Godliness with contentment is great gain"* (1 Timothy 6:6). If you don't expect something, and you do get something, how do you respond? With great excitement and gratefulness! Give your expectations to the Lord, so that there is not a demand on your husband. Then when he comes through, you will be delighted!

- Trust in the Lord, not your husband. When you trust in your husband, and he fails you, you will be upset, and it will cause division in the relationship, all because you trusted in the wrong thing!

- Believe that God will work in your husband and through your husband to fulfill His goals in you. God will work His purpose in you.

- Set your goals, and for the next three months, build up your husband. In front of him, tell others how "blessed you are because you married a genius."

- You want him to be known at the gates (Proverbs 31:23). Make that your goal.

- He is your ministry. Know his moods, and then be supportive and do what needs to be done.

- Look to him to be your spiritual leader, even if you think you can do it better. Look to him for spiritual truths.

- Bring him good and not harm (Proverbs 31:12).

4. **Romance your husband.**

    - If you don't love him and give to him, then someone else will!

    - Go on a date once a week.

    - Make phone calls and send text messages that show you care.

    - Feed kids early if needed so you and your husband can spend time together.

    - All the verses in Proverbs that warn against the adulteress woman are actually things you are allowed to do with your husband. Or you can get some ideas from Song of Solomon.

    - Check out *A Celebration of Sex* by Douglas Rosenau.

**Tips from *Love Life for Every Married Couple* by Ed Wheat (in a nutshell):**

Do the **BEST** method daily:

**Bl**ess him verbally.

**E**dify. Do something special or say something nice about him to others in front of him.

**S**hare thoughts, ideas, plans, dreams, day-to-day, etc.

**T**ouch — this means love pats and holding hands, not only sexual touches.

This picture is an illustration of what does *not* work in cultivating a relationship with your man.[7] Whatever happened; I guess Mrs. Lion should have learned to trust in the Lord and not her husband! I heard author Eddie Smith explain it this way:

"In all relationships, trust the Lord, and love people. If you trust people, they will disappoint you, and that is how offenses occur."

Remember, your husband will fail you, and you will be upset — all because you trusted in the wrong thing. Trust in the Lord and not your husband!

**True North**

Before closing out this chapter, I would like to share a treasure of truth that a friend of mine, Kathy Bailey, sent to my son, Pete, and his wife, Andrea, for their wedding celebration:

*"As I meditated on both Pete and Andrea, I felt a sense of 'home' — coming home to each other. Being a light for each other and listening for the sound of the voice that leads us to safety in Christ. Together you are one in Christ. Your home is in Him and each other.*

> *When we find someone we love, we find our one 'True North.' We become 'home' for each other over time.*

*Be light. Be like a beacon of light in a dark place for one another. When one is lost, may the other shine as light. I was lost, but now I am found in you.*

*I once saw this movie called 'Message In A Bottle.' In it, a woman finds a love message written by a man totally in love with his wife. He called his wife, his 'True North.' When we find someone we love, we find our one 'True North.' We become 'home' for each other over time.*

*Christ and His Bride, the Church, are like a husband and wife (see Ephesians 5:25-27). Jesus illustrates this concept. He is like the man who sent the message in the bottle to the bride. Jesus loves the Church. He is calling her, beckoning her to come 'home' to Him. Though there are storms of life, there is a light that shines brighter than all. He is the light of the world. When it gets dark, and we feel lost, we listen for the sound of the foghorn. The foghorn is like Christ calling to His bride to come home when she cannot see clearly. As she listens to His voice, He will lead her safely home. Even when it is dark, and you are feeling lost, listen for the sound, and focus on the light of His love. Over the storm-tossed waves, you will see His light shining and leading you onward — homeward bound.*

*As you go through the world, there will be many voices, but you must attune yourself to the one true voice that is able to steer your ship in the right direction —- 'True North.'*

*I pray you become 'home' to each other — comfortable, a safe harbor in the storm. I pray that you understand through your relationship the relationship of love you have with Christ, the one who came to give you His life so He could lead you home safely to the Father.*

*John 8:12 says, 'When Jesus spoke again to the people, he said, "I am the light of the world. Whoever follows me will never walk in darkness, but will have the light of life."*

**Poem: *You Are My Home***

*By Kathy Bailey*

*When I walk in darkness, and I feel alone*

*I set my compass to True North, for you are my home*

*Though the waves thrash at my boat, and
I cannot see the shore*

*I listen for your soft sweet voice, which guides me
safely to the shore*

*For you are my beloved, I have found my home in you*

*You are my love; I am your husband — you are my bride*

*In the light of your love there is comfort, and in your heart is
where I hide*

*When God created me, I know He thought of you*

*He planned for us a future and a family; I have found
my home in you*

*Pete and Andrea have found their home in each other, and may they and all the family God has given them be cherished and honored always."*

**Family Discussion with Pete, Relating Kathy's True North Analogy**

As we prepared for the wedding, Pete and I discussed this beautiful devotion, and I told him that it resonated with me because I experience his dad as my home, and that was one reason I have been able to move so often with my husband's career path. He is my "home," and so it didn't matter where we lived or what I was leaving behind when we picked up and relocated.

Pete then asked me, "What about when he retired from business after 32 years and started a farm?"

I replied, "Pete, that is the ultimate proof that 'home' for me is with your dad. He is my 'True North.' You know the lifestyle changes we made, and I am very happy and content because I am with him. Of course, he considered me in the decision process and has met the requests I needed to get behind this new adventure 100 percent."

**Your Husband Is Your North Star**

Moms, God want your husband to be your "True North" star. Let me encourage you; I have the advantage of looking back over 36 years and seeing the long view back. You might feel stuck in a moment, holding a child on each hip while your feet are mopping up a spill and your hands are wiping a nose. Your imagination thinks your husband is at a cushy job, enjoying lunch, and you wish he could "be home" with you! I know, I relate. Been there and felt that. Now, I am the "older woman" that Titus 2 is talking about when it says, "Older women… admonish young women to love their husbands."

Just as I am now looking back, let me suggest that you look forward toward the goal of growing old together with your "True North." Don't focus on the frustrating moments of the here and now. Each stage of life has its ups and downs, and one way to get through the challenging times is to focus on the love that brought you together and the goal of being one in Christ and sharing your children and grandchildren together in the later years.

I will be transparent here and explain that there were some frustrating times. Let me explain. Gene and I met as summer missionaries. I became an R.N. to bring together two goals: mission work and nursing. When we married, Gene was also interested in missions. We had both planned to go to seminary. Soon after we were married, Gene was given an opportunity to accept a management promotion. We took a day off to pray and talk. One of his goals was to also be a Christian businessman, bringing the influence of Christ and principles to the workplace. I agreed and gave him my support.

Fast forward a few years, and I was a young mom with three kids on my hips! My heart still felt the tug of missions and, after taking mission trips, my frustration of not fulfilling a dream was disturbing me. I cried out to the Lord, asking Him about this, knowing that my priority was to my family before my dream. The Lord spoke to me clearly in only the way He can comfort and guide. He said, "Whether you are in Timbuktu or a city in the States, your job would be the same, tending to your husband and these three precious kids, raising them to love Me. You would not be working in mission hospitals any more than you are doing now." Oh! Aha! I had made a choice to be a stay-at-home mom so that I could be the one who influences and trains my kids. That decision would remain the same no matter where I was.

The Lord has been so good. Gene continued to move up the corporate ladder, thus all the moves. And I saw each new city as a new mission field and quickly got involved with church work, whether in children's ministry or women's ministry. Through it all, my number one priority after God was to Gene, and my number one mission was to my three kids. The Lord provided through His hand on Gene so that I could be a stay-at-home mom and work in the church. Through the Lord's provision, I have been able to travel the world on many short-term mission trips and support many missionaries.

Young moms, it's all perspective. We can focus on the challenges, or we can focus on divine strategy through our walk with Him. We can focus on the frustration of the moment, or we can focus on the goals and dreams and see God's hands doing what He said, *"promising to complete the good work that He has begun in you."* And, *"The steps of a good man are ordered by the Lord, and He delights in his way."* (Philippians 1:6, Psalm 37:23NKJV)

Fight for your family through the specific strategy of prayer. Learn to fight His way, with Him fighting for you while you "rest" and trust Him. As you pursue the Lord as your "True North," your husband will become your "True North," and you will be able to weather any storm or lifestyle changes. You will be at home in Him.

## *Prayer Corner*

**Reality check:** At the end of the day, have you been able to have a conversation with your husband? Have you found a way to demonstrate some love or respect through a positive attitude? Have you prayed for him? What is your tone toward him as you go about your day?

**Prayer:** Lord, I love my husband, but it seems I rarely have time to show it. Help me to be able to give him the focus and the love he needs. You said in Your Word that You order our days. I need You to help me with time management. Keep me aware of times when I need an attitude adjustment that will give him the respect he needs. Lord, I would love a date night each week, but we need someone we trust to help with the kids. You are the Master Networker; help provide this for us, please. Father, remind me that sometimes it doesn't take extra time to give respect, but merely a respectful attitude that will be reflected in my tone.

Lord, I now pray for my husband. Help him to be the man You created Him to be. Help him to walk out the destiny and future that You have for him, according to Your Word in Jeremiah 29:11. Lord, I want to honor him as the leader of our home. I declare that he is the priest, the king, and the prophet of our home.

Today at his work, he needs wisdom. Give it to him. This evening, he needs to relax and enjoy the kids. Help him to be able to. Help me to give him a place of honor through my attitude at the dinner table. May we have peace and harmony. And Lord, I do want him to be known at the "city gates." Give me wisdom on how to brag about him to others (Proverbs 31:23). Lord, I desire for our marriage to be "True North." In Jesus' name. Amen.

# Part 2:
## *All Aboard the Training of a Temple*

*"Train up a child in the way he should go,
and when he is old he will not depart from it."
(Proverbs 22:6 NKJV)*

*"Do you not know that your bodies are temples of
the Holy Spirit?"
(1 Corinthians 6:19a)*

### Preface to Training

In order to validate the "how to" training, this session will be full of personal stories. There are times when this might seem cumbersome for some, and for others it will give them their "Aha!" moment. I pray this will be an encouragement for young moms everywhere to declare, "I can do this!"

This is one of the most challenging parts for me to write, because when I teach this series to young moms, I am full of expression and drama. I am challenged to get the stories across in written words in the same way that I relate them to a live audience.

> *The bottom line of this whole book is training your kids to understand that the choices they make matter.*

I also want to make it clear that I am writing success stories. I am not here to air out our family's dirty laundry. We are not a perfect family, and I am not a perfect mom. However, since the time of having my firstborn, I have set my eyes like flint to the goal of learning how to train and activate my kids in godly character qualities and spiritual disciplines.

I come as a grandmother who is now on the other side of raising kids and can say, "Been there, done that." I can tell you that what sometimes felt like the worst of times or occasions when I totally blew it — those periods are but a moment in time. With determined and prayerful focus, those times can be reversed and redeemed. I can say that with the advantage of looking back.

It is important as a parent not to be in denial of problems and to face each one prayerfully and head on. I have seen when parents are in denial or blind to problems that continue to grow and affect their child later in life. Keeping an honest but noncritical outlook is important.

The bottom line of this whole book is training your kids to understand that the choices they make matter. They will learn that obedience brings blessings and disobedience brings discipline or consequences. This truth is throughout Scripture and specifically in Deuteronomy 28 and Leviticus 26. We will talk about this more in Chapter 15.

Now, sit back and enjoy the ride! Remember, there is no condemnation as you read this and make comparisons. This book is written by someone who also experienced life and didn't always hit the mark, but who learned the secret to training, redemption, and restoration.

**The Family Business**

This is Abraham, holding the promised baby. Can you guess who the baby is? I bet most of you thought of Isaac. Rethink.

Genesis 22:18 says, *"In your seed all the nations of the earth shall be blessed, because you have obeyed My voice"* (NKJV).

Galatians 3:16 says, *"Now to Abraham and his Seed were the promises made. He does not say, 'And to seeds,' as many, but as of one, 'And to your Seed,' who is Christ"* (NKJV). The promised baby is Jesus!

In my hands is the genealogy of all the generations between Abraham and Jesus. God needed a family to carry on the family business — the business of teaching and training their kids to worship the one true God and to live according to His laws and promises. Abraham took on the challenge, and the promise was passed on for 2,000 years. This family had its share of ups and downs and times when the enemy tried to corrupt the seed. Through it all, the promise and the covenant of God prevailed.

We as believers are tied to the promises through adoption (Romans 8:15-23, Romans 9:4, Galatians 4:5). Have you caught a key word in this segment? Promise. Abraham was the father of the Jews, and we typically think of laws and more laws and that we are set free from the law. He is also the father of the promise that includes us!

Will you pick up the baton and take it to the next generation? Will you accept the challenge, as Abraham did? In studying Judges, one can see the constant cycle of generations *"doing what was right in their own eyes"* then cycling back to crying out to the Lord (Judges 17:6, Proverbs 21:2, Judges 3:9). Apparently, parents and grandparents did not pass the baton of faith on to the next generation, or the younger generation dropped it. Commit to picking up the baton and securely placing it into the hands of the next generation![1]

> *We are training the next four generations. We are raising temples!*

*"Therefore know that the Lord your God, He is God, the faithful God, who keeps covenant and mercy for a thousand generations with those who love Him and keep His commandments"* (Deuteronomy 7:9 NKJV).

---

### *Prayer Corner*

**Reality check:** Are you ready to take on the "family business?" Are you ready to pick up the baton of faith and securely place it in the hands of the next generation? Yes, they might rebel, but are you willing never to give up and keep up with the praying and creative ideas to make them thirsty for God?

**Prayer:** Dear heavenly Father, with faith, I take the baton of faith, and my desire is to place it into the hands of my kids, _____. Train me. Show me. Give me creative ideas on how to run this race with endurance and not give up and to keep my eyes on the prize: kids serving you! I pray this in Jesus' name. Amen.

# Chapter 7
# *What Does It Mean to Train?*

*"Train up a child in the way he should go,
And when he is old he will not depart from it."
(Proverbs 22:6 NKJV)*

As mentioned earlier, terrorists know how to train. They immerse their kids in an entire lifestyle of being comfortable handling guns and experiencing hate. These pictures of kids training with rifles at terrorist training camps probably send a chill down the backs of most of the moms reading this book.[2]

What could be worse than these images? How about pictures of 3-year-olds playing with ammunition belts strapped around their torsos, just to get them used to wearing a gun or other destructive devices? What are the terrorists doing? What are they thinking? Lord knows we can't get into their minds and understand them, but there is no doubt that they have learned what the word "train" means.

In our Western culture, we have minimized the word "train" to simply mean teaching or dropping our kids off at children's church or Christian school. Training is so much more than expecting the church to do it.

We can see from this picture that training is an indoctrination of lifestyle and mindsets through activities. Check out the definition from an online dictionary: "To teach a person or animal a particular skill or type of behavior through practice and instruction over a period of time; cause to be sharp, discerning, or developed as a result of instruction or practice."

As we work through this book, you will discover that the Jewish culture of Jesus' day also had the lifestyle of total immersion of their belief system. They understood the value of training. We can learn practical insights on how to take their methods and apply them to our modern culture.

**Training involves three steps:**

1. **Teach**: Instruction about what is expected

2. **Train**: An activity with coaching; practice

3. **Trust**: Blessing or discipline. Either positive or negative reinforcement of the expectation. Never trust before teaching and training.

A very obvious example of this that most parents can relate to is potty training. Think about the process. What do we do?

**Teach:** First, we explain to little Johnny or Susie what we are going to do and what we expect from them. We teach them by demonstrating the process, perhaps through a doll or storybook.

**Train:** Next we create lots of opportunities to practice what has been taught. We might spend a whole day or two giving lots of juice and water. Nearby would be a little potty seat, just the right size and special for the occasion. We make a game out of it. We "try" to have fun with it (big smile and wink), and we keep our eye on the goal, continually thinking of new ways to teach and activate what has been taught.

**Trust:** The day finally comes when we know we can trust little Johnny or Susie with their new ability to use a bathroom. We trust them to let us know when they need to go. We trust them to wear their brand new big boy or big girl underwear and keep them dry and clean. Eventually, we are out of the picture, and they are so trained that they can go without discussion or help.

Now, we would never take a diaper off a 2-year-old and put on underwear and then just trust her to keep her pants dry and clean. Likewise, with most things we are training our children in, we never trust before we train, and we don't train before we teach. We need to work the process. Sometimes the process is quick, and they get it with very little training, and sometimes it takes a much greater effort.

Training often involves a period of time. When teaching a character quality, a good starting point is over the course of three months, the same as a season. I suggest this because God speaks to us often with gardening terms, such as "we reap what we sow." Seasons are usually three months. If something is not learned through training in three months, then start over, asking the Lord for fresh ideas on training. Usually, the most intense time and effort are at the beginning of the training process. You will know when the trust phase begins.

**Example in Training Gratefulness**

When Ann was in the first grade, I realized that we needed to do some training on gratefulness. Before school started, we had shopped together for her school clothes, and in her new wardrobe were three dresses that she had picked out but now did not want to wear to school. She made comments such as, "Oh, that old thing" or "No, I am not going to wear it" or "I hate that dress."

We talked about gratefulness. We read stories about gratefulness. We memorized some Scripture on gratefulness. We reviewed examples of people who demonstrated appreciation and contentment. All of this discussion did not seem to change her heart.

I prayed and asked the Lord to show me a way to train Ann in gratefulness. At the time, I was also volunteering at a migrant center where people came to receive donated food and rummage through a barn full of donated used clothing. I made a plan to take Ann on a field trip to the migrant center so that she could see how others had their provisions of food and clothing supplied.

Her Sunday school teacher, with whom I had talked about our planned trip, donated $20 to us to go shopping and buy a week's worth of groceries for one family. The typical meals consisted of rice, beans, and flour to make tortillas. With the $20, Ann and I were also able to add some chicken, sugar, and vegetables. We added a box of cookies and other things we thought would be an added blessing.

On the day of the field trip, Ann was to take her three dresses that she wouldn't wear along with a favorite dress to give to the migrants. To model the experience, I also gave one of my favorite dresses to someone who I knew needed it. We prayed that we would find a family that had a little girl who wore a size 6x. The day we were going was not the typical day of distribution, so we had no guarantee that anyone would even come to the center that day.

Praise Jesus. One family came, and of course, they had a little girl who wore a size 6x. She was thrilled with Ann's gift of clothes. We gave the family the groceries we had selected, and they were blessed beyond words. I had a Spanish-speaking friend go with us to interpret. We included in our discussion the story of Jesus and how He is the reason that we were there and that He had impressed upon us to bring things on this day. We discovered that this family was not able to come on distribution day and had been praying that something would be left on the day they could come. We all had answered prayer that day.

Before leaving, I took Ann into the barn of donated clothes and she discovered how other kids "shop" for their outfits. Many things were in bad condition! We both learned and grew from the experience. I became much more attentive to any clothes that I might want to pass along as donations. I purposed to only give what we would be willing to wear — clothes that are clean and without need of mending.

Ann is one of the most grateful and appreciative young ladies I have ever known. She demonstrates gratefulness for any gift or deed done for her or her family. To this day, she is faithful with thank-you notes, even for the little things, putting me to shame in comparison. That one day of training has reaped a lifetime of fruit.

**Gratefulness Leads to Appreciation**

Let me share something else that training in gratefulness does. When my kids demonstrate gratefulness and appreciation, Gene and I are so willing to give to them. They lack nothing as far as we can control or provide for. Likewise, I have learned through this that as we give our heavenly Father gratitude — as opposed to grumbling — then He is also willing to meet our needs. However, just as when our kids' grumbling turns us off from blessing, so it is with our heavenly Father when we grumble.

---

### *Bonus Box*

Training in gratefulness is preparation for receiving truth and the blessing of God. To better understand the importance of training in gratefulness, read Romans 1:18-32.

What was the result of not thanking God (verse 21)?

List the progression of the sin cycle by working through these questions or statements:

It all began when man stopped _____ God and _____ Him (verse 21).

What happened to their thinking and their hearts (verse 21)?

What exchange did they make (verses 22-23)?

This spiraled into _____ (verse 24).

Another exchange: They worshipped _____ instead of _____ (verse 25).

How did the downward spiral continue (verses 26-27)?

They were given over to a _____ (verse 28).

The "new normal" continued. Take the time to write them out (verses 29-31).

Finish verse 32: "Although they know God's righteous decree that those who do such things deserve death,

_____.

Have you ever watched the news and scratched your head at the thought process and actions of politicians? Rioting protestors? I am not talking about people with a different opinion or strategy to reach a common goal. I'm referring to some calling what seems to be wrong "right" and believing the end justifies the means. Romans 1 helps explain how a society gets to this place — and it all starts with parents training or not training their kids.

Go back and look at verse 17. How is righteousness revealed?

(Rabbit trail alert! Read Matthew 24:12 <lawlessness> and Titus 3:1-2 <authority>, watch the news and put two and two together. Did I mention the condition of man's heart as the end times approach?)

**Prayer:** Lord, forgive me for not being thankful in all circumstances as You have asked me to be. I realize the deeper issue is not trusting You with Your provision or with the outcome. I purpose to trust Your hand in my circumstances. Now, Lord, I want to train my children in trust, thankfulness, and gratefulness. I know You are faithful. Partner with me and give me strategies to impart these truths. In Jesus' name. Amen.

**Three Key Areas to Train: Spirit, Soul, and Body**

There are three key areas we need to consider training. Paul says that we should be found blameless in our spirit, soul, and body: *"May God himself, the God of peace, sanctify you through and through. May your whole spirit, soul and body be kept blameless at the coming of our Lord Jesus Christ"* (1 Thessalonians 5:23).

*We are preparing the heart of the child for the Holy Spirit. Then after the child chooses to believe, as parents we continue to train and mentor them.*

The Word of God differentiates the spirit, soul, and body and is powerful, sharp, and alive to pierce the division between all three. Read this verse again, as if for the first time, recognizing the power and life of the Word along with its ability to divide spirit, soul, and body: *"For the Word of God is living and powerful, and sharper than any two-edged sword, piercing even to the division of the soul and spirit, and of joints and marrow, and is a discerner of the thoughts and intents of the heart"* (Hebrews 4:12 NKJV).

1) **Spirit:** Worship - principles for living, praying, Bible reading, and even fasting

2) **Soul:** Social - (attitudes, manners, and interaction with peers and authority), mental (soul and emotions), wisdom

3) **Body:** Physical - exercise, housekeeping, environment, normal growth process

This concept is familiar to all of us, but often our understanding is blurred, especially in differentiating between spirit and soul. I am going to explain it similar to the way I explain it to kids.

While holding up an astronaut figure,[3] I ask the kids, "What do you see?"

They quickly yelled out, "An astronaut!"

I ask again, "Seriously, how many of you see the astronaut?"

Again, there are shouts of, "Me!" or "I do!"

Once again, I would say, "think about it, what do you really see?"

With puzzled looks, they would say, "An astronaut."

After playing around with this question-and-answer game, I finally tell the kids, "Y'all are not really seeing the astronaut. You can't see him. All you can see is the suit the astronaut is wearing. The *real* astronaut is inside the suit!"

I go on to explain that astronauts wear a suit to help them breathe in outer space. There is no oxygen there, and the suit helps them live and work safely. That is how God made you and me. He gave us a suit that we call our body. We need our body to live on this earth. We breathe, see, hear, touch, and smell with our body. But our real self is deep inside. God also gave us a spirit and a soul.

The Bible says that God created man in His own image. God has a body (John 5:37) and a spirit (John 4:24) and a soul (Leviticus 26:11). First, God created a body, as a potter shapes the clay, out of the dirt of the ground. He then breathed life into man, giving him a part of Himself. The breath of life allowed the body and soul and spirit to live and function together.

Notice that this creation process is totally different than the way God created animals. Furthermore, God never breathed His life into the animals. Man is distinctively different than all other animal life. This foundational truth is so important for us as believers to understand. This truth will make a difference in:

- Our identity — how we view ourselves
- Our walk — how we make decisions
- Our relationship — how we relate to God, the Father, Son, and Holy Spirit
- Our understanding of Scripture, since it will be enhanced.

The body is the outward part that we see, like the astronaut suit. The soul and spirit are the invisible inner parts. The soul is what feels, and the spirit is that which knows (1 Corinthians 2:11). Each part has a distinctive role and can be differentiated: "*For the word of God is alive and active. Sharper than any double-edged sword, it penetrates even to dividing soul and spirit, joints and marrow; it judges the thoughts and attitudes of the heart"* (Hebrews 4:12).

The body is temporary, but the soul and the spirit are immortal and will live forever. The soul is our mind, where thoughts are formed, and our personality. The spirit is the part of us that becomes "born again" when we get saved. Our spirit is the part of us the Holy Spirit speaks to when He leads and guides us. We hear, see, and know in the spirit — in our belly (John 7:38).

When teaching your kids, have them say, "I am created in the image of God. God has three parts, and I am three parts. God is the Father, Son, and Holy Spirit. I am body (touch body), I am soul (touch head), and I am spirit (touch upper abdomen)."

When we explain this to children with Kids in Ministry,[4] we have three kids, each holds a poster of what they represent. One represents the soul (mind, personality). The second represents the body (flesh), and the third represents the spirit (spirit).

Together they represent one human being who does not know Jesus, with the mind, body, and spirit all headed in the same direction. The mind, body, and spirit cooperate with each other. When a person believes what the Bible says about Jesus and becomes born again, it is the Holy Spirit that enters into the spirit of the person. The person's spirit is joyful and full of hope, and the person's life changes.

**Inner Conflict Between Our Three Parts**

In the demonstration with the three kids, the one representing the spirit turns and faces the opposite direction. The body and the soul don't get saved, and they still want to do and think as they always have. Only the spirit that is reborn wants to go God's way. This explains the conflict that Paul spoke of in Romans 7:15-20: *"I do not understand what I do. For what I want to do I do not do, but what I hate I do. And if I do what I do not want to do, I agree that the law is good. As it is, it is no longer I myself who do it, but it is sin living in me. For I know that good itself does not dwell in me, that is, in my sinful nature. For I have the desire to do what is good, but I cannot carry it out. For I do not do the good I want to do, but the evil I do not want to do — this I keep on doing. Now if I do what I do not want to do, it is no longer I who do it, but it is sin living in me that does it."*

How do we solve this problem? We need to build up the spirit. The spirit needs to get stronger through praying, worshipping, and reading Scripture. This is in essence what this whole book is about. As parents, we can begin strengthening the spirit of our child while he or she is still in the womb. We are preparing the heart of the child for the Holy Spirit, and then after the child chooses to believe, as parents we continue to train and mentor them.

## Examples of Parents Training Body, Mind, and Soul from Scripture

### Mary and Joseph

What we know about Jesus's babyhood and childhood is summed up in these verses: *"When they had performed everything according to the Law of the Lord, they returned to Galilee, to their own city of Nazareth. The Child continued to grow and become strong, increasing in wisdom; and the grace of God was upon Him."* Later as a teenager, this verse describes Jesus: *"And Jesus kept increasing in wisdom and stature, and in favor with God and men"* (Luke 2:39-40, 52 NASB).

From these verses we see that Jesus's training followed the pattern:

1) **Spirit:** The grace of God was upon Him; He grew in wisdom and obedience.

2) **Soul:** He increased in favor with God and man; obedience.

3) **Body:** He continued to become strong and grow in stature.

We have no idea what it was like to raise a perfect little boy or teenager, but we do know that Mary and Joseph were strong in faith and took their training seriously. Jesus was raised according to the Jewish faith and traditions. A study in Jewish culture reveals that the indoctrination of faith is deliberate and part of everyday life. "Jewish law, halakhah, governs not only religious life but daily life, from how to dress to what to eat and how to help the poor. Observance of halakhah shows gratitude to God, provides a sense of Jewish identity, and brings the sacred to everyday life."[5]

True to the general characteristics of Jewish values, Jesus grew up reciting prayers and Scripture three times a day and more often on the Sabbath and holidays. He was brought up practicing the Sabbath every week and with the rhythm of Jewish holidays throughout the year. By the time He transitioned from boyhood to adulthood at 12 years old, He knew His identity as clearly seen right after a Passover celebration in Jerusalem. He was passionate about His faith and yet left the Temple, a place that brought Him much joy, in obedience to His parents (Luke 2:41-52).

Typically, a child would begin to study Scripture at about 5 years of age. The written word was rare; so much of the training would come from memorization. It is possible that Jesus committed huge portions of Scripture to memory. Jesus would have learned from His father and from local rabbis. Debating contemporary issues of the day was a common practice and part of the training. Typically, a question would be answered with another question. Jesus became a master of teaching using this method. One of the many examples of this is when He healed the paralytic in Luke 5:17-26. He perceived the scribes' and the Pharisees' questioning thoughts. He then asked a question: *"Which is easier: to say, 'Your sins are forgiven,' or to say, 'Get up and walk'?"* (verse 23) As you read through Scripture, look for questions being answered with a question.

The family business was also passed on to the children, so much training on being a master carpenter was passed along to Jesus.

## Timothy's Parents

Paul gave Timothy's mother and grandmother the credit for training Timothy in the faith (his father was Greek, see Acts 16:1, 3 and 2 Timothy 1:5). His faith was strong enough to withstand the evils of the day. Paul charged him to continue what he had learned from infancy. He was trained in the Holy Scriptures, making him *"wise for salvation through faith in Jesus Christ"* (2 Timothy 3:14-15). The conditions of the world were evil and deceptive.

Paul was writing from a dungeon, where he was jailed for his faith. Yet Timothy's godly training enabled him to make a difference in an ungodly world.

Let's look at how Timothy's life fits into the model of training we have outlined.

1) **Spirit:** Salvation came at a young age through the training of Scripture. His personal conviction continued as he was convinced of the truth.

2) **Soul:** He was wise, relying on the absolutes of Scripture and not humanism.

3) **Body:** Timothy was strong enough to become a co-worker of Paul and go on many mission trips, as indicated throughout the book of Acts.

I know some of this has already been answered, but take the challenge and see how much more you can fill in this chart. Some might not be cut and dry but more speculative. Some may show the result of negative training.

|  | **Spirit** | **Soul** | **Body** |
|---|---|---|---|
| 1 Thessalonians 5:23 | worship, principles for living, praying, Bible reading, and fasting | social, attitudes, manners, interaction with peers and authority, mental, emotional | physical, exercise, housekeeping, environment |
| **Jesus** Luke 2:40 boy |  |  |  |

|  | **Spirit** | **Soul** | **Body** |
|---|---|---|---|
| **Jesus** <br> Luke 2:52 teenager | | | |
| **Timothy** <br> 2 Timothy 3:14-15 | | | |
| **Samuel** <br> 1 Samuel 2-3 | | | |
| **Samson** <br> Judges 13 | | | |
| **Ishmael** <br> Genesis 16 | | | |
| **Ishmael** <br> Genesis 21:8-21 | | | |

|  | **Spirit** | **Soul** | **Body** |
|---|---|---|---|
| **Ishmael** Galatians 4:21-31 | | | |
| **Isaac** Genesis 21:1-7 | | | |
| **Isaac** Genesis 22 | | | |
| **Isaac** Genesis 24 | | | |
| **Isaac** Galatians 4:21-31 | | | |
| **Jacob** Genesis 25:19-27 and ff | | | |

|  | Spirit | Soul | Body |
|---|---|---|---|
| **Esther**<br>Esther 1-9 | | | |
| **Daniel and three friends**<br>Daniel 1 | | | |
| **Moses**<br>Exodus 2:7-10 | | | |

## *Prayer Corner*

**Reality check**: What type of training have you been doing? Has it been purposeful and intentional? Do you incorporate it into your lifestyle? Do you include training for all three of your parts; the spirit, soul, and body? Do you live a grateful lifestyle?

**Prayer**: Lord, I may not have understood and still don't understand training as a lifestyle, but I am willing to learn. Please open up my eyes and ears to see and hear what You want to teach me. Help me keep a teachable spirit and learn to look for opportunities to train my kids. Father, I am only just now beginning to understand the difference between spirit and soul and want to train both with wisdom. I know Your Word is sharp, active, alive, powerful, and able to help me divide the spirit, soul, and body (see Hebrews 4:12). Alert me to the opportunities.

Father, we are so thankful for all of the blessings that You have given to us. I commit to living a grateful lifestyle and demonstrating thankfulness to my kids. In Jesus' name. Amen.

## Chapter 8

# Why Train? What's the Big Deal?

*"Have nothing to do with godless myths and old wives' tales; rather, train yourself to be godly."*
*(1 Timothy 4:7)*

*"For lack of discipline they will die, led astray by their own great folly."*
*(Proverbs 5:23)*

*"As dog returns to his own vomit, so fools repeat their folly."*
*(Proverbs 26:11)*

*"I saw that wisdom is better than folly, just as light is better than darkness."*
*(Ecclesiastes 2:13)*

What's the big deal about training? This might seem like a silly question. On the surface, of course, we think it is a good idea to train our kids. Isn't it common sense, after all, we train our pets? If we don't, they become unruly. A puppy that weighs five pounds is cute when it takes a running leap on people, but it is annoying and even dangerous when that same puppy turns into a fifty-pound playful

> *Weeds grow without training. Fools grow without understanding and discernment. Discernment comes from training.*

dog and does the same thing. Do we want to take away the playfulness? The fun? The laughter? No. But we want to train so that both the pet and people enjoy the growth, the maturing, and the experience.

Likewise, if we do not purposefully train our children, they become unruly. What seems cute and laughable at age 2 is not cute at age 5. I remember times when I had to hide my giggles while putting on a stern front to instruct and guide more appropriate behavior. I bet you can relate and are remembering some of your stories of stifling a giggle while needing to discipline. If training when they are so cute at age 2 is ignored, what happens? If this is a pattern, I believe they lose the ability to instinctively develop the difference between right and wrong. Proverbs 5:23 says, *"He shall die for lack of instruction, and in the greatness of his folly he shall go astray"* (NKJV). Unruly behavior and confusion dominates a household. This happens to good, well-meaning parents.

We live in a society where it is not politically correct to correct misbehavior. The PC crowd has put the fear of ruining a child's self-esteem into society, and parents seem to have unknowingly adopted it by osmosis. Parents often confuse protecting a child's self-esteem with protecting his or her self-worth.

A child's self-esteem comes from knowing clearly what is expected and meeting the challenge. Furthermore, when a parent is vague or brushes off misbehavior with light-hearted excuses or redirection without explanation, then the child's ability to discern right from wrong is reduced. Let me explain with two simple examples.

**Heart Condition**

Have you ever heard someone say that people are basically good and that, if raised in a healthy, safe environment, adult kids will choose what the parents want? I have heard that said, and did you hear me now scream "Fallacy!" and pull my hair? Let's look at what the Bible says about this myth:

*"Then the LORD said in His heart, 'I will never again curse the ground for man's sake, although the imagination of man's heart is evil from his youth"* (Genesis 8:21b NKJV).

*"The heart is deceitful above all things and beyond cure. Who can understand it?"* (Jeremiah 17:9)

Who would want to take a chance on not training when you have these truths straight from the infallible word of God? Enough said.

**Lack of Training**

Think of the consequences of lack of training. Weeds grow without training. Fools grow without understanding and discernment. Discernment comes from training.

> *When training does not start early, the ability to instinctively develop the difference between right and wrong is potentially lost. Proverbs 19:20 says, "Listen to advice and accept discipline."*

Though I was well aware that I was in the company of an unruly child, my mouth dropped when I witnessed a 5-year-old child walk up to a stranger's baby stroller and give it a push to see what would happen as it bumped down a curb. The stroller with the 9-month-old baby inside tumbled sideways. Thankfully, no one was hurt. The parents of the 5-year-old laughed it off, saying, "Boys will be boys. He is curious about everything, always experimenting." The only comment to their son was, "Did you know a baby was in there?" There was no instruction or discipline.

There are two things that bother me: 1) I think a well-trained 5-year-old would be able to discern that this was not a wise thing to do. 2) Training would have included a complete discussion and encouragement to apologize to the mother of the baby. The 5-year-old should have been in the "trust" stage for this circumstance. The Bible says, *"Whoever has no rule over his own spirit is like a city broken down, without walls"* (Proverbs 25:28 NKJV).

Another example of an immature ability to discern is commonly seen when children see gifts. A beautifully wrapped gift is a temptation to any child, and a 2-year-old would be drawn to unwrap one without any thought. A well-trained 6-year-old should know to ask when it is appropriate to unwrap a gift. Why would a 6-year-old unwrap one without a thought? It is because the same child at age 2 was redirected without instruction. The opportunity to train at age 2 would be to explain gift unwrapping protocol and then redirect to an interesting activity. The child being redirected would know why he is being redirected rather than blindly starting another activity. He would begin developing his sense of right and wrong. *"But solid food is for the mature, who by constant use have trained themselves to distinguish good from evil"* (Hebrews 5:14).

**Inconsistency**

My brother and I have often analyzed a source of frustration and confusion for us. While growing up, we never knew precisely what was expected of us from our parents. Some days a certain activity would be okay or even laughed at. Other days, the response would be screaming, accusations, and punishment. Frustration and confusion are saying it lightly; sometimes we would live in fear of the unknown. I now believe that our mom loved us very much and had no idea the frustration she was causing with her mixed messages.

Why did she do that? I really do believe that she would never have knowingly hurt any of us. Perhaps the first time we did something, it was funny or even cute — in the privacy of our home. The same activity later would be embarrassing, either because we were older or because it was done in front of others in public. Correction starts at home, with even the little things. We train by our responses, starting at a very early age. But now I realize that it is so important for the adult to train with consistency and be without excuse.

Mixed messages and inconsistency create poor self-esteem and a feeling of unworthiness. Again, without consistent proper training, the child's ability to discern right from wrong is reduced. When a consequence is not given consistently, then a child, especially a strong-willed child, will always look for the loophole or the opportunity to experience the temptation.

The Bible says that foolishness is sin, so we want to correct foolish behavior just as we would want to correct our perceived obvious sin. The Bible says, *"O God, You know my foolishness; and my sins are not hidden from You"* and *"The devising of foolishness is sin"* (Psalm 69:5, Proverbs 24:9a NKJV).

**Benefits of Consistency**

Ann was only 6 months old when we discovered we were pregnant with Pete. Do the math. Pete would be a newborn when she was only 15 months old. I shared a big concern with my pastor's wife. I had been observing the 2-year-old next door jump the backyard fence and run off while the mother was busy nursing or tending to her newborn. I was concerned for her safety while her mother had other "mommy" duties. My wise pastor's wife pointed out to me that it would not "ruin" the baby to stop what I was doing, even if he was nursing, to give consistent training to my toddler. Furthermore, if I were consistent, it would not take more than two or three times for my toddler to realize that following instructions were important and the temptation of testing the opportunity would diminish. She was right. It only took two or three times to train Ann that just because I was nursing or busy with the baby, that did not give her permission to misbehave. Often, as time goes on, there are new opportunities to test and, again, be consistent.

This principle continued to be a lifesaver when I soon found out I was pregnant with my third child. When Mark was born, I had three kids 3 years old and younger. Most would agree this balancing act would be challenging for the best of us. I am not the "best of us," but I followed the principle of being consistent, no matter how inconvenient, and it paid off in the long run.

I had crazy "how to" thoughts while having three kids 3 and under. How do you safely get three kids out of the car in a public parking lot? Reason with me. If I take the youngest out first, it did not seem safe to put a baby carrier on the ground while still working car seats and seat buckles with the other two. If I let the 3-year-old out first, she would be out of sight in a parking lot! The next couple of years, there would be two in diapers at the same time. Fast-forward a few years, and there would be three learning to drive at approximately the same time, and then there would be three in college at the same time. It was not always easy, but a little extra effort in training at critical and inconvenient times paid off. Today, my three kids and their families continue to be the joy of my life.

**Grace**

Let's get real, girlfriend. Sometimes, it is literally impossible to be consistent — yet we can't let our little ones know what those loopholes are. Believe me; they will take advantage of it. They may not be able to articulate any thought processes, but they instinctively know when they can get away with something. This gives us another opportunity in training.

Suppose you are in traffic and late for an appointment and

something is going on in the backseat that would typically require discipline. You can threaten to do it when you are able to stop the car or later when you are home, but that is not as effective. One reason is because it is easy to forget, and then inconsistency pops its ugly head again. It is also better to deal with an issue at the moment it is happening.

Say, "Johnny, what you just did deserves _____. You have been told not to do _____, and I am going to give you grace. Do you know what grace means?" If you have done this before, little Johnny will say, "I deserve _____, but you are going to give me grace." You will say, "Yes, Johnny, and that is what Jesus has done for us."

At another time, perhaps during devotions, give a good explanation of grace and favor and how we are saved by grace. Giving grace saves the day in a predicament without being inconsistent, and it gives you the opportunity to teach one of God's principles.

One time when Ann was about to receive her discipline, she hollered out, "Give me *grapes*, please!" Now how can you help but giggle? Nonetheless, consistency is necessary.

Be wise with giving grace. If you do it too often or with the same situation, it will cease to be effective.

**Making a Respectful Appeal**

Another time when it might be tempting to not be consistent or to follow through with something you requested is when a decision was made quickly without much thought, or you didn't understand the whole picture. Let's face it, we can change our minds, and that is okay. The trick is being sure that your mind is not being changed based on bad behavior.

Typically, when children don't get their way, they cry, argue, plead, stomp their feet, or in some way demonstrate a bad attitude. None of this is good behavior. The temptation for the adult is to wear down and give in. Guess what that does? It reinforces the behavior that is not pleasing. When I am with a group of kids, it does not take me long to know which ones get their way based on bad behavior or have never been taught to respond appropriately to authority.

**The Value of an Appeal**

We taught our kids how to be respectful and make an appeal. The principle comes from the story of Daniel and his three friends, Shadrach, Meshach, and Abednego. They were being groomed for the king's service and were given the best foods that the king had to offer. However, the banquet meat and wine went against their Jewish laws. Daniel went to the chief eunuch and requested that they not be required to eat the food served but rather vegetables and water only. The eunuch's concern was that their preference would not be healthy for them. Daniel respectfully asked for him to test their request for ten days. At the end of the ten days, Daniel and his friends appeared healthier, so their request was granted. This story is from the first chapter of Daniel.

We taught our kids that when they did not like an answer or a request we made of them that they were to say, "Mommy (or Daddy), may I make an appeal?" We, of course, would say, "Yes." The child was given the opportunity to make his or her case. This gave us an opportunity to reconsider and possibly change our mind. The rule was that if we did not change our mind, then the final answer must be accepted. Any whining or demanding would end with discipline.

We taught our kids that when they did not like an answer or a request that we made of them that they were not allowed to whine, cry, or have an attitude. In fact, an attitude or misbehavior would never get them their request.

This was an excellent way to teach them to follow the same pattern with others in authority, whether a teacher, a coach, or eventually a boss. Over time, with further training, they would learn some techniques from the story in Daniel. Notice that Daniel had a good relationship with the eunuch. It is important to be well mannered and develop relationships with those in authority. When a need to make an appeal arises, then teach them to pray for favor.

Next, notice that Daniel explained his convictions without condemnation to others. Your children will be learning how to make their case in a respectful, non-threatening way.

Through the discussion with the eunuch, Daniel discovered the goals that the eunuch had and was able to make a suitable suggestion.

Another illustration of making a respectful appeal is with Timothy, Paul's protégé. He was in the position of pastoring and had authority over people in his congregation. Timothy's church was troubled with false teachers, and if older men were wrong, then Timothy would need to deal with them in a very respectful way. He was to exhort or appeal to them as he would his own father. (See 1 Timothy 5).

In the South, we call this diplomacy. This process will teach your kids the art of diplomacy, the skill of dealing with people tactfully. Negotiating tactfully will bring favor and open doors throughout life. Respecting authority with these guidelines will be well served.

## *Prayer Corner*

**Reality check:** Do you excuse misbehavior? Are you consistent? Do you take the opportunity to correct? Are your expectations made clear? Do you train on how to respect authority?

**Prayer:** Lord, sometimes it is downright hard to be consistent, and sometimes I just don't know what to do. I ask You to take me by the hand and teach me, guide me, and show me how to do proper corrections. I pray for my child to grow up with wisdom and not foolishness. In Jesus' name. Amen.

# Chapter 9
# *When to Start Training*

*"But even now .... gather the children,
even the nursing infants."
(Joel 2:12a, 16b GW)*

The spirit is with the child at conception. This was explained in detail in chapter seven. Let's review. Humans are created in the image of God (Genesis 1:26). The human spirit is what differentiates humans from animals. Babies are born with a body, soul, and spirit. The Bible supports this: *"Now may the God of peace Himself sanctify you completely; and may your whole spirit, soul and, body be preserved blameless at the coming of our Lord Jesus Christ"* (1 Thessalonians 5:23 NKJV). Just as the body and soul grow and develop, so does the spirit. The spirit is the power behind the body and soul and is influenced by either light or darkness or, in other words, from God or Satan.

The embryonic ear develops between the third and seventh week. The spirit of the child is ready to receive. Where does faith come from? *"Faith comes by hearing, and hearing by the word of God"* (Romans 10:17).

John the Baptist leaped in Elizabeth's womb when she heard Mary's greeting, and she declared, *"For indeed, as soon as the voice of your greeting sounded in my ears, the babe leaped in my womb for joy"* (Luke 1:44 NKJV).

Another example of a young spirit receiving from the Lord is Jeremiah: *"Before you were born I sanctified you; I ordained you a prophet to the nations"* (Jeremiah 1:5b NKJV).

I heard a story of a third-grade girl refusing to color a witch in school on Halloween. When the teacher spoke to her father about it, he was perplexed, because they had never taught her about witches. Later, her parents realized that since she was conceived, they had been reading the Scripture out loud. They concluded that the Spirit of God began working on their little one even before she was born.

When Ann was 3, she insisted on praying the prayer of salvation. We had been telling her about Jesus since she was born. Gene led her in a prayer, and her countenance began to shine, and she was full of joy. On one occasion, my Bible study teacher kept her while I had an appointment. Upon returning and thanking her, she said, "No thanks needed. We had a delightful time. Ann told me all about the latter days, including the rapture, tribulation, and second coming. I have never seen one so young know so much about the Bible."

You see, long before a child can speak, they can hear and understand. Long before they can articulate a single concept, they have understanding. It is never too early to begin training.

We have seen examples from Scripture and modern day examples of starting our training early. Let me encourage you to also meditate on this passage to draw your own conclusions: *"Whom will he teach knowledge? And whom will he make to understand the message? Those just weaned from milk? .... For precept must be upon precept, precept upon precept, line upon line, line upon line, here a little, there a little"* (Isaiah 28:9-10 NKJV).

I have worked in children's ministry for years, and as the director of the department, I was able to interact with a variety of age groups. I could honestly see child-like faith change as a child grew older. For those with nominal training, the child-like faith turns into skepticism very early. For those with purposeful training, the child-like faith continued to develop and strengthen.

Preschool is a great time to speak truth to children. Sadly, what do most churches do? They babysit and offer coloring pages or videos.

Preschool kids have a short attention span. Repeat simple sentences over and over. For example, if you are teaching them that God created everything, then as you read a picture book say over and over, "God created the (say picture image, like trees)." As you take a walk, repeat the phrases. If your preschooler has started talking, ask, "Who made the trees? Who made the sun?"

You can apply this idea to other themes, such as "God loves you. God loves (say family name)." Later ask, "Who does God love?"

Let your baby, toddler, or child - *hear* you pray and *see* you read Scripture. They learn by watching, and soon you will see them doing what you do.

Little ones learn by using all five senses. If you are telling the story of Jericho, start marching and make it fun. Try to do it silently as the Israelites did. Blow your pretend trumpets. Pretend to run over the flattened walls (Joshua 6).

### Taste and See

Psalm 34:8 says, *"Taste and see that the LORD is good."* Taste-test a variety of fruits. Incorporate a teaching on the fruit of the Spirit: *"The Holy Spirit produces this kind of fruit in our lives: love, joy, peace, patience, kindness, goodness, faithfulness, gentleness, and self-control"* (Galatians 5:22-23a NLT, second edition).

- Admire the shape of an apple, and think about **love** as you taste it.
- Together, pop a grape in your mouth and say, "Oh! This tastes like **joy**."

- Gently chew on a banana, and reflect the softness of **peace**.
- Dramatically have a hard time opening a pineapple, and say, "Opening this pineapple takes **patience**!"
- Carve a watermelon, and **kindly** share it with one another.
- Grab a handful of blueberries or strawberries, and delight in their **goodness**.
- Divide up an orange, and say, "Orangcha glad God is **faithful**?" Have some fun, and put the peeled wedge in your mouth, covering up your teeth.
- Rub the skin of a peach on your skin, and declare, "This is **gentle**."
- Put your toddler's favorite fruit in front of him and say, "Let's wait five minutes before eating to practice **self-control**."

**Character Qualities**

I came up with some character qualities that animals or insects have, and put them on 3x5 cards. I would build an object lesson around these character qualities. When we would see the animal, we would repeat the character quality and Bible verse that went along with it. I was able to find some songs or jingles that also went along with the character qualities. Below is a picture of the front and back of a few cards, and the text is some examples of what is on the cards. I kept these handy in a decorated 3x5 card box, for quick and easy use.

 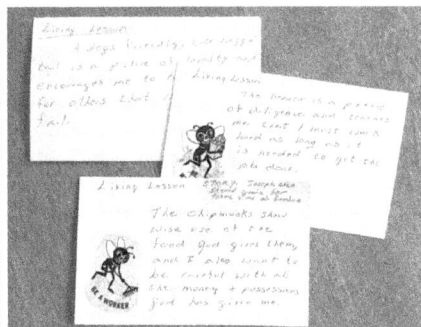

- **Dogs:** Dogs are **loyal**. A dog is always there to meet me and happy to see me. His friendly, wagging tail is a picture of loyalty and encourages me to have **loyalty** for others that will never, ever fail. Proverbs 21:21 says, *"Whoever tries to live right and be loyal finds life, success, and honor"* (NCV).

- **Cows:** Cows are so **generous**; they give us milk to drink. *"A generous person will prosper; whoever refreshes others will be refreshed"* (Proverbs 11:25).

- **Ants:** Ants are **wise**, **self-motivated**, and strong laborers. *"Take a lesson from the ants, you lazy fellow. Learn from their ways and be wise! For though they have no king to make them work, yet they labor hard all summer, gathering food for the winter"* (Proverbs 6:6-8 TLB).

- **Sheep:** Sheep are **good listeners** and can hear the voice of their shepherd. The Bible says, *"The sheep hear his voice; and he calls his own sheep by name and leads them out"* (John 10:3 NKJV).

- **Beaver:** The beaver is **diligent** and teaches me to work hard as long as it is needed to get the job done. Proverbs 13:4 says, *"A sluggard's appetite is never filled, but the desires of the diligent are fully satisfied."*

- **Chipmunks:** Chipmunks are **thrifty** and wise in gathering their food. I want to be careful will all of the money and possessions God has given me. *"It is required that those who have been given a trust must prove **faithful**"* (1 Corinthians 4:2). Story: Joseph stored grain for future time of famine.

- **Bees:** Just as I love to get another bite of honey, so do I love to get more of God's Word. The Bible says, *"How sweet are your words to my taste, sweeter than honey to my mouth!"* (Psalm 119:103) This is one of my favorite sayings, and I would often say it and offer a little honey treat before teaching Bible study for both adults and kids.

The sky is the limit for ideas of using things that are common to teach the spiritual to babies, toddlers, and preschoolers. Let these ideas be a springboard for your creativity, and expand this list. If you homeschool, you can take this to a whole new level with your teaching.

**Promises**

Make a Rainy Day Box to have meaningful fun on rainy days. Fill it full of promises.

Talk about:

- Promises. Fill the box with Bible verses that are God's promises, and pick one out.
- The rainbow, the Covenant we have with God (Genesis 9:8-17).
- How God sends rain to the just and the unjust (Matthew 5:45).
- Noah (Genesis chapters 6-9).
- Anything the *Rainy Day Box* reminds you of.

**News Flash!** Children do not have a junior Holy Spirit. They have the same one that adults do. Their spirit can be developed and trained.

---

## *Prayer Corner*

**Reality check:** Have you been ignoring the spiritual development of your baby, toddler, or child, thinking they don't understand? Are you reading this at just the right time and having an Aha! moment as you understand more of what to do?

**Prayer:** Lord, I confess that I didn't understand how to train my child when he/she was a baby or toddler. I ask You to restore the years of ignorant neglect. Give me wisdom and a strategy to make up for lost time and to make the most of every opportunity. I approach this with trust in You as my guide and not out of anxiety from the neglect.

Lord, _____ is still young enough for me to implement these ideas. I know these ideas are simply a springboard for You to give me creative ideas on any topic we want to impart. I am listening, Lord. Give me fresh ideas and activities for Your Word to be fun and exciting. In Jesus' name. Amen.

# Chapter 10
# How to Train Jesus' Way

*"Take My yoke upon you and learn from Me, for I am gentle and lowly in heart, and you will find rest for your souls."*
(Matthew 11:29 NKJV)

We can learn how to train through the way that God trains us, His children. The Bible says, *"Here is what I want you to know in your hearts. The LORD your God guides you, just as parents guide their children"* (Deuteronomy 8:5 NIRV). And, *"Since my youth, God, you have taught me, and to this day I declare your marvelous deeds"* (Psalm 71:17).

Do you feel totally inadequate for the job? Most parents do! They come home from the hospital with their little bundle of joy, not having a clue how to begin raising a godly young man or woman. No worries! Give all your weaknesses to the Lord, and He will be your strength. We can't train in areas we are not strong in, so praise God for His promises: *"For when I am weak, then I am strong"* (2 Corinthians 12:10b NKJV) and *"... whose weakness was turned to strength"* (Hebrews 11:34b). That is good news. If we are honest with ourselves and with God, He can work through us as we become mighty and adequate in spirit.

Jesus and God's Word do not change. Therefore, teach godly principles from Scripture. Don't teach standards. Standards change over the years along with the culture. I heard a conference leader say, "What one generation accepts in moderation, the next will accept in excess." It doesn't take a sociologist to see that this is true. The history of TV programming validates this maxim. One of the most popular shows of the 50s, "I Love Lucy," had married couples in twin beds and

> *Principles stay the same, but standards change.*

could not use the word "pregnant." Need I point out the comparison of what is accepted today?

**Object Lessons**

Object lessons are so valuable that it is worth repeating a principle from part one, chapter 4. I am currently a director for Kids in Ministry International, and we dedicate a whole class in our school to object lessons called "Thou Shall Do Object Lessons."[6]

We have heard it said, "You can lead a horse to water, but you can't make him drink." Skilled teachers will add this: "*But* you can give him a salt tablet to make him thirsty!" Jesus was a Master Teacher, and He knew how to create a thirst and develop curiosity. Let's learn from His example of using stories, parables, and the familiar to explain the unfamiliar. I have already pointed out that as a children's ministry worker, we call this "object lessons." As you study Jesus, pay attention to His teaching techniques, and ask the Holy Spirit to give you creative ideas to imitate His methods. With Nicodemus, He pointed to the wind to explain the spirit. With the woman at the well, He related physical thirst to give hope for eternal satisfaction. With the familiar traits of salt and light, He made clear their destiny.

What about with you? How does He draw you in? Notice He used parables to conceal truths to the unbelievers *and* to create curiosity with the disciples. When the disciples didn't understand, they came a little closer and asked questions (see Mark 4:1-20, note verse 11). Fellowship happened. You see, when He gives you a vision or a dream or a thought that you don't understand, He wants you to come and talk to Him about it. He loves conversation. If you understood everything, would you have a need to "come a little closer?" Hint: This is another thing to train your kids in — to continue to press into Jesus for answers when He gives your children dreams and visions. When they come to you with questions, point them to Jesus for the answer. Keep the discussion open as you share what Jesus is saying.

I am going to state the obvious here: Jesus was born a Jew, and He was raised Jewish, with all of the typical Jewish customs, ceremonies, and traditions of the day (Luke 2:22, 42; 4:16). We see this many times as Jesus and His disciples prepared for Passover or Hanukkah or Feast of Tabernacles. He wore the typical prayer robe, participated in the synagogue, practiced the trade of his father; his disciples were Jewish, and they called him "Rabbi." The disciples sought Him because they believed the Torah and the prophets (Luke 4:17, 21:37; John 1:45-47, 4:31).

As soon as children could speak, they were taught the Shema (pronounced "shuh-maw"). The Shema was a call to worship and prayer and was recited every morning upon awakening and upon retiring at bedtime. From an early age, children understood the Jewish confession of faith. The example we have from Jewish culture is to train children to worship and to pray from the very beginning of life.

Dedicated Jews took the idea literally to involve their whole body, soul, and spirit, so they would bob back and forth from the waist as they recited the Shema and prayed.

Another custom from the Shema is for Jewish men and boys to wear the phylacteries, little leather boxes with Scripture verses inside.[7] They strap them on their foreheads and arms when praying. It reminds them to keep God first in their thoughts and minds. This recognition of the constant presence of God helps remind them to stay pure and away from sin.

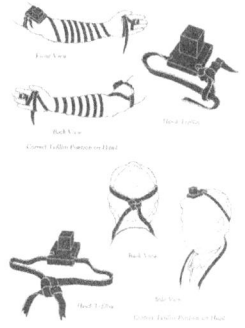

Knowing all of this, teach the Shema to your children and, like the Jewish people, put your whole heart and body into it. Bob back and forth as you recite it. Make it a fun experience.

**Shema**

*"Hear, O Israel: The LORD our God, the LORD is one.*
*Love the LORD your God with all your heart*
*and with all your soul*
*and with all your strength.*
*These commandments that I give you today*
*are to be on your hearts.*
*Impress them on your children.*
*Talk about them when you sit at home*
*and when you walk along the road,*
*when you lie down, and when you get up.*
*Tie them as symbols on your hands*
*and bind them on your foreheads.*
*Write them on the doorframes of your houses*
*and on your gates."*
*(Deuteronomy 6:4-9)*

We can see from the Shema and Jewish tradition that the time to train is *all the time*. When my kids were growing up, I used these verses as a guide to model how to incorporate teaching godly principles in our everyday life. At that time, I did not understand the importance of teaching them to recite the Shema.

A more modern way to interpret verses six and seven would be: "These commands I give you today should be in your heart. Teach them diligently to your children, and talk of them when you sit in your house, when you drive to school or shopping or wherever you are going, when you prepare for sleep, and when you get up in the morning."

Likewise, as you go about life, take advantage of the activities you are doing with your kids to teach them godly principles.

**Putting It into Practice**

How do we put this into practice? The sky's the limit with ideas!

1. When gardening, teach about reaping and sowing.

2. When cooking, teach about "a little yeast leavens the whole batch."

3. When bathing, teach about being washed in the Word of God.

4. When a commercial comes on while you're watching TV, talk about the message. What do they want you to believe? Is it true? Can you discern and decide for yourself?

5. When life happens, is there a lesson? We had a little friend who broke her leg and was hospitalized for surgery and needed traction. The accident occurred because she ran into the street after being instructed not to. I privately used her misfortune to point out to my kids the importance of obedience. This really made an impact on my kids when they saw the consequence of her disobedience. We also used the opportunity to learn how to minister to one another. We visited her in the hospital with a gift and prayed with her.

More on the Shema in chapters 12 and 14.

**Teach Bite-size Truths**

Isaiah 28:10 says, *"For precept must be upon precept, precept upon precept, line upon line, line upon line, here a little, there a little"* (NKJV).

My mother-in-law was a first-grade teacher. She used to tell me that we can teach kids anything; we just need to do it in small segments. She was speaking academically. The same principle is true with spiritual training. There are so many concepts that I have taught my kids and many others that most adults don't think are possible. It seems that most believe that one must be an adult before he or she can learn to pray for the sick, have discernment, hear the voice of God, give an encouraging or comforting prophecy to another, and much more. Just like you teach a child how to wash the dishes or make a bed by following step-by-step instructions, so you also teach the spiritual concepts.

This summer I taught my 5, 6, and 8-year-old grandkids how to "can." Yes, I said "can" — as in blueberry jam and bread and butter pickles. What could be more fun than to smash blueberries or slice cucumbers? They were so proud to give their own creations later to other family members. Here are some of the small steps that they learned and the corresponding pictures.

- They had a blast smashing the blueberries (1). Yes, they washed their hands first. And yes, as an adult I use a potato smasher. But why not do it this way?
- This is so fun for them to learn new techniques and a few math skills along the way.
- They learned to zest. (2)
- They learned to be precise (3) and give it a quarter-inch headspace and wipe the rim before putting the lid on — all preparation for sealing the jars.
- The joy is the finished product as a special gift for other family members (4).

 1.
 2.
 3.
 3.
 4.

**Training Stage, Not Trusting Stage**

Could they do it alone next time? No, we are still in the training stage, not the trusting stage. However, a few more times with guidance, and they will have this!

**Plead the Blood of Jesus Training**

Now it's time for an example of step-by-step training in pleading the blood of Jesus. I have heard other teachers or parents say that they don't think kids can handle a teaching on the blood because it is so gory and scary. When I hear them talk and see the expression on their faces, I realize that they think of blood in the "Halloween version."

When I teach the kids, my attitude is one that reflects that Jesus' blood is priceless, imperishable, incorruptible, and used as a love gift to me! (See 1 Corinthians 15:50, 1 Peter 1:23.)

Every year we do the Passover with our family along with several other families. It is a story full of symbolism, so they have learned that Jesus is our Passover lamb. The story of Exodus is told, and everyone understands that the Israelites had to sacrifice a lamb and apply the blood to the doorposts for protection. The power of the blood of the lamb/Christ is explained.[8]

Symbolically and for the purpose of teaching, we hung a red (blood) drape on our doorposts with the cross in view. *"Defend my cause and redeem me; preserve my life according to your promise"* (Psalm 119:154). These terms are taught:

**Plead:** A legal term meaning "argue" or "declare"

**Cause:** A bad situation in which a person finds himself

**Redeem:** To set free

**Activation:** The children then applied what they learned and prayed for protection over themselves and their families.

Their prayer may have gone something like this:

- For someone sick: "I plead the blood of Jesus over _____ and command the disease to go in the name of Jesus."

- For someone not saved: "I plead the blood of Jesus over _____ so that she will desire to say 'yes' to Jesus."

- For someone in danger: "I plead the blood of Jesus over the soldiers who are at war and pray for protection."

The Kids in Ministry curriculum, *The Blood of Jesus,* can be used for family devotions.[8]

Prayerfully, you can see that kids can learn what adults can learn, just in smaller bites. What do you want to teach your kids?

---

## *Prayer Corner*

**Reality check:** Have you limited what you are teaching your children? Have you thought they were too young to learn or to actively apply what they are learning? Have you been inspired by new possibilities? Are you open to what the Holy Spirit can do through you and your kids?

**Prayer**: Father, forgive me for not understanding or purposefully teaching my kids some of the deeper truth of Your Word. Forgive me for not knowing how to activate them into practicing the things that Your Word says that a believer can do. Give me creative ideas, and show me the opportunities that are waiting for us. Help me to break down the deeper truths into bite-size steps so that they can understand and apply it. In Jesus' name. Amen.

## Chapter 11
# *Who Is This Kid?*

*"Be sure you know the condition of your flocks, give careful attention to your herds."*
*(Proverbs 27:23)*

One of the foundational verses that we are using throughout this book is Proverbs 22:6: *"Train up a child in the way he should go, and when he is old he will not depart from it"* (NKJV).

**Additional Advice from Carol Kohl:** *Listen*

Recently, I contacted Carol Kohl, my mentor, to let her know that thirty-some years later, her words to me were almost in book form. She wanted to be sure that everyone understood the importance of Proverbs 22:6 — phrase by phrase. Her emphasis was on the importance of *"in the way he should go,"* meaning one must understand the personality characteristics of your child. This chapter is valuable in giving you tools and tips for understanding the "way" of each one of your kids and, therefore, adapting your training to their specific God-given personalities and giftings.

Understand that "the way" in Proverbs 22:6 indicates characteristics or personality. It is the same word used in Proverbs 30:19: *"The way of an eagle in the sky, the way of a snake on a rock, the way of a ship on the high seas, and the way of a man with a young woman."* Training involves knowing what makes your child tick. God created him or her this way before birth, and it is up to you to discover your child's individuality. Understanding this will give you much wisdom in the growing-up years.

Carol emphasizes this because the approach to training will be different for each child, and understanding each child will help in their training as well as preventing hurtful comparisons.

**Knowing Your Child**

All three of our kids have different personalities, temperaments, and interests. I have seen families with eight kids, and no two are the same. Even identical twins have their own individual style. In his book *You and Your Child*, Chuck Swindoll emphasizes the importance of getting to know your child: "The effectiveness of training your child is in direct proportion to the extent you know your child."[9]

Why is this important? It is important because you will train each child differently according to his or her interests and personality. The three main areas that we are training in — social, physical, and spiritual — will be different for each child. We have one child with a one-track mind in sports. Pete was "Mr. Baseball." Knowing that, we did all we could to help him succeed in the sport. We had another one who tried everything — swimming, golf, soccer — and changed sports every season, enjoying the variety. Our daughter pursued gymnastics, cheerleading, and stunt acting.

As he grew older, Pete developed a carbon copy of his dad's business skills. His education and career continue to reflect that. As they discuss business strategies, they are often on the same wavelength.

Sometimes your children's "way" may not be yours or even part of your own instincts. Don't force them to be like you or follow your dream. You know the saying, "You can't put a square peg in a round hole." Mark has an artistic personality and pursued photography and graphic arts. His thoughts for combining the arts and business are instinctively different than a mainstream business person. In order to understand the thought process that was so different than our instincts, we sought out other successful artists. This led to useful discussions and valuable strategies. We wanted Mark to be free from who we are and free to be Mark.

From the time Ann could communicate, she has always loved the role of "mommy." She didn't just play with her dolls; she took every child younger than her under her wing to nurture. She loved teaching and organizing. Today, she lives her dreams as a great mommy to three precious kids and is the director of her homeschool organization. There were so many natural occasions to help encourage her desires, but we also helped her seek out educational opportunities at appropriate times.

Allowing your child to chase his or her interests has other benefits, too. If they are busy with activities that they enjoy, then they will be less likely to get into drugs and alcohol. There are more people such as coaches, teachers, other parents, and even teammates who are also looking out for your child's interests. Unspoken accountability goes a long way!

Knowing how your child responds to blessings and discipline will also help you be a more effective and loving disciplinarian. Much more of this will be discussed in chapter 16.

**Gifts of the Spirit and Personality Traits**

I found it fascinating and helpful to consider what the motivational spiritual gifts were of my kids and their personality types. The more understanding we have of who our kids are and what makes them tick, the better. With both the gifts and the personality traits, there are strengths and weaknesses. Knowing this helps one capitalize on the strengths and compensate for the weaknesses. I will give a brief summary of these. For more information, there are plenty of good books specializing on these topics.

**Motivational Spiritual Gifts**

There are many ways to unpack the spiritual gifts that are available to believers. I choose to look at them this way: We each have a motivational gift given to us by God (Romans 12:3-8). This gift is what makes us tick. It motivates us to do ministry, given to us by the local Body, and it can be manifested in several different ways. Are you confused yet? Bear with me, and let me explain. My motivational gift is exhortation. I will do almost any ministry where I know that someone will be encouraged. It can look like teaching, helping, and even administration. It could manifest as a word of wisdom or knowledge, faith, healing, discerning of spirits, and more. From my example, you can see that I am using a variety of gifts, but only one motivates me. Believe me, administration is not my motivational gift — it is a learned skill — so I use it when needed to encourage or to accomplish another ministry.

The motivational gifts are what I am going to explain. I am taking the stance that there is one motivational gift. Your little Susie or Johnny might be very gifted in other ministry gifts, but this is for the purpose of discovering motivation. The Bible says in 1 Peter 4:10 that one gift is to be used for service: "Each of you should use whatever gift you have received to serve others, as faithful stewards of God's grace in its various forms."

Paul said that *"it is God who works in you both to will and to do for His good pleasure"* (Philippians 2:13 NKJV). This implies that as the motivational gift is used, God gives power and ministry gifts manifest.

Let's look closer at each of the motivational gifts. They are found in Romans 12:3-8: *"For I say, through the grace given to me, to everyone who is among you, not to think of himself more highly than he ought to think, but to think soberly, as God has dealt to each one a measure of faith. For as we have many members in one body, but all the members do not have the same function, so we, being many, are one body in Christ, and individually members of one another. Having then gifts differing according to the grace that is given to us, let us use them: if prophecy, let us prophesy in proportion to our faith; or ministry, let us use it in our ministering; he who teaches, in teaching; he who exhorts, in exhortation; he who gives, with liberality; he who leads, with diligence; he who shows mercy, with cheerfulness"* (NKJV).

Of course, Jesus has all seven of these gifts. We don't all have the same gift, but together we complete the Body of Christ. We can learn the skills of each other's gifts and enhance our own ministry. What fun it is to understand them and know who has what gift! You can capitalize on the gift to your advantage. At the same time, understanding the weakness helps you be more forgiving when someone with a different gift does something that would normally annoy you.

For example, we have a close friend who has the gift of organization. Sometimes, her obsession with details would drive me crazy. I would just want to get on with it. (I am sure that likewise, my relaxed approach drove her crazy) Once I understood her gifting, I asked her to help me organize my kitchen and some other things. All the while, I encouraged her on. I would say I got the better end of the deal!

You can see from this example that when we understand gifts, there is a paradigm shift in our attitude, and we become gifts to one another.

A simplistic test for trying to figure out what your motivational gift is would be to ask yourself what other believers do that annoys you. Very often, the very thing that you do so naturally is what makes you want to "pull out your hair" with other people when they don't operate the same way. However, the more you understand yourself and others through their giftings, the more you will begin to appreciate their gifts, and you will tolerate their perceived weakness.

The next two illustrations come directly from *Research in Principles of Life, Advanced Seminar Textbook* and explain motivational gifts in a nutshell. See if you can find yourself and your loved ones.[10]

**Understand the Basic Motivation of Each Spiritual Gift**

If each of the seven motivational gifts were represented in a family, and someone dropped the dessert on the floor, here is what each one might say and why they would say it.

1. **Prophet:** "That's what happens when you're not careful" (motivation: to correct the problem).

2. **Server:** "Oh, let me help you clean it up" (motivation: to fulfill a need).

3. **Teacher:** "The reason that it fell is that it was too heavy on the one side" (motivation: to discover why it happened).

4. **Exhorter:** "Next time, let's serve the dessert with the meal" (motivation: to correct the future).

5. **Giver:** "I'll be happy to buy a new dessert" (motivation: to give to a tangible need).

6. **Organizer:** "Jim, would you get the mop. Sue, please help pick it up; and Mary, help me fix another dessert" (motivation: to achieve the immediate goal of the group).

7. **Mercy:** "Don't feel badly. It could have happened to anyone" (motivation: to relieve embarrassment).

**Understand How Each Gift Responds in a Situation**

If seven Christians representing each of the motivational gifts visited a sick person in the hospital, here is what each one might say, based on the perspective of his gift.

1. **Prophet:** "What is God trying to say to you through this illness? Is there possibly some sin you haven't confessed yet?"
2. **Server:** "Here's a little gift! Now, I brought your mail in, fed your dog, watered your plants, and washed your dishes."
3. **Teacher:** "I did some research on you illness, and I believe I can explain what's happening."
4. **Exhorter:** "How can we use what you're learning here to help others in the future?"
5. **Giver:** "Do you have insurance to cover this kind of illness?"
6. **Organizer:** "Don't worry about a thing. I've assigned your job to four others in the office."
7. **Mercy:** "I can't begin to tell you how I felt when I learned you were so sick. How do you feel now?"

**Definition of Each Gift**

To continue to illustrate the definition of each gift, I will describe it through our family or friends. See if you can pick out yours and your loved ones' gifts from some of these descriptions. Keep in mind, we all have a little bit of all the gifts, and we learn to develop others. This exercise is looking for the bottom line — what makes a person tick.

1. **Prophecy:** Pete and our grandson Haynes have the motivational gift of prophecy. It looks a little different as one grows, but the basic traits are incorporated in the personality of the child. They want to do things right and are very alert to dishonesty. They see things in black and white, right or wrong. They have an ability to discern the truth and analyze a situation and to them, there are no gray areas.

**A clue to why this is their gift:** People who compromise or operate in the "gray" area bug them. They don't understand people who are not "all in" or who, in other words, do not have a wholehearted commitment.

**Today**, as an adult, Pete is able to use this gift in the business world to make wise decisions. Haynes is a child, and I am amazed as he picks up on things in his world and can discern truth. With both, they are also open to their own faults. They both have a gift of persuading others with the truth. The weakness of a prophet is the tendency to condemn himself. They are loyal friends. In fact, I marveled at Pete's wedding when I realized his lineup of groomsmen dated back to fourth grade. He had a friend from each place we had lived. Pete is a great motivational speaker and writer. (This motivational gift of prophecy is not to be confused with the prophet who declares, "Thus saith the Lord" or is able to prophesy over people. That type of prophet is a ministry or manifestation gift).

2. **Serving:** Ann is a server. At first glance, everyone would say she is a teacher because that is what she does. Teaching is not her motivation, but it is her ministry gift. Ann is quick to see and meet needs without regard to her time or strength. She has difficulty saying "no" when she sees another in need. The weakness is the tendency to serve beyond her own time and energy capacity. Ann can pick out great gifts for others because she is observant to their likes and dislikes. It frustrates her to see other people not notice or ignore obvious needs.

   **A clue to why this is her gift:** She is aware of others who do not step up to the plate and serve when there is a need. As a server, she will go out of her way to meet a need, and that is not everyone's gift. Of course, in her maturity and growth in her gift, she understands and now sees the other valuable gifts others have to offer.

**Today:** As a server, Ann often goes the extra mile, knowing that the extra touches will bring joy to the one receiving. The frustration side of this is "never having enough time for excellence." If you are on the receiving end of her service, you are blessed!

3. **Teaching:** We have a friend who is motivated by teaching. She has the need to check out all information and confirm it. She is quick to be able to pick out the false teachers who have a gift of communication but do not speak the truth. When teaching, her method is often very methodical. We can see that Dr. Luke liked it best this way when he wrote, *"Since I myself have carefully investigated everything from the beginning, I too decided to write an orderly account for you"* (Luke 1:3).

**A clue to why this is her gift:** As a teacher, she is not able to accept experience as a validation of truth. What irritates her are people who put experience over Scripture. She is a person who is always validating information through Snopes or more careful research.

**Today:** She has learned to put the Holy Spirit over her intellect and find the balance to following the Spirit over logic. She is also very quick to clarify misunderstandings and help others understand the sequence that led them from the right path. Proverbs 3:5-6 says, *"Trust in the LORD with all your heart, and lean not on your own understanding; in all your ways submit to him, and he will make your paths straight."*

4. **Exhorting:** My gift is exhortation. Before I learned these principles, I would have guessed teaching. I love to teach, but bottom line, my motivation for teaching is that it brings me joy when I see people's eyes get bright as the light goes on in their minds and spirits. Watching people grow spiritually is a delight. In fact, I still struggle with one of the weaknesses of this gift and keep my family waiting while I am still ministering. I can often see what the hindrance to spiritual growth is and prayerfully address it. I had to learn that I don't always have the answer, and it's not always up to me to make spiritual growth happen. As an exhorter, I encourage others to take some practical steps to accomplish the goals (do you see that throughout this book?). I will use my mistakes or bad situations as an opportunity to teach others not to repeat or to discover the positive. So, there is transparency with the encourager to share while training. I have had to learn to not "*cast my pearls among swine*" (see Matthew 7:6).

**A clue to why this is my gift:** It really bothers me when people do not do what it takes to grow spiritually or lose their desire to grow. I have learned not to take it personally. I clearly remember a day when a new person in our church came to one of my Bible studies and in the midst of it, pushed her Bible to the center of the table and said, "I do not like studying the Bible." I kept my composure and prayed. It didn't take long before we couldn't slow this person down with her spiritual growth. Almost 30 years later, she continues to love the Lord and serve Him wholeheartedly. I go to her for spiritual fellowship!

**Today:** My favorite way of exhorting is to be with a person or people and have a lively conversation with facial expressions and all the drama! It can be through a conference or lunch with a friend, but that personal experience is important. That is one reason I have struggled with writing this book. I much prefer the parenting classes or the one-on-ones with a young mom.

5. **Giving:** A giver is not necessarily wealthy. A giver has a unique ability to be able to use resources to multiply or invest in what they do have. They are usually very frugal and content with the basics. Often the giver is the one who is offering matching funds in order to encourage others to experience the joy of giving. They will also give sacrificially and usually anonymously. One of the misuses of the gift is having difficulty learning when to say "no" and giving into pressure from others who might take advantage. An example of a giver in the Bible is the little boy who gave his lunch to feed 5,000 (John 6:4-14).

**A clue to why this might be your gift:** Givers are annoyed when they see people are not trusting God in their finances.

6. **Organization:** My husband, Gene, has the gift of organization. He used it powerfully in the business world, and now our farm is in tip-top shape. He is able to visualize the end of a project and then create the steps needed to accomplish it. We can see this same trait in Nehemiah as he set his sights on repairing the walls of Jerusalem (Nehemiah 2). He is resourceful and knows the art of delegation. Gene can think through and spot details that will help complete a project. Another trait that served him well as a businessman was his ability to make quick and decisive decisions.

**A clue to why this is his gift:** It annoys Gene to see someone not set goals and make a plan to accomplish the goals.

> **Skill to learn:** I have discovered that organization is a learned trait. It is not my gift, but I use what I have learned. Friends have taught me how to organize my time and my laundry! I have learned skills that are not natural to me, but the tasks help me to operate more efficiently.

7. **Mercy:** Mark has the gift of mercy. He always has a tender heart toward others. Someone with this gift is able to relate to the feelings of others. He has a desire to remove hurts, which sometimes manifests with generosity and sometimes with helps. I have seen him give when no one was looking, just to meet needs or to give joy.

   **A clue to why this is his gift:** It bothers Mark when someone is in need, and no one is comforting or trying to meet the need. He can spot an insincere person quickly.

   **Today:** Interestingly, merciful people are often attracted to prophets, and Mark married someone with the characteristics of a prophet. They are opposites and balance one another out.

As you understand this for yourself, then you will be able to discern the gift that motivates your child. Hopefully, your appetite to learn more has been whetted. It is fun, and spiritual growth happens as one recognizes the weakness of each gift. (There I go again, practicing my gift of exhortation and wanting to see each of you discover your gift and your kids' gifts so you can grow through the weaknesses of them!)

**Personality Traits or Temperaments**

There are lots of books and tests on personality traits. In the 70s, I learned a lot about others and myself when I read *Spirit-Controlled Temperament* by Tim LaHaye. More recently his wife, Beverly LaHaye, has written *Understanding Your Child's Temperament*. Today, some of the names have changed, and teachings can be complex or simple. Since there is so much available both in books and on the Internet, I am not going to take the time to describe the varieties of temperaments. However, I would like to encourage you to look into it. For each one there are strengths and weaknesses. Again, this information helps you understand yourself and your loved ones. Knowing the weaknesses also helps one overcome them.

**Vision**

The Bible says, *"Where there is no vision, the people perish"* (Proverbs 29:18a KJV).

Once you know who your kids are and what makes them tick, give them vision. Believe in your children, and never doubt that God is working.

There will be a time when your kids will come up with their own dreams and visions, and when they do, if possible, encourage and edify them. In the meantime, while they are developing, begin planting seeds of what you believe about them.

For example, when Ann played with her dolls or took another child under her wing, I would tell her, "Someday you are going to be the best teacher ever!" or "Someday you will be the greatest mommy!"

When she was taking piano lessons, I would think of a great pianist. We had gone to a Bill Gaither concert and of course in the 80s Sandy Patti was amazing, and Ann could relate to her. As she practiced her piano, I would say, "You are going to be able to play as beautifully as Sandy Patti!"

Ann did not stick with the piano, but that is okay. She had seeds of affirmation and encouragement placed in her, and those same seeds could later be transferred to the next dream being explored. So, the same type of edification would continue while she tried gymnastics, dance, stunt acting, and cheerleading.

Pete was Mr. Baseball. This little guy had radar for balls. He could spot a ball in the most hidden places, and from the time he could crawl was finding and pitching them. I can't resist telling this story: We often moved with my husband's career and somehow missed the typical baby dedications at appropriate ages. So when Ann was 3, Pete was 2, and Mark a toddler, we dedicated all three. Ann and Pete were old enough to be standing on the stage. The gift from the pastor was a tiny Bible. Since they were old enough to hold their own, the pastor gave our "babies" their Bible. We were standing behind the pastor when he turned to address the congregation. Pete's Bible felt just right in his hands, and he threw out the greatest pitch to the middle rows! I was red-faced, but I knew in my heart that I was raising a pitcher!

We would take Pete to baseball games, and Gene spent a lot of time doing backyard baseball with Pete. I remember watching baseball on TV the day Pete Rose made his record number of hits. The game stopped, the stadium cheered, and Pete Rose's mom came running down from the stands to hug and congratulate him. So I would often say, "Pete, when you become a famous baseball player, I am going to be there just like Pete Rose's mom was there for him!"

Mark tried lots of different things, and we did the same thing for him by encouraging him in his interests. Seeds of edification can be transferred, and different interests are explored. He loved golf for a long while, and we would say, "Watch out, Tiger Woods!" He loved landscape photography and cameras, and our way of edifying him was to hang his art in our house and giving him opportunities to discover landscapes.

As young parents, we were visiting one of Gene's relatives. Their daughter had a large display of trophies and ribbons from being a champion baton twirler. As we were admiring the photographs that reflected her talent, her dad unknowingly gave us some great advice that we took to heart. He said that he wanted his daughter to be the best she could be, and they invested in lessons and coaches as she showed a willingness to practice and improve. We thought that was a great idea, so to the best of our ability, we also tried to provide excellent training for our kids' interests. Sometimes it was a friend with the same passion, and other times we hired coaches.

**Forever-changing Dream**

The most important thing is to encourage your child in his or her dream. It could be a forever-changing dream. That's okay. Go with the moment! Those seeds of encouragement will transfer to the next thing, and so will any other investment.

While I was writing this book, my daughter, who has three preschool kids, called and asked, "How do you figure out what to put your child in that will be the most effective? To do more than one thing is expensive." We were watching the Olympics and realized that just to achieve in one sport is sacrificial and costly.

The expense is a challenge, and figuring out the right one is not easy with every child. Lessons and paid activities don't have to start at a young age. In the beginning, pick out something that looks like fun for all, and just enjoy it. Like I said, Pete was obvious with his love for baseball, but Mark tried lots of different things before he settled on golf in high school. The Lord will give discernment on what is best for you and your family. The important thing is having an interest in what your children like and encouraging them.

Speaking of encouragement, sometimes as they grow older and are trying to refine their skills, encouragement could be hearing the "tough words." Gene and Pete would often analyze every detail of baseball plays. Understanding how to improve always improved his game. Casting the vision and encouraging also include tough love, and, done with the correct tones, it is healthy.

**The Giants in the Land**

*"There we saw the giants ... and we were like grasshoppers in our own sight, and so we were in their sight"* (Numbers 13:33 NKJV).

*"Caleb ... said, 'Let us go up at once and take possession, for we are well able to overcome it'"* (Numbers 13:30 NKJV).

What do you see? Do you see God's promises, or do you see "giants in the land"? This well-known picture of a kitty seeing a lion when he looks in the mirror[11] helps illustrate that success depends on what you see and how you "see" God.

> *I believe Joshua and Caleb had parents who intentionally taught them about God and helped them recognize His sovereign hand in their life experiences.*

You may be familiar with the story in Numbers of the Israelites entering Canaan, God's Promised Land. Moses first sent in twelve spies, one from each tribe. Ten came back with a great report of how the land was as wonderful as promised, flowing with milk and honey, and gave a "show and tell" of the fruit. The grape clusters were so big that two men had to carry them on a pole. However, in spite of the fact that God had said He was going to give them the land, they did not believe they were able to because they also saw "giants" in the land.

On the other hand, two spies, Caleb and Joshua, believed the Lord and said, "The Lord is with us. Do not fear them." Sadly, as the story goes, because of the lack of faith of the majority, they wandered for forty years, and only Joshua and Caleb were ultimately able to enter the Promised Land (Numbers 13).

I am about to step on some religious toes, but I would like to speculate that the faith of Joshua and Caleb had not just automatically sprung up because they were God's favorites. I believe they had parents who intentionally taught them about God and helped them recognize His sovereign hand in their life experiences. All twelve spies saw the same thing with their physical eyes. Ten saw giants because their spiritual eyes were not developed, and two saw God's promises through developed spiritual eyes.

I am reminded of another Bible character that also saw a giant and was able to reason that he could take on the giant. He based this not only on his faith in God but also on his belief in himself. Remember David and Goliath? David had faith in God, and, based on application from life experiences, he also believed God would work through him. Here he makes his case to King Saul: *"Your servant has been keeping his father's sheep. When a lion or a bear came and carried off a sheep from the flock, I went after it, struck it and rescued the sheep from its mouth. When it turned on me, I seized it by its hair, struck it and killed it. Your servant has killed both the lion and the bear; this uncircumcised Philistine will be like one of them, because he has defied the armies of the living God. The LORD, who rescued me from the paw of the lion and the paw of the bear, will rescue me from the hand of this Philistine"* (1 Samuel 17:34-37).

The time for the duel came, and Goliath started mocking the young Israelite coming to him for the challenge. David responded with faith in God and the trash talk typical of a young competitor — similar to what I have seen with baseball players: *"You come against me with sword and spear and javelin, but I come against you in the name of the LORD Almighty, the God of the armies of Israel, whom you have defied. This day the LORD will deliver you into my hands, and I'll strike you down and cut off your head. This very day I will give the carcasses of the Philistine army to the birds and the wild animals, and the whole world will know that there is a God in Israel. All those gathered here will know that it is not by sword or spear that the LORD saves; for the battle is the LORD's, and he will give all of you into our hands"* (1 Samuel 17:45-47). We all know the rest of the story — David did just as he declared!

**How Does This Apply to Casting a Vision?**

As parents, we need to be purposeful and intentional in building the faith of our kids. We should not only teach them the Bible stories, but as life happens, we should also look for God and see His hand. Doing this, you will not only build their faith in God, but their inner character will also be strengthened. Chuck Swindoll said, "Wisdom is simply looking at life from God's point of view. It is the ability to apply biblical principles to everyday life."[12]

Life does happen, and our Mr. Baseball had a big blow to his dream. His freshmen year of high school, he had trained and was ready to try out for the high school team. His little league career had proved valuable for him. You know the drill: The list is posted, and one by one the boys go and look for their names. Boys left the post either thrilled and confident or deflated. It was a sad day, not only for our Mr. Baseball but also for us. Moms suffer the heartbreak as well. It was a day spent in much introspection.

The next day, Pete dusted off his hurt and put his eyes on the prize for the next year. He spent a year continuing to play little league. He continued to work hard at training and had a successful year. His little league accomplishments were written in a local newspaper. And yes, he then had a successful and fun final three years of high school baseball.

Pete is a gifted thinker with business. My husband, who is also a businessman, has many discussions with Pete and always marvels at his natural instincts and his great attitude when "life happens." We give God all the honor and glory for the man Pete has become, but we also recognize that intentional training through life's ups and downs helped develop character and instincts.

No, he is not a professional baseball player. But all of the vision casting done as he worked hard at his baseball goals and the seeking of God in the midst of life circumstances, contributed to the successes and character he experiences now as an adult.

**Mighty Man of Valor**

The Lord has a plan for each of us and for our kids. He casts a vision and gives one identity and authority to fulfill His planned destiny. Often, His vision seems very unlikely. Consider the story of Gideon, a farmer who was hiding from the Midianites in the winepress, beating and separating the wheat. The angel of the Lord appeared to him and said, *"The Lord is with you, you mighty man of valor!"* (Judges 6:12b)

Picture the scene: Gideon and all of Israel were being terrorized by the Midianites, and they were crying out for help. The Lord found Gideon hiding and called him a *"mighty man of valor"*! If you were an Israelite you might be thinking, "Huh? Can't you do better than this, Lord? We were hoping for a superhero, not someone hiding and shaking his knees in fear!" Gideon saw himself as timid and was doing his best to be unnoticed and unassuming. But the Lord saw him as a mighty warrior.

The story continues, and the Lord worked with Gideon's doubts and fears and brought the best out of him. He was able to lead a small army to victory against a mighty multitude of Midianites (Judges 6-8). Casting a vision was the beginning of Gideon understanding his identity. Once he understood his identity, he was able to walk in his God-given destiny.

If the Lord uses the technique of casting a vision, in spite of what is apparent, how much more do you need to do the same with your young warriors for Christ?

What does the Lord call you and each of your kids (1 Peter 2:9)? Identity gives authority and confidence. Authority and confidence lead to destiny. Again, *"Where there is no vision, the people perish"* (Proverbs 29:18a KJV).

## *Prayer Corner*

**Reality check:** Do you know your child? Do you know what makes him tick? What is his personality type with strengths and weaknesses? What are his gifts? Have you noticed how he uses or misuses the gift he has been given? Have you used affirming words to cast a vision and help him to dream?

**Prayer:** Lord, help me to see the treasure that You have placed in my child. Help me to be able to participate in fashioning him to be all that you created him to be. Give me fresh ideas and strategy. In the areas where I do not relate, help me to understand him better. Lord, show me when I might be forcing myself or my desires on him. I want my kids to be free to be who you created them to be. May my words always be pleasing to You. In Jesus' name. Amen.

# Chapter 12
# *Where to Train*

Again, the Shema holds the key.

> **Shema**
>
> *"Hear, O Israel: The Lord our God, the Lord is one. Love the Lord your God with all your heart and with all your soul and with all your strength. These commandments that I give you today are to be on your hearts. Impress them on your children. Talk about them when you sit at home and when you walk along the road, when you lie down, and when you get up. Tie them as symbols on your hands and bind them on your foreheads. Write them on the doorframes of your houses and on your gates"* (Deuteronomy 6:4-9).

**We Teach Everywhere, All the Time**

In other words, impressing our kids with the truth of God's words and principles has no boundaries. We teach everywhere, all the time. Our faith is our lifestyle.

Being able to do this - starts with asking the Lord to show Himself to you in the everyday parts of your life. If He is part of your thoughts and heart, sharing His principles will be a natural part of your talk. *"For out of the abundance of the heart the mouth speaks"* (Matthew 12:34b NKJV).

After learning the Shema, Jewish children learn to "bless" at every opportunity. They have a prayer for every part of their lives, including when they are about to experience something new or even when they see the beauty of a flower or a sunset. It starts off like this: "Blessed are you, O Lord our God, King of the Universe, who has kept us in life and sustained us and allowed us to reach this moment …"

You don't have to say the prayer, but take every opportunity to express the beauty or specialness of God's creation. We have also taught our kids and now teach our grandkids to pray when we see an accident or hear an ambulance. They are alert to when someone says they are not feeling well and offer to pray for that person. Sometimes, with our grandkids, we have prayed for our restaurant server.

In other words, there are no limits to where you train. I know if you are reading this book, you already know not to limit their training to only dropping them off for Sunday school or VBS in the summer. Have fun with it, and explore God sightings and possibilities.

Where do we train? Everywhere, as we look for God-training opportunities!

**Practicing Discernment**

Philippians 1:9-10 says, *"And this is my prayer: that your love may abound more and more in knowledge and depth of insight, so that you may be able to discern what is best and may be pure and blameless for the day of Christ."*

Train your children in discernment, to be wise in that which is good and to be innocent of that which is evil.

We were on vacation in a mountain community, enjoying shopping and experiencing all of the sights and sounds of quaint mountain boutiques. We walked into one gift shop, and I suddenly felt a different spirit. I looked around to discern why and realized we were in a "New Age" shop that sold paraphernalia related to that belief system or lifestyle. My kids were elementary age. I had two choices: walk out and move on to the next store or use this as a teaching opportunity. I chose the latter.

The feeling I sensed was subjective. Each person discerns spirits differently and needs to learn how to read their own signals. As we walked outside to the sidewalk, I prayed for some wisdom and prayed the protective blood of Jesus over each of us for what we were about to do. I gave my kids some instructions: "Kids, while we were in that shop, I felt a spirit that was not the Holy Spirit. Who can tell me the source of other spirits?"

One of them piped up, "The devil."

I continued, "Yes, and for me, when I sense this, my nose feels like something is on it. Sometimes I feel a tightness in the air, and my body feels a slight pressure. For you, it can be totally different. If you are not aware, you might not feel anything at all. I want you to learn how the Holy Spirit in you shows you that there is a different spirit. For you, you could feel a knot in your tummy or a roughness inside. Just be aware. You have nothing to be afraid of as Jesus is part of this teaching lesson and we have prayed for His protection."

After our walk through the store and back out on the sidewalk, I asked the kids if they could put words to their discernment. We talked a bit more and then proceeded with our shopping.

About a week later, we were in a small fast food restaurant. Ann said, "Mom, I feel that other spirit. I think we need to get out of here." I paused for a second to increase my awareness, and I did not sense a thing. However, I wanted to respect and honor the discernment that Ann was experiencing. We gathered up our food and walked out to the car to finish our meal. The discussion and teaching of discerning strange spirits and what to do about it continued.

**Source of Power**

Fast-forward about 20 years. Gene and I took our 7-year-old grandson to the fair for a special day of fun. We were walking from one area to another when that discerning feeling suddenly hit me strongly. I thought, "What? Huh? Where is this coming from?" I began to look around. We had just walked past a fortuneteller. I led Haynes over to some nearby picnic tables to talk to him about it. We discussed that both God and the devil have supernatural power. The Lord wants us to discern and use the power that comes from the Holy Spirit but not the devil. We need always to be careful about the source of power.

I then explained to Haynes that we had just passed a vendor who was a fortune-teller and that I was first aware of the sensation of evil in my spirit before I saw the vendor who was practicing supernatural abilities using the devil as the source. I explained to Haynes how to begin developing discernment — about the same as I had with my kids 20 years earlier. With a prayer, we purposefully walked past the fortune-teller and once inside the next building, we again sat down to talk. After further discussion, it was evident that Haynes had a good understanding of the experience. Of course, we gave a full report to his mom. Later that week, Haynes and his mom were able to continue discernment training.

**Spirit of Knowledge, Spirit of Wisdom**

I hear someone saying, "We are to love everyone and not discriminate!" You are so right! Loving someone into the Kingdom should always be on our mind. But first, we need to learn to discern. The next step in any circumstance would be to pray and ask for the leading of the Holy Spirit. Of course, pray for the person and for his or her eyes to be open. Next, ask the Lord if there is a next step that involves you. You see, discernment is part of having the spirit of knowledge. After receiving that, ask for the spirit of wisdom. "What do I do with this knowledge?" Don't assume anything. Always ask the Lord, and train your youngsters to do the same.

From my experience, most adults don't think that children are able to learn about the discerning of spirits. We can teach kids anything we understand. We just have to break it down into bite-size segments. The world knows that kids can learn about the supernatural, and that is why we see so many media outlets cover the topic. Look around, and notice the best-selling Harry Potter books and the movies on vampires and witchcraft. These things are giving our kids a thirst for the supernatural, and they are going to seek it. Who will get to them first --the church, or the world?

**Challenge:** Are any of you writers? Storytellers? Media savvy? Let me challenge you to write the next supernatural best-selling novel — with a young believer in Christ with the power of the Holy Spirit as the star. This can be a teaching tool on how the unseen warfare is all around us, and our weapons of warfare are practicing discernment, using prayer, and hearing His voice. All the gifts of the spirit can be included in the storyline. The Harry Potter series has proven to us that kids are willing to read large books and that they are hungry for the supernatural. Who wants to go for it?

## *Prayer Corner*

**Reality check:** Do you take the time to see God in life's circumstances? Are you using every opportunity to glorify God and make His presence known?

Have you thought your children were too young to learn to discern? Have you thought they were too young to take authority in the spiritual realm? Have you let the world train them about witchcraft through the media? Kids are interested in the supernatural. The question is, who is going to get to them first to train them in the supernatural? The world? Or those who love Jesus?

**Prayer:** Lord, open my eyes and my ears so that I can see what Your Spirit is doing throughout my busy day. Give me eyes to see and ears to hear. Give me a strategy on how to make the most of every opportunity, with training my kids in mind. I love You, Lord, and I want to raise kids that see You in their lives and experience Your presence.

Lord, forgive me if I have only allowed books and movies to train my kids in the power of the supernatural. Give me insight, and strengthen my own ability to discern. Show me how to help activate discernment in my kids. In Jesus' name. Amen.

# Part 3:
## *What to Train*

# Chapter 13
# Wisdom and Godliness

*"By wisdom a house is built, and
through understanding it is established;
through knowledge its rooms are filled
with rare and beautiful treasures."*
*(Proverbs 24:3-4)*

Let's think about the structure of the house we are creating. We are raising a temple. What does it look like? Solomon was in the temple-building business, and we can learn much from him on how to raise the ideal temple in which the Holy Spirit will dwell.

The rooms are filled with the knowledge and understanding of God. What is inside is what really makes the house; it is full of pleasant and precious riches. As a mother, you build into your children the understanding and knowledge of the Savior, and that is how they obtain wisdom. Let's look further into how to raise our temple in which the Holy Spirit will dwell.

**Wisdom: The Five Ds**

Wisdom is the walls and roof, so we can see things from God's point of view. Solomon knew he needed wisdom (2 Chronicles 1). We need wisdom, too, and we need to train our little temples on how to get wisdom.

1. **Declare:** "I don't know it all! I need wisdom." Cry out to God.

2. **Depend:** Confess that you depend on Him for wisdom.

3. **Desire**: James 1:5 says to ask for wisdom if you desire it.

4. **Delight:** You delight in wisdom, and then God delights. He was delighted that Solomon asked for wisdom.

5. **Discover:** *"If you look for it [wisdom] as for silver and search for it as for hidden treasure, then you will understand the fear of the LORD and find the knowledge of God"* (Proverbs 2:4-5). Treasures of wisdom are hidden in Christ Jesus (see Colossians 2:3).

A fun gift that I would give to the girls using this verse was a purse filled with lots of fun things that little girls would delight in. I would say, "Just as you are having so much fun discovering the treasure in this purse, we need to search for God's wisdom." For a little boy, you can do the same using an appropriate type of bag.

Encourage daily readings of Proverbs. There are 31 chapters, one for each day of the month. Younger children could do smaller portions. Proverbs is rich in wisdom and was written by King Solomon, the wisest man in the Bible.

**Affirmations:** Say often at applicable times, "You are as wise as Solomon" and "That was a wise decision that you made." Talk about wisdom. Also, discuss how Solomon forgot his first love and got wrapped up in materialistic things.

**Foundation: Jesus Christ and Knowing Him**

The foundation of our house is Jesus Christ and our knowledge of Him. Let's take a look at 2 Peter 1:2-7 to see how to build our foundation:

*"Grace and peace be multiplied to you in the knowledge of God and of Jesus our Lord, as His divine power has given to us all things that pertain to life and godliness, through the knowledge of Him who called us by glory and virtue, by which have been given to us exceedingly great and precious promises, that through these*

*you may be partakers of the divine nature, having escaped the corruption that is in the world through lust. But also for this very reason, giving all diligence, add to your faith virtue, to virtue knowledge, to knowledge self-control, to self-control perseverance, to perseverance godliness, to godliness brotherly kindness, and to brotherly kindness love"* (NKJV).

**Recipe for a godly life: It all starts with faith.**

A. Where do we get everything we need for a godly life? Through our _____ of Him (hint: see verses two and three).

A godly life is having a focus on our living God, living with Christ-like attitudes, using Christ-like words, and having Christ-like actions. *This is what a "temple of the Holy Spirit" looks like.* This is our goal.

B. Pray as Paul prayed in Ephesians 1:16-23 for your little ones to *know God*. Remember, your most powerful prayers are in agreement with God's Word. Praying His Word is powerful and valuable. Insert your child's name into this prayer. Notice that to really *know* God the Father, the Holy Spirit is also involved. We are not praying for natural human knowledge but for spiritual, special insight. We are also praying for revelation, meaning that your child is "seeing" beyond the physical. The Holy Spirit is the one who opens our "eyes of understanding." To have *knowledge* only puffs up (see 1 Corinthians 8:1).

*"[I] do not cease to give thanks for you, making mention of you in my prayers: that the God of our Lord Jesus Christ, the Father of glory, may give to you the spirit of wisdom and revelation in the knowledge of Him, the eyes of your understanding being enlightened; that you may know what is the hope of His calling, what are the riches of the glory of His inheritance in the saints, and what is the exceeding greatness of His power toward us who believe, according to the working of His mighty power which He*

*worked in Christ when He raised Him from the dead and seated Him at His right hand in the heavenly places, far above all principality and power and might and dominion, and every name that is named, not only in this age but also in that which is to come. And He put all things under His feet, and gave Him to be head over all things to the church, which is His body, the fullness of Him who fills all in all"* (Ephesians 1:16b-23NKJV).

C. Let's see what else our recipe for godly living requires. Add each of these qualities to faith to build your foundation. Each one is an opportunity for training. Ask the Lord for creative ideas on how to impart each of these steps to godly living.

| | | |
|---|---|---|
| Faith | Romans 10:9 | Salvation |
| Virtue | 1 Peter 2:9 | Moral excellence, doing the right thing |
| Knowledge | Romans 12:2 | Dedication |
| Self-control | Titus 1:8; Galatians 5:22-23 | Fruit of the Spirit |
| Endurance | 1 Peter 4:12 | Fixed in one direction, even through suffering (going through the fire) |
| Godliness | Romans 8:29 | Desiring what God wants, the fear of the Lord |
| Brotherly kindness | 2 Corinthians 1:4 | Being alert and available to share |
| Love | Colossians 1:27-29 | Evangelism and discipleship |

D. *"For if these things are yours and abound, you will be neither barren nor unfruitful in the knowledge of our Lord Jesus Christ. For he who lacks these things is shortsighted, even to blindness, and has forgotten that he was cleansed from his old sins"* (2 Peter 1:8-9 NKJV).

1. I love promises in Scripture. We can really hang our hat on them and know that God's Word is true and faithful. Many have a condition to them. You can be alerted to the conditional promise when you see the "if" and then look for the condition.

If _____

Then   1. _____   2. _____  of  the

_____

Lack: 1. _____   2. _____

2. Do you agree that using this sequence is a powerful tool to build into the temple you are raising? Ask the Lord for creative ideas and increased awareness of opportunities to build from faith to love. In doing so, your child, the temple you are raising, will be a star witness for Him.

**Understanding Virtue**

Virtue or moral excellence seems to be something that is slipping away from our society. In the current atmosphere of our nation, knowing what is right or wrong is confusing, even for adults. Let's spend a little bit more time learning how to build this part of our foundation. One of the warnings in Scripture is that "even the elect" can be deceived, especially with the approach of the end times (Matthew 24:24).

The Bible says in 2 Peter 1:10, *"Therefore, brethren, be even more diligent to make your call and election sure, for if you do these things you will never stumble"* (NKJV). We have a promise with the "if" word. Notice another word that should always catch your attention: "therefore." Always go back and see what the "therefore" is there for. In this case, it is the "recipe for godly living" that we just spent time reviewing. This is a powerful promise! Write out the last four words of this promise from 2 Peter 1:10.

Y_____ W_____ N_____ S_____

Let's claim this promise for our kids!

**Building Virtue Exercises**

Some additional ideas to build virtue in little Johnny or little Susie:

- Train them to understand any and all authority and how to respond properly to authority, including making an appeal (see chapter 8).
- Train them to respect the rights of others.
- Train them on how to have a forgiving spirit, even when they don't feel like it.
- Expose what is wrong by asking, "Was that right?" or "Did you do the right thing?" While training, they may not always choose what is best, but God knows that and encourages us with this verse: *"The godly may trip seven times, but they will get up again. But one disaster is enough to overthrow the wicked"* (Proverbs 24:16 NLT, second edition).

- When age appropriate, teach sons about the adulteress woman and how sin leads to death (Proverbs 5).

- When age appropriate, teach daughters to recognize the hot-tempered man.

- Train them to look into the eyes of others and discern. The eyes are the windows of the soul: "The lamp of the body is the eye. If therefore your eye is good, your whole body will be full of light. But if your eye is bad, your whole body will be full of darkness. If therefore the light that is in you is darkness, how great is that darkness!" (Matthew 6:22-23 NKJV)

- Give affirmations. Say, "You are so special!" If children do not feel good about themselves, they will have doubts about God.

## *Prayer Corner*

**Reality check:** Have you considered the power of training your children in these steps of godliness? Are you living according to these steps? Do you recognize that we need both the Word and the Spirit to work through us and our children, to give supernatural insight and to "see" as God sees? *"Because our gospel came to you not simply with words but also with power, with the Holy Spirit and deep conviction. You know how we lived among you for your sake"* (1 Thessalonians 1:5).

**Prayer:** Lord, I lift up my kids to You. I want to train them in wisdom and how to obtain it. I also ask You to help me impart faith, virtue, knowledge, self-control, endurance, godliness, brotherly kindness, and love to my children. Give me the wisdom and the strategy to know how to do this. I claim that my kids will not be deceived or stumble. In Jesus' name. Amen.

## Chapter 14
# *Worship and Love God*

*"'Teacher, which is the greatest commandment in the Law?' Jesus replied: 'Love the Lord your God with all your heart and with all your soul and with all your mind.' This is the first and greatest commandment. And the second is like it: 'Love your neighbor as yourself.' All the Law and the Prophets hang on these two commandments."*
*(Matthew 22:36-40)*

**Spirit:** Let's look a little closer at what Jesus pointed out as the greatest commandment. He says to worship with all your heart (spirit): *"God is Spirit, and those who worship Him must worship in spirit and truth"* (John 4:24). This is obvious, as usually when we worship, we tend to naturally have our spirit engaged.

**Soul:** As we discussed in chapter 7, the soul is part of our emotions and our personality. Sometimes we may not "feel" like worshiping for a variety of reasons. Take a moment and relate to your own reasons when you have not been in the mood but worshiped anyway. This is what we also need to train our kids to understand.

Hebrews 13:15 says, *"Through Jesus, therefore, let us continually offer to God a sacrifice of praise — the fruit of lips that openly profess his name."* When I praise Him, even when I don't feel like it, then I am giving Him a sacrifice of praise. I intentionally turn my mood into worship and ask Him to receive it in spite of how I feel. Teaching to be *intentional* is the key to this type of worship.

**Mind:** The mind is part of the soul. Let's get specific on what this implies. How many times have you purposed to worship and your grocery list or to-do list keeps flashing through your mind? This is when you get to practice taking your thoughts captive: *"We demolish arguments and every pretension that sets itself up against the knowledge of God, and we take captive every thought to make it obedient to Christ"* (2 Corinthians 10:5).

Practice "renewing your mind" (see Romans 12:2). Again, be intentional in your thoughts, and worship the King of Kings, who has everything under control! Train your children on how to be intentional with their thoughts. *"Whatever is true, whatever is noble, whatever is right, whatever is pure, whatever is lovely, whatever is admirable — if anything is excellent or praiseworthy — think about such things"* (Philippians 4:8b).

**Singing and Music**

We talked about the Shema in chapters 10 and 12. Let's dissect the Shema a little more. We see that it includes the first commandment to love and worship God with all your heart. Worship and love of God should be one of the first things we train our children. I knew a music minister who told me that he values spending time in worship every evening with his kids as much as most value the habit of brushing teeth before bed. I must confess, I understood, but, not being a singer, I misunderstood worship and did not practice or train worship with this kind of dedication. If I were to do it all over again, I would find a way to incorporate worship as a habitual practice. My understanding was limited at the time.

With my experience as a children's minister and not always having a worship leader in my children's church, I have learned how to lead worship without using my singing voice. For those of you who are in my category, here are the tips I have learned and wish I had known when my kids were growing up:

1. **Worship recordings.** Obviously, we can use a quality CD or DVD or digital files. Listen to the song for sing-ability. The artist might sound anointed and fabulous, but if you can't sing along, then it becomes a listening time and not an interactive time.

2. **Declare the names and attributes of God.** Use your speaking voice, and begin declaring the names or attributes of God. Make it interactive by taking turns with your kids. For a change-up, take the challenge and encourage the kids to declare His names or characteristics in alphabetical order. Remember, God inhabits the praises of His people (Psalm 22:3).

3. **"Drum up" the supernatural.** I learned a huge tip from my friend, Pamela Ayers, when she taught "Understanding Children and Worship" for the School of Supernatural Children's Ministry. She suggested using drums. Anything can become a drum. The beat of a drum, when done under the anointing, invites the supernatural. Many cultures use percussion in worship. Perhaps because of the rhythm, it works in a similar way that dance expresses worship.

*"Praise Him with timbrel and dance; praise Him with the stringed instruments and flutes"* (Psalm 150:4 NKJV) (A timbrel is similar to a tambourine.)

I followed this example and combined it with some Scripture memory techniques, and the results were amazing.

I would pick out a verse and begin to clap out a beat. For example: *"The LORD is my light and my salvation; whom shall I fear? The LORD is the strength of my life; of whom shall I be afraid?"* (Psalm 27:1 NKJV) Everyone would join in, either clapping or tapping a makeshift drum. Within a few minutes, the presence of the Lord was evident. I would often ask one of my child singers to take it to the next level and sing the verse, using the beat we had established. Again, after a couple of rounds, everyone would join in. The result was worship, and often a new song would emerge.

I teach this when I do Kids in Ministry training for Power Clubs. One time in Mexico, we did this, and it developed into a powerful worship experience. That night, as I was leaving the facility, the pastor of the church said, "Lori, listen to the youth. They are practicing what you preached on this morning." I looked back at the front of the church where the youth ministry had started and began watching and listening to them worship by developing a song through Scripture and rhythm. I was puzzled and asked, "How did they know? They weren't in here." The pastor explained that the youth pastor had been in the sound booth that morning. Wow! I was so blessed to see how God works! He used someone (me) who used to think worship was all about music (ability to sing) to lead and train a group in worship — a small segment of worship but a breakthrough nonetheless! (If you could see me, I have big smiles now, knowing that if you are like me, you can do this with your family now and won't have to wait a lifetime to discover it!)[1]

Let me challenge you to train your children in the importance of worship; in fact, make it as important as brushing their teeth. I didn't do this, based on a poor understanding of worship. You can do it — with no excuses!

**Added Bonus**

When we are worshipping, we are ministering to the Lord. That is such a precious thought to me that it motivates me to intentionally spend more time in worship. Most children love to please, so be sure to include this in your training on worship. They are ministering to *Him*.

The phrase "ministering to the Lord" is often used in Scripture. When the Lord separated the tribe of Levi to be priests and carry the Ark of the Covenant, it was to *"stand before the LORD to minister"* (Deuteronomy 10:8).

Anna, the prophetess who was blessed by seeing baby Jesus, served God with fasting and prayers night and day (see Luke 2:36-38).

When Mary anointed Jesus' feet with costly oil and wiped His feet with her hair, she was ministering to the Lord (John 12:3). A fragrance filled the room. Likewise, we can minister to Jesus the same way — in the spirit.

This book is about preparing a temple for the Holy Spirit because the body of the believer is His temple. What happens in the temple? Continual praise and worship.

*"For by Him all things were created that are in heaven and that are on earth, visible and invisible, whether thrones or dominions or principalities or powers. All things were created through Him and for Him. And He is before all things, and in Him, all things consist"* (Colossians 1:16-17 NKJV).

## *Prayer Corner*

**Reality check:** We are told that the greatest commandment is to love Him with all of our heart, soul, and mind. What type of training have you done with your kids that help them learn to worship with all their heart (spirit)? All their soul? And with all their mind? Have you relied on the church to teach worship? Have you only relied on the time your child is at church to give him his worship experience?

**Prayer:** Dear heavenly Father, I confess that I didn't understand the importance of training in worship. I also didn't differentiate the training of worship that included the spirit, the soul, and the mind. Thank you for Your love toward us. You are the one who taught the Israelites to worship. Now, will You teach me how to worship in a deeper way and how to impart worship to my kids? Cause my kids to love You with all their heart, soul, and mind. I lift them each up to You and ask that You draw them in closer to You and baptize them with Your love. As they experience Your love, I know they will in turn fall in love with You and worship. You are the King of Kings, the Bright and Morning Star. You are the Creator of all things and the Mastermind of the whole universe — yet You look down upon my family and love us personally. We worship and adore You! In Jesus' name Amen.

# Chapter 15
# *Honor Your Father and Mother*

*"Honor your father and your mother,
so that you may live long in the land
the LORD your God is giving you."*
*(Exodus 20:12)*

*"Children, obey your parents in the Lord,
for this is right. 'Honor your father and mother' —
which is the first commandment with a promise —
'so that it may go well with you and that you may
enjoy long life on the earth.'"*
*(Ephesians 6:1-3)*

Honor seems like a lost art. We have become a society of "What's in it for me?" Honoring someone is a higher form of respect; it's giving a person great value. The Bible exhorts us to honor others, specifically our parents, the elderly, widows, the poor, and those in authority. Honor is a gift we give with our words and our actions. Giving someone high value and worth communicates that he or she is important to us.

Why is honor so important — and specifically to parents? Obviously, it is more pleasant to be in an environment where there is mutual respect and honor as opposed to disdain or mocking. Is it something we can choose to do or not do depending on the circumstance? (My answer will be addressed later.)

Let's get a deeper understanding. Consider where this commandment — the first one with a promise, the one specifically for children — is located in the sequence of the Ten

Commandments. The first four commandments point to God. The last five commandments are how we treat others. The commandment to children to honor their father and mother is sandwiched between these two threads. To small children, the parent is "their god." They love and worship the voice, the smile, the being of those two who have brought them into the world and take care of them. As they grow older and become aware of who God is, they can make the transition of the love they have for their parents to the one who created them and is due all honor and glory.

Honoring our parents is also part of the foundation of the last five commandments on how to treat our neighbor. Remember what Jesus said about the greatest commandment? *"Love the Lord your God with all your heart and with all your soul and with all your mind. This is the first and greatest commandment. And the second is like it: 'Love your neighbor as yourself.' All the Law and the Prophets hang on these two commandments"* (Matthew 22:37-40). How does all the Law hang on these two commandments?

The first four commandments relate to loving and honoring God, and the last five relate to loving our neighbor. In the middle is a transitional commandment for children to honor their parents. I propose to you that this is the cornerstone for all of our laws — connecting the divine with the human law. With this revelation of its importance, can you see why it has a promise of long life and that it will go well with you if you obey?

Later, when Jesus reaffirms the commandment, He includes a curse for not following it: *"'Honor your father and mother' and 'Anyone who curses their father or mother is to be put to death'"* (Matthew 15:4).

Training your child to honor and hold parents, authority, widows, and others in high esteem is part of being the *"temple for the Holy Spirit."* Paul exhorted the Ephesians, *"Do not grieve the Holy Spirit of God"* (Ephesians 4:30). Home life is much more pleasant with honor, and so is our temple where the Lord dwells.

**Teaching Respect at an Early Age**

It is important to begin teaching respect at an early age. Where does it begin? It begins with you! This is one of those characteristics of which it could be said, "What goes around, comes around" or, as the Bible says, *"A man reaps what he sows"* (Galatians 6:7). Create an environment of respect and honor in the home. It's easy to do that when all is going well and yet difficult when you feel like chewing someone's head off! Yes, deal with misbehavior, but in a respectful way. In the process, you are not only modeling honor but also self-control.

Manners are also tied to honor and respect. I said earlier that honor is becoming a lost art. Not giving people courtesy or proper respect shows very little concern for their feelings and cultivates selfishness. Manners are an important part of temple raising!

Giving honor is tied to obedience. Notice from the verses at the beginning of this section that in Exodus, it says "honor" and in Ephesians, it says "obey." Children are born with free will, and it is up to the parent to cultivate an environment of love and respect to bring that free will under submission to first the will of the parent and then to the will of God.

Earlier in this section I asked the question, "Is honor something we can choose to do or not do, depending on the circumstance?" I believe that circumstance does not dictate our choice to give honor. There are times when boundaries must be placed, but honor can still be given.

God gave us our parents; therefore, He picked them out knowing their personality traits and values. He knew that as we follow His rules and seek after His wisdom, we would ultimately be shaped into the image of His Son. As believers we often quote Romans 8:28 when giving comfort to someone. We don't always remember the purpose that is given in verse 29: *"And we know that all things work together for good to those who love God, to those who are the called according to His purpose. For whom He foreknew, He also predestined to be conformed to the image of His Son, that He might be the firstborn among many brethren"* (NKJV).

Some principles to consider as an adult include the following: The Bible says we are to give honor, so that is the choice we must make. That is the goal, even if we are not perfect. We honor the position, even if the person seems unlovable or dishonorable. We can honor someone but still set boundaries.

As a teenager, I fell in love with Jesus. I was raised in a "Christian home" where we were regular attenders of church. I learned the Bible stories, yet my mom continually told me not to become too "spiritual." She said it would turn people off, and I would never find a man that way. She complained I read the Bible too much, so I wouldn't let her see me reading. But it was more difficult than that. My mother was what is referred to today as a rage-aholic. It kept me walking on eggshells.

Because God gave us our parents, I tried to trust that the Lord would work through them to guide me. But that wasn't always easy. For instance, when they said "no" to me going on a youth retreat, I was disappointed but chose to trust God to bless me in other ways. That same weekend, we had a surprise visit from my favorite aunt and uncle, who were missionaries and filled with the joy of God. I was delighted and saw God's hand at work in spite of how things seemed.

Over the years, I tried to give honor to my mother as best I could, looking past her accusations and verbal abuse, trying to remember she was a child of God and loved by Jesus. But it was a struggle for me to know how to respond appropriately in standing my ground and giving honor. I would ask the Holy Spirit to help me walk in instant forgiveness. I made mistakes, but I slowly learned to stay sensitive to the Holy Spirit and to respond to God's guidance and not just my circumstances.

**Parents Are Our Inheritance**

After I was married, we were visiting my parents' home with our two small children, and my mom went into a rage that was so bad, we packed up and left the next morning. I purposed in my heart that I would never take my kids to her home again and expose them to that type of behavior. My heart was broken, because I always wanted to do the right thing, and I felt defeated.

But God brought Carol Kohl, the mentor I spoke of earlier, into my life. She lovingly counseled me. She taught me many of the principles in this book. She told me that I should make peace because parents are our inheritance, and they are my kids' inheritance. She taught me how to be honorable yet set boundaries. For instance, she suggested I choose a neutral place, like a motel between our cities, and invite them for a weekend visit. She said to take a small gift because *"a gift opens the way and ushers the giver into the presence of the great"* (Proverbs 18:16).

We made the trip, and my parents continued to be part of my life until the day they each went to be with the Lord. It was not easy. There is value that comes through a struggle, and I am grateful that we made the trip.

Here is a side note for the end of the story. My mom died of Alzheimer's, a very cruel disease. For the last three years of her life, she was in assisted living or a nursing home. I had a goal of traveling to see her every month for a few days. Those last few years were peaceful. She continued to remember me but never brought up anything negative or bad. We spent many times talking and chatting. Nothing deep, under the circumstances, but we enjoyed sharing pictures and meals.

When she died, I can honestly say that I did all I knew to do at the time. Was I a perfect kid or adult? No. But through forgiveness, redemption, and continually seeking the Lord, I have peace. I am glad that all three of my kids were able to spend time and get to know both of my parents. Honor with boundaries was in place.

I can't close this chapter without sharing one more tip that Carol Kohl gave me that got me through many potentially frustrating moments. When my mom would come visit, she would rearrange my furniture, change the thermostat, and other things that seemed intrusive. Carol said to ask myself each time, "What does it matter in eternity?" That thought calmed my nerves, and I would accept the changes, knowing they were temporary. *"If it is possible, as far as it depends on you, live at peace with everyone."* Romans 12:18

Why is this important in a book on training kids? Because mom, you need to be at peace in order to create the atmosphere in your home. With other personalities, other methods would make since. If a simple discussion or confrontation is not possible without creating rage, then remember this thought, "What does it matter in eternity?"

> *If a simple discussion or confrontation is not possible without creating rage, then remember this thought, "What does it matter in eternity?"*

## *Prayer Corner*

**Reality check:** Take an honest look at your heart. Do you give honor to your parents? This is not about a possible need for "boundaries." It's a heart issue. Ask the Lord what this needs to look like for you and your family.

Are you training your kids to give respect and honor to authority, even when they disagree?

**Prayer:** Dear heavenly Father, (if your parents are living) I bless my parents and ask You to pour out Your grace and peace upon them. Alert me to ways I am not being honorable, and help me to give them honor.

I want to show honor to my parents, and I want to train my kids in how to be respectful. I pray that my children will be respectful and obedient to us, their parents, for this is just and right. This is the first commandment with a promise, and so I pray that it will go well with them, and they will live long as they fulfill honor and respect. I also pray that as parents we won't provoke them or irritate them. Let our training be tender, consistent, and uplifting. We ask for Your guidance and help. In Jesus' name. Amen.

## Chapter 16
# *Breaking Family Curses*

*"For I, the Lord your God, am a jealous God, visiting the iniquity of the fathers upon the children to the third and fourth generations of those who hate Me, but showing mercy to thousands, to those who love Me and keep My commandments."*
(Exodus 20:5b-6 NKJV)

Moms, I hate to tell you this, but just as you have passed on to your children your pretty blue or brown eyes or cute freckled nose, you have also passed down your family sins! The good news is that you have also passed along your family's positive qualities. The even better news is that Jesus has come to set us free: *"Then Jesus said to those Jews who believed Him, 'If you abide in My word, you are My disciples indeed. And you shall know the truth, and the truth shall make you free"* (John 8:31-32 NKJV). Did you catch what the key is to this good news? It's "abiding in His Word." It's the truth that you know that sets you free.

Our Western minds don't easily relate to sins being passed along from generation to generation. In the Middle East, this concept was and is accepted and understood. That is why when Jesus and the disciples walked by a blind man, they asked, *"Rabbi, who sinned, this man or his parents, that he was born blind?"* (John 9:2 NKJV)

Let's take a look at some Bible families we are all familiar with and follow the sin line. Keep in mind that as we look at the sin for the purpose of this discussion, every one of them was redeemed and part of the great Hall of Faith in Hebrews 11. Abraham, the father of the Jewish faith, lied twice about Sarah being his sister. He rationalized that his life was in danger because Sarah was so beautiful. Abraham's son, Isaac, grew up and married Rebekah, and they had twins. The Bible says that Esau came out first, but Jacob came out grasping Esau's heel. The family blessing belonged to Esau. Rebekah and Jacob conspired together to trick Isaac into giving the blessing to Jacob. But then Jacob was later deceived by his sons when they lied to him and said that wild animals had killed Joseph. The root sin being passed along was deception. It manifested in different ways and seemed to grow through the generations (see Genesis 25ff).

**Look for the Root**

When considering generational sins, look at the root, rather than how it manifests. For example, one generation may have alcoholism and another may have drug problems. The root sin is addiction.

Take a look at Exodus 20:4-6: *"You shall not make for yourself a carved image—any likeness of anything that is in heaven above, or that is in the earth beneath, or that is in the water under the earth; you shall not bow down to them nor serve them. For I, the LORD your God, am a jealous God, visiting the iniquity of the fathers upon the children to the third and fourth generations of those who hate Me, but showing mercy to thousands, to those who love Me and keep My commandments"* (NKJV).

What is the commandment associated with family curses and blessings?

Commandment #3 (verse 4):

_____


The bottom line is that idolatry is the root of all the generational sins. Let's look at one more thing before we proceed. Go further back in Exodus 20 to verse 2: *"I am the LORD your God, who brought you out of the land of Egypt, out of the house of bondage."*

Do you see what sin does? It keeps us in bondage. If sin is not broken, we become a slave to the sin. Our precious Lord gave us the Ten Commandments to set us free!

So, for the sake of your kids, let's roll up our sleeves and get to work on discovering the truth and breaking the power of any generational sin that is in the family bloodline.

Please keep in mind that the purpose of this chapter and the exercises in it are not to dwell on bad memories or to make anyone feel condemned. The purpose is to see clearly what needs to be forgiven, broken, and stopped. We will go on to victory over the influence of the enemy, and through this restoration, you and your kids will experience spiritual growth.

*"They will rebuild the ancient ruins and restore the places long devastated; they will renew the ruined cities that have been devastated for generations"* (Isaiah 61:4).

I saw a chart similar to this in Beth Moore's *Breaking Free* workbook,[2] however, this is a typical outline of recording and figuring out the generational sins and blessings. Prayerfully fill this out. If you do not know your birth family, then substitute in the parents who raised you.

| Mother | Father |
| --- | --- |
| Positive influences | Positive influences |
| Negative influences | Negative influences |

| **Paternal Grandparents** | |
| --- | --- |
| Grandmother positive influences | Grandfather positive influences |
| Grandmother negative influences | Grandfather negative influences |
| **Maternal Grandparents** | |
| Grandmother positive influences | Grandfather positive influences |
| Grandmother negative influences | Grandfather negative influences |

The past is done. We cannot change it. Now we are going to prayerfully change the future!

**Prayer for Forgiveness**

The first thing to do is release forgiveness:

Prayer of forgiveness: Lord, I forgive _____ for the influence of sin in his/her life and the way it affected me. I can see how I am a product of this bad influence, and I can see how I am repeating the cycle. I forgive him/her and pray that you will bless my _____.

Next, we break the cycle: Lord, I want this cycle of sin stopped (name specific) and for it to no longer operate in me or be passed down to the next generation. I take the sword of the Spirit, the Word of God, and cut all generational sin off me and through the blood of Jesus, declare it impossible to be passed on to my kids. I ask that the Holy Spirit would fill the void with the fruit of the Spirit and that I would right now experience God's love, the height and width and depth of it as described in Ephesians 3:14-21.

Moms, I have kept this very simple, and some of you may be confused or have questions. Another whole book could be written on this very subject, and my purpose has been just to awaken your awareness and give you some simple help to address it. If you would like more information or feel a need to work through the process more, I would like to suggest Beth Moore's book, *Breaking Free*. The generational study is specifically in week 4. It is an excellent study and should be done with a group, including her videos.

Another excellent book is *Breaking Generational Curses* by Marilyn Hickey. Marilyn gives a very thorough and Scriptural teaching on generational curses, from identifying it to the process of breaking and overcoming. It's almost as if she is holding your hand step by step through the process.

Romans 12:2 says, *"Do not conform to the pattern of this world, but be transformed by the renewing of your mind. Then you will be able to test and approve what God's will is — his good, pleasing and perfect will."*

We have just been dwelling on generational curses based on Exodus 20:5. Do not lose heart; remember the good news and what the emphasis of this book is, *"Therefore know that the LORD your God, He is God, the faithful God who keeps covenant and mercy for a thousand generations with those who love Him and keep His commandments"* (Deuteronomy 7:9).

Yes, that's right — we can influence up to 1,000 generations! Let's go for it!

**Praise God for Setting Us Free!**

Back to my testimony that I started in the last chapter: The last thing I would ever want to do would be to raise my children in an atmosphere of rage or confusion. I was aware of family curses from studying the Bible and had learned in nursing school that cycles of abuse continue through the generations. Even secular professionals recognize the cycle of sin. Over time, I learned that the core of cyclic sin was spiritual, thus it needed to be dealt with spiritually and then with thoughtful choices.

I prayed a prayer similar to what is above and continued to work out the process. You see, once set free, the temptation or other factors might come into place, but the key is that one is no longer held in bondage. Now there is the freedom to make a choice. It is the enemy who takes away the free will that God has given to us. So the work continues after the prayers.

The Lord is so good. I remember a specific time when Ann was dealing with my oldest grandchild, who was about 2 years old. Through the interaction, I saw love, kindness, and discipline. The Holy Spirit whispered in my ear, "The cycle has been broken." I had to excuse myself to go worship, with tears of joy and gratitude to the One who came to break the chains of the enemy off of each of us! I rejoice that we serve such a Savior, who came to not only pave the way to Heaven, but to also give us abundant life during our Earth walk. Allowing Him to work through us to victory is sweet!

**Generational God**

*"For I, the LORD your God, am a jealous God, visiting the iniquity of the fathers upon the children to the third and fourth generations of those who hate Me, but showing mercy to thousands, to those who love Me and keep my commandments"* (Exodus 20:5b-6).

The good news is that we can pass on the blessings to generations that will come after us, and that is what I am after! We may live long enough to see the fruit of our labor to possibly the next two to three generations — but in Heaven, we will see our influence for generations to come!

Let me share an amazing story. I went on a genealogy retreat with my cousin, who was really into investigating our heritage as far back as possible. In one of the workshops that included some of our distant cousins, we heard about a relative named Penelope who lived in the early 1800s. She would prayer walk and call out for the salvation and spiritual walk for all her relatives, including future generations. She was known as the prayer walker.

I have good news for Penelope, and I am sure she realizes the power of her prayers as she sits in Heaven, enjoying fellowship with many. Just from the family members we know, we have pastors and missionaries. Many are walking with Christ in their secular jobs and influencing others. As my cousin and I looked at her genealogy record, we saw many more committed believers, including circuit riders and more pastors. They are — and I am — the fruit of Penelope's prayers! Your prayers are also making an impact!

*"I will sing of the LORD's great love forever; with my mouth I will make your faithfulness known through all generations"* (Psalm 89:1).

## *Prayer Corner*

**Reality check:** Have you looked at the good, the bad, and the ugly on your family tree (not for the purpose to accuse or condemn)? Remember, the instant you repent of your sins or family's sins, the curse is broken. Have you noticed a series of negative patterns from your family history? Take a moment and prayerfully ask the Lord how to pray. Look forward to the impact that your blessings will have for generations to come.

**Prayer:** Dear heavenly Father, I have considered the traits on my family tree, and I break the power of the negative ones (state them). I want to claim and pass down Your blessings, and I ask that You will show Your salvation power to all in my family and my seed. Bring them all to Your saving power. Help all of us to live according to Your principles and give You glory and honor. I am committed to nurturing, watering, and even pruning that seed until we see the fruit. In the name of Jesus, Amen.

# Chapter 17
# Hearing the Voice of God

*"The sheep hear his voice; and he calls his own
sheep by name and leads them out ....
They will hear My voice."
(John 10:3b, 16b NKJV)*

It is vital that our kids learn to hear the voice of God. He says that we can, just as the sheep can hear the voice of a shepherd. I remember after Pete was told the story of little boy Samuel hearing the voice of God, he asked me if he could hear God's voice too. I said "Of course! Let's practice" (see 1 Samuel 3). I had Pete sit down with his hands in his lap, pointing up, as if in receiving position. I prayed that the Lord would speak to Pete just as He had spoken to little boy Samuel. We recognized that God does not show favoritism, and what He did for Samuel, He would do for Pete (see Acts 10:34).

We sat quietly for a few minutes, and then Pete got a big grin on his face. I asked him, "What did the Lord tell you?" He said, "When I am on the playground, and someone is mean to me, I am not to punch him." I smiled and confirmed that word.

I wish I knew then what I know now about teaching children how to hear the voice of God. I spent a whole year teaching my children's church using *Hearing God's Voice* and using the KIMI curriculum.[3]

## MaryBelle's Farm

I mentioned in chapter 6 that my husband retired from the business world, and we bought a farm. We raise goats, sheep, and chickens. We have learned so much from the animals.

One of the first things we learned was the reality of John 10. Verses 3 and 4 refer to a shepherd and say, *"The sheep hear his voice; and he calls his own sheep by name and leads them out. And when he brings out his own sheep, he goes before them; and the sheep follow him, for they know his voice."* Jesus explained that He used this as an illustration so that we could understand our relationship with Him, and he continued the illustration in verse 27. This time, He is the Great Shepherd,: *"My sheep hear My voice, and I know them, and they follow Me."*

MaryBelle is a goat, and though John 10 is about sheep, the characteristics referred to in this passage are the same for all grazing animals. During the transition time of purchasing the farm, the owners told us a special story about MaryBelle. She was born on Christmas Eve and was the runt of triplets. She was so small that she measured about the size of the palm of an adult hand. The owners took MaryBelle into their laundry room to bottle feed and care for her until she was strong enough to join the herd.

With the amount of nurturing MaryBelle received, she learned her name. The previous owners asked us, "Do you want to meet MaryBelle?" Of course we did. We went out to the fence line of the pasture, where about 20 goats were grazing. They called, "MaryBelle! MaryBelle!" MaryBelle lifted up her head and came trotting over to us like a little puppy dog. We were so delighted realizing the power in the illustration of John 10, that we named the farm after MaryBelle.

We enjoy sharing farm life with other families and schools. During birthing season, we are usually busy with visitors. I enjoy taking the opportunity to teach the kids about hearing the voice of God. I ask all of them, "Who wants to hear the voice of God?" They  all raise their hand. I share a couple of verses from John 10 and tell them that Jesus is using the illustration of little lambs and sheep hearing the voice of their shepherd as an example to demonstrate to us that we too can hear His voice. I ask them, "So if these little lambs can hear my voice and respond, do you believe you can hear God's voice as well?" They all agree. I instruct them that our spirit ears are not *these* ears, pointing to my ears. I then point to the lower part of my sternum and tell the kids that we "hear" from God inside, about right *here* in our gut. Sometimes, He speaks some words, maybe a Bible verse, sometimes we see a picture, or sometimes we sense a feeling.

I then tell the children that we are going to get real quiet for about a minute and listen for the Lord to speak into each one of our hearts. Since we are on a farm, under shade trees and with animals all around, we don't rely on music or atmosphere.

**God Loves Me**

I ask the children, "Who would like to share with me what the Lord said?" If this is the first time kids have experienced this, I often get answers like, "He told me that He loves me." I validate this to the child. Then, to the parents, I assure them that I know their little ones have heard this from them and their Sunday school teachers, but now they have heard it from Him, and it will be forever imprinted on their heart.

Many times children cannot yet articulate what they experienced, so I ask them if they had a different feeling or noticed anything else while we listened. One time a young boy practicing this for the first time told me that he felt so much peace and comfort. I later found out that his grandmother had just died, and they were going to the funeral the next day.

With kids I have had the privilege to work with on a regular basis, there is more complex communication between God and the child. Recently, I taught some kids how the Holy Spirit sometimes tugs on our heart to go pray for someone specifically. During the activation, I expected the kids to be pulled to one another and pray. One felt led to pray for a young mom. She prophesied that the young mom would have more children. I later found out that this young mom desired this very much but had difficulty with fertility. It's been a little over a year since this encounter, and a new little bundle of joy has been born!

I could give lots of similar testimonies I have seen, not only with kids in the U.S. but when I take this message to other places as well. I remember one time being in a hot, overcrowded room in Mexico and inviting the Holy Spirit to speak to the kids. I must confess that in my mind, I thought, "It's too hot and crowded in here for us to focus." It was not too hot for the Lord to move, and those kids saw some amazing visions and had some great words of encouragement to share with others. They only needed to be taught, trained, and trusted.

**Listening Prayer Takes Practice**

Like anything, listening prayer takes practice, and I encourage parents to have listening prayer as part of their daily routine. I have learned so much from the KIMI *Hearing God's Voice* curriculum that I incorporate principles and object lessons from it spontaneously as I communicate with children, even for a few minutes. Though this is a curriculum, an eager mom would be able to break it down for family devotions.[3]

One of my favorites is to use the traffic light to teach kids how to know when they get a green light from God or a red light from Him. Just think, if your kids learn to talk to God, including listening, they will learn to be guided to what party is going to be "okay" and which ones the Lord gives a "red light" to. It will soon become some of your "inside lingo" when having discussions. You can say, "Did you get a red light or a green light?"

Sometimes we don't know why we get a red light — or as us adults call it, "a check in the spirit." This is our opportunity to trust the Lord and not lean on our own understanding. I remember getting a strong red light about Ann going to a slumber party. It was difficult to say "no" as I knew it would offend the family. We offered a lunch date. A few months later something was exposed that gave us great relief that we had learned to listen to the voice of the Lord and not lean on our own understanding. (See Proverbs 3:5-6)

Another available source for learning and teaching principles on hearing God's voice is a book by Becky Fischer called *The Adventures of Ivy and God*.[4] This book is a true story about a little girl named Ivy who applied many of the principles from the KIMI curriculum, including the traffic light illustration, and saw answers to her prayers. Ivy is now a grown woman, serving the Lord. The book is a storybook with pictures and is written for children.

**Eyes Behind My Head**

Many people hear God's voice and just don't recognize it as that. They might call it women's intuition, the conscience, or "having eyes behind your head." Speaking of that, one time when

Pete was young, I went outside to give some safety instructions on using the trampoline. As I walked back in, I had a second thought and went back out to warn the boys, "I will be watching, so do as I have asked."

Pete's little friend responded, "I know, I know. You have eyes behind your head. You can see everything!"

I had to smile at Pete's comeback statement: "No, my mom does not have eyes behind her head. She is filled with the Holy Spirit, and He tells her everything!"

Well, I don't want to use the Holy Spirit as a tattletale, but it is helpful to be sensitive to the leading of the Holy Spirit, a treasured tool to train our children. In fact, Scripture says, *"Do not grieve the Holy Spirit of God, with whom you were sealed for the day of redemption"* (Ephesians 4:30).

**Other Voices**

When I talk to adults who are not used to practicing the art of listening to God's voice, they lack confidence, because there are other voices we internally hear, and they have not learned how to differentiate the voices. Perhaps you relate. I have good news for you: You are never too old to learn. With practice, your confidence will soon soar. You will develop a spiritual intuitiveness or a "knowing" of the voice of the Holy Spirit. Romans 8:16 says, *"The Spirit Himself bears witness with our spirit"* (NKJV).

First, let's narrow down the possible inner voices:
1. Your thoughts (Proverbs 14:12)
2. God thoughts (Job 32:8)
3. Enemy thoughts (2 Corinthians 11:13-14)

**Your thoughts:** God's thoughts do sound a lot like your thoughts, so it is essential to slow down. Psalm 46:10 says, *"Be still, and know that I am God."* Also 1 Kings 19:12 says that the Lord speaks to us in a *"still small voice"* (NKJV). That still voice is often drowned out with the busyness of life.

Often our thoughts have their own agenda, so it is also important to be aware of your own agenda. When we desire a particular answer with passion, it confuses the peace process. So you might have to pray, "Lord, I want to hear Your voice above my voice, so I submit my agenda and emotion to You and ask that You will clearly lead me in peace. I am willing to be satisfied if the answer is not what I know to be my thoughts."

In other words, get yourself out of the way — as best you can!

**God's thoughts:** Remember, according to John 10, a believer is able to genuinely distinguish and recognize the voice of God. Your "God thoughts" originate from your inner being (heart or belly): *"He who believes in Me, as the Scripture has said, out of his heart will flow rivers of living water"* (John 7:38 NKJV). God is a Spirit, so we listen to Him with our spirit. Take time to be quiet before the Lord so you can begin to be aware where thoughts originate and the tone of the thought.

Remember, *"There is a spirit in man, and the breath of the Almighty, gives him understanding"* (Job 32:8 NKJV).

Since we are relating God's voice to John 10 and sheep, let's think for a minute what sheep hear when they hear the voice of their shepherd. They hear love, encouragement, safety, security, and correction that are not condemning.

The tone of a God thought could be:

- Powerful but not demanding or with pressure (Isaiah 30:21, 2 Timothy 1:7).

- Correction with conviction but never condemnation (Romans 8:1, 1 John 1:9).
- Peaceful, without confusion (Isaiah 55:12, 1 Corinthians 14:33).
- Gentle, not harsh (Matthew 11:29-30, James 3:17).
- Loving encouragement (Psalms 37:23-24, Jeremiah 29:11, John 10:27).
- Safe and secure (Proverbs 18:10, Romans 8:31).

It's hard to explain, but God thoughts come from your core and not your brain. Once you take a thought captive, your mind and heart will think it through together.

**Enemy thoughts:** The enemy's thoughts originate from the mind or the soul (not as deep). It's as if he injects the thoughts into our minds. Have you ever had a thought and said to yourself, "Where did that come from? I would never …" It was probably an "injected" thought.

Learn to discern — increase your awareness — of where the thoughts come from. Besides John 10 assuring us that we can hear the voice of God, it also assures us that we will recognize the voice of the enemy: *"But they will never follow a stranger; in fact, they will run away from him because they do not recognize a stranger's voice"* (John 10:5).

Remember, God's Word will help you distinguish between the soul and the spirit: *"For the word of God is alive and active. Sharper than any double-edged sword, it penetrates even to dividing soul and spirit, joints and marrow; it judges the thoughts and attitudes of the heart"* (Hebrews 4:12).

The tone of enemy thoughts could be:
- Demanding and full of pressure
- Condemning, with no hope

- Confusing
- Harsh

Enemy thoughts seem to come through the mind, often causing a flood of words. Command the words to STOP, and then focus on the Prince of Peace and the voice of the Lord (Isaiah 9:6, Psalm 29:4).

**Test the Spirit**

The Bible says in 1 John 4:1 to "test the spirits." I bet you already know these, and now you just need to apply them to your own ability.

1) God's thoughts will never contradict Scripture (see 1 Peter 1:24-25, Acts 17:11).

2) Ask for confirmation in Scripture.

3) God's voice convicts, with instant understanding of how to redeem. Conviction is wrapped in love, faith, and hope, whereas the enemy condemns and gives hopelessness. If you feel condemned, ask yourself, "Where did this come from?" and then take authority over the enemy!

4) God's voice is confirmed by the Holy Spirit: *"But the Helper, the Holy Spirit, whom the Father will send in My name, He will teach you all things, and bring to your remembrance all things that I said to you"* (John 14:26 NKJV).

5) God's voice brings peace: *"But the wisdom that comes from heaven is first of all pure; then peace-loving, considerate, submissive, full of mercy and good fruit, impartial and sincere"* (James 3:17). Do you sense

peace? Sometimes we have to put ourselves in neutral in order to do so (see also Colossians 3:15, Philippians 4:7, John 14:27).

6) Does this help or hurt my witness for Christ (1 Corinthians 9:22-23)?

7) Does it glorify God (1 Corinthians 10:21)?

8) Can the spirit say that *"Jesus Christ has come in the flesh"* (1 John 4:2)? "How is that done," you ask, "since we do not often speak to spirits, if ever?" Practice, and ask the Lord to give you discernment as you do this. Remember, we hear from the spirit from within our belly, and we hear from the enemy with our mind. When a thought comes that you want to test, say, "Spirit that gave this thought, say, 'Jesus Christ has come in the flesh and is from God.'" Listen, and if this thought is from God, your inner being will be able to say this sentence. *If* this thought is from another source, you will feel a check, and the sentence will not form. Frankly, this takes practice, and it is not widely practiced. It is in the Scripture as one of the tests, so use it, practice, and ask the Lord to train you so you can train your kids.

Take time to read and meditate on Scripture. Listen. Journal what you hear. With time, you will be reading and sharing what the voice of God said to you and the acts of God He did through your obedience.

**One More Stumbling Block**

I want to address one more argument I have heard. Sadly, some say that God does not speak to man today because "we have the complete Word of God, and He does not need to. We test everything by the Word, and that's it." This grieves my spirit because then the believer is only open to a partial relationship with the Lord. It's no wonder many don't take the time to listen — they don't think there is anything to listen to!

Let's consider some New Testament believers who heard and were directed by the Lord speaking to their spirit man.

- Paul, as a prisoner, was on a voyage to Rome when he said, *"Men, I perceive that this voyage will end with disaster and much loss, not only of the cargo and ship, but also our lives"* (Acts 27:10 NKJV). His perception (or knowing from the Holy Spirit) was ignored, and they were shipwrecked.

- Peter perceived and declared in Acts 10:34-35, *"In truth I perceive that God shows no partiality. But in every nation whoever fears Him and works righteousness is accepted by Him"* (NKJV).

- The woman at the well had a clear perception from her spirit: *"The woman said to Him, 'Sir, I perceive that You are a prophet'"* (John 4:19).

If you have been taught that modern-day believers cannot hear the voice God, please consider the following Scriptures. There are many more. May the Lord illuminate them to you as you read through the Scripture.

*"See that you do not refuse Him who speaks. For if they did not escape who refused Him who spoke on earth, much more shall we not escape if we turn away from Him who speaks from heaven"* (Hebrews 12:25 NKJV).

*"Do not quench the Spirit"* (1 Thessalonians 5:19).

Listen to what Jesus told the disciples during His farewell speech to them: *"But the Advocate, the Holy Spirit, whom the Father will send in my name, will teach you all things and will remind you of everything I have said to you"* (John 14:26).

*"However, when He, the Spirit of truth, has come, He will guide you into all truth; for He will not speak on His own authority, but whatever He hears He will speak; and He will tell you things to come. He will glorify Me, for He will take of what is Mine and declare it to you"* (John 16:13-14 NKJV).

**Frame Your Prayer Time**

Another way to increase your confidence is to frame your prayer time with this prayer based on verses from Luke 11:11-13.

Pray, "Lord, I want to frame this time of prayer with Your words. You said, 'if a son asks an earthly father for bread or for fish that he would not give him a rock or a serpent, then how much more can we trust You, our heavenly Father, to give good gifts!' In this prayer time, I want Your thoughts to be my thoughts. I trust You as I listen to my spirit."

Then begin praying and listening. If it helps you, write down what you are hearing.

**Practice**

Pray for someone, and ask the Lord how He would like you to pray for that person. Ask Him for His thoughts for the person; talk to Him. Then share this with your friend to encourage him or her. You can say something like, "I was praying for you. May I share an impression I had?"

Listen to your friend's response. You will often hear how much the very words that the Lord gave you touched that person's heart. Why does this work? Because God's Word works! He says, *"But the one who prophesies speaks to people for their strengthening, encouraging and comfort"* (1 Corinthians 14:3).

Okay, now I *hear* someone saying, "I can't do that. I'm not a prophet!" Relax. Neither were most of the people who read this Word when it was still only a "letter" and not the Bible. This is a general Word for all readers. Besides, verse one from this passage says, *"Pursue love, and desire spiritual gifts, but especially that you may prophesy"* (NKJV). I'd say the Lord says, "Go for it!"

For clarity, prophets receive directional words for people, but everyone who has the Spirit of God in them can listen and hear the heart of God to encourage, edify, and comfort. Try it! As you do, you will build up your confidence, and then you can encourage your child who has "child-like" faith and does not need all of this coaxing!

Practice listening to the voice of God, in the variety of ways He speaks. It is all part of *"exercising our spiritual senses and training them to maturity"* as it says in Hebrew 5:20.

## *Prayer Corner*

**Reality check:** When praying with your kids, do you take the time to listen? Have you given them plenty of opportunities to hear the voice of God? Have you taught them how recognize the other voices?

Have you questioned whether *you* can hear from God? Do you lack confidence in your ability to hear the voice of God? Have you been taught against it? Are you willing to explore this part of your relationship with the Lord?

**Prayer:** Dear heavenly Father, open up our eyes and ears so that we can see and hear what the Spirit of God is saying to us. I lift up my kids to You and ask that You will speak clearly to them. Help them to learn to know your voice. You said in Your Word that sheep hear the voice of the shepherd, so we are ready. Sometimes it's hard for us to know which voice is Yours. Help me train my children to know how to differentiate.

Lord, I have lacked confidence, and yet I do believe that if little lambs can hear their shepherd, then I too can hear Your voice. I am even confused because I have heard all of my life that it is not possible to hear from God apart from the Scripture. Train me, and keep me in Your will. I believe as I ask for this that You are not going to give me a "rock or a serpent." In Jesus name, Amen.

# Chapter 18
# *Words Are Powerful*
*"The tongue has the power of life and death."*
*(Proverbs 18:21a)*

**Name Calling**

Have you ever been out in public and heard a parent angrily call her child a monster or some other awful name? That makes me cringe. Our words have meaning, and they do hurt! The saying, "Sticks and stones may break my bones, but words will never hurt me" is not true!

When you are frustrated with the behavior of your child, never call them names! They stick, and they hurt. It breaks the spirit of the child, not his or her will. Say something like this firmly: "I am disappointed in the *act* that you did."

Let's take this "name calling" a step further. Eventually, your child will be saying descriptive words about himself. "I am so dumb" or "I am ugly" or "I'm a klutz." How can we expect anything different if they have heard horrible descriptions of themselves from a parent or caretaker? Truthfully, we have all made similar mistakes, and we need to stop speaking this over ourselves as well (yes, I am pointing a finger back at me!).

As a young mom. I remember reading a book called *Children Are Wet Cement* by Anne Ortlund. The premise of the book is that what you say makes an impact. The book encourages parents to speak lots of kind words, giving the child a positive identity.

Here are some examples that you can whisper in the ear of your child over and over: "I believe in you." "I love you always, and you don't have to do a thing to get my love!" "Go for it! You can do it!" "I am so happy that the Lord gave you to me!" "Don't worry about it. There is always tomorrow." "The Lord has an assignment for you that only you can fulfill." You get the idea. It won't hurt to say these and other affirmations over and over again.

## Our Tongue Has the "Power of Life and Death"

Proverbs 18:21 says, *"The tongue has the power of life and death."*

I have already talked about casting and creating a vision through the words and encouragement we give our kids. Now I want to take it a step further, acknowledging that our tongue has the "power of life and death."

Creation was started with the sound of God's voice, and we are made in His image. So far, I haven't been able to create something out of nothing as God did. However, we do create our environments and even our future by the words we say.

What are the most powerful prayers we can pray? They are the ones where we use God's Word and His promises. As we pray something using God's Word, we need to be careful of how we use our words after the prayer so that we are not negating what we just prayed.[4]

Let me give this example. I have observed people pray for the sick, using Scripture to declare their healing. Shortly after the prayer, when walking away with a friend, the conversation is about how sick the person is and what typically comes next in the disease process. These words negate the prayer!

We all have this tendency to state the facts as we see them with our physical eyes. We need to train ourselves to see the truth with our spiritual eyes. So what is the difference, you ask? Facts are the tangible things that can be seen, heard or felt with our physical senses or an event that actually happened. Our tendency is to think facts cannot be changed.

Truth is based on our belief system. Truth is subjective and uses our spiritual senses. For example, if you go to the doctor and hear that "you have terminal cancer, and you need to get your affairs in order," then you have been presented with a fact. At the same time, you remember a truth from Scripture, *"by whose (Jesus') stripes you were healed"* (1 Peter 2:24b NKJV). The truth can change the facts.

Facts are part of this real world that we live in, but we are citizens of heaven, and as we have already discussed, we have spiritual senses that need to be trained (see Hebrews 5:14). The spiritual world holds more truth and trumps over the physical world. The Bible says that the "truth will set you free" — but notice it is the truth you know (or believe) that sets you free (see John 8:32).[5]

To this day, I catch myself stating facts over truth and need to say in prayer, "Lord, please break the power of the words I just spoke. Instead, I declare Your promise that says _____ " (I quote a verse with a promise that is applicable). For example, using the above scenario of walking away from a hospital room and saying, "Did you see all those tubes and wires? I don't see how Ted is going to make it through this sickness." You immediately get a "check in the spirit" and know those were not faith words. Now say, "I break the power of the words I just spoke, and I agree with the faith prayer we just prayed in the room. Ted is going to be healed through the blood of Jesus" (see Isaiah 53:3, 1 Peter 2:24). Praying this way is praying truth over facts and activating the spiritual.

**Self-Condemnation**

Another example of applying this is when we call ourselves names! Have you ever said, "Oh, I am so stupid. Why did I do that?" Maybe something does need to be fixed, but don't let those words create atmosphere or power. Say, "I break the power of my own words with the Sword of the Spirit, which is the Word of God, and I declare that I have the mind of Christ. Lord, I ask You for Your wisdom on how to fix this". Or have you ever said something like, "Ugh. I am so unorganized! My laundry room and kitchen are a huge mess, and I can't find anything!" Now, say, "I break the power of my words and, using the Word of God, I speak order into my house. Father, You said, 'Let there be light' into a dark world, and light and order were established. I speak order into my household. Give me grace to work through this, and please reveal to me where my missing _____ is." (Be sure to give Him thanks as soon as you find what you are looking for!)

**Facts Vs. Truth**

This concept that I have been talking about might seem like a foreign idea if you have not thought about it prior to this discussion. Let me try and explain it further by sharing a biblical illustration. Facts are what we see and understand with our physical eyes and our own understanding. Truth is seeing through God's eyes and His Word. A biblical story that illustrates this is when Joshua was tricked by the Gibeonites. They pretended to be ambassadors from a far-away country, wearing old, torn clothes and carrying stale, moldy bread and torn wineskins. Their craftiness convinced Joshua and the elders to make a treaty with them. Joshua's mistake was that he did not inquire of the Lord and he trusted in his own understanding (see Joshua 9, Proverbs 3:5-6).

**Words Are Seeds of Faith**

The Bible says in 2 Corinthians 4:13, *"And since we have the same spirit of faith, according to what is written, 'I believed and therefore I spoke,' we also believe and therefore speak"* (NKJV).

There are hundreds of kids out there who have learned the power of the words we speak and the value of praying God's promises because of the testimony of a little dog we owned. Let me share it with you, and you can use it, too. Soon, you will have a whole list of your own testimonies.

We had two dogs, a Brittany named Cooper and a Miniature Pinscher named Rocket. One day my husband came in and asked if I had let the dogs in the garage that day. I said, "Yes, it started raining during our walk, and I wanted them to dry off. Why do you ask?"

He said, "I had some mouse poison behind the furniture, and it is gone" (we lived in front of a field on a hill). My guess was that somehow Rocket was the culprit because he was smaller and could get to the poison. I doubted he shared it with Cooper. We took both dogs to the emergency vet and, sure enough, Cooper was clear, but Rocket's blood tests came back positive.

We were told that poison is a slow death, causing the victim to bleed slowly to death, and that we would gradually see signs and when it got too difficult for us to bring Rocket back to be put down gently. He said it might take about a week. The vet did give him a vitamin K shot to help. In the meantime, we were told to go home and enjoy him and say our goodbyes. I sadly called all my kids, who were off at college, to give them an opportunity to come home if possible.

The next day, after having my quiet time and praying for several family members, I got a determination inside of me that "enough was enough" and I was going to fight this in prayer. I called a couple of my good prayer friends, and while Mark held Rocket, we anointed him with some oil and started praying and confessing Bible verses. Of course, we prayed for all of our families who needed prayer that day, but Rocket was the focus of this particular event.

As one of my friends left after a visit, she advised me, "Lori, use your tongue powerfully. Every time you pass Rocket say, 'I bless you Rocket. You are going to live and not die.'" I came up with a couple of other statements to say over Rocket and was faithful to speak God's Word over him.

A week went by, and Rocket was just as energetic as usual. We took him back to the vet for a checkup and told the vet we saw no sign of him slowing down; in fact, we believed he was healed. I further explained how we anointed Rocket with oil and prayed. As the doctor examined Rocket, he asked me, "What kind of oil did you use?" (He thought it was medical oil, but we had used anointing oil that is used when praying for the sick!)

The doctor could also see no difference in Rocket and wondered if the poison had been long-acting rather than short-acting, which would be twenty-one days versus seven. We knew it was the short-acting poison.

Rocket continued to live a vibrant life for many more years. I used his testimony in children's church several times and would often hear a child praying, "Lord, if you could heal a little dog like Rocket, then you can heal my grandmother …" Rocket's story increased the faith of many and encouraged kids to use their words wisely.

**Angels Are Waiting to Be Busy**

Did you know that our angels are waiting for us to declare the Word of God so that they can get busy? I imagine that when we negate God's Word with our words, they are just sitting around bored (speculation and imagination at work in my thoughts)!

Psalm 103:20 says, *"Bless the LORD, you His angels, Mighty in strength, who perform His word, obeying the voice of His word!"* (NASB)

Delight with me as I tell you this story. One time, we had several relatives who needed visits due to age or illness. There is only so much cash and frequent flyer miles to go around. To make a long story short, I felt compelled by the Holy Spirit to go see my mom the next day. Due to the cost of a quick trip, the best way to do it was with frequent flyer miles. If there was a seat available, they will let you use them. I did not have enough points available. I could have said the negative: "I don't have the money. I can't use the frequent flyer points. How am I supposed to do this?"

Instead, I declared, *"My God supplies all my needs according to His riches in glory"* (Philippians 4:19). "Lord, if You want me on a plane tomorrow, You need to help me figure this out."

Within ten minutes, a friend of mine called and said, "Lori, I feel compelled by the Lord to give you a frequent flyer ticket." I joyfully thanked her, explaining the prayer. I was on the plane the next morning for the needed visit. Our God reigns!

**Train to Be in Agreement with God**

*"Can two walk together, unless they are agreed?"* (Amos 3:3 NKJV)

We need to train ourselves and our children to be careful when speaking. To agree with God is to use His words. We need to agree that we are who God says we are, and we can do what He has called us to do. This can be done in at least two ways. One way is for everyone to be careful how they use their words. It is a difficult habit to develop. Make a deal with your kids. When they hear you saying something contrary to God's Word, ask them to give you a gentle reminder. And you do the same thing for them.

Another way to train using God's Word is to practice praying God's Word. Give your child some of God's promises, and practice praying them. For example, this morning I reminded my grandkids of a Bible verse they already knew: *"I can do all things through Christ who strengthens me"* (Philippians 4:13 NKJV). They have already learned how to use it to pray for themselves when frustrated with an assignment or project they are working on. In that case, they would pray, "Lord, your Word says that I can do all things through you and that you strengthen me. I am asking for your strength and your help to complete my assignment."

This morning I asked them to use that verse and pray over me as I write this book. So each one of them practiced by saying, "Lord, Ghee Ghee (that's me) would like some extra strength and wisdom today as she works on her book. Please give it to her and work through her."

There is nothing more powerful than praying the Word of God or declaring it in conversation. With the verse illustrated here, we get rid of the "I can't" and replace it with "I can through Christ."

The prophet Joel encouraged the Israelites during a war cry to say, "Let the weak say that I am strong" (Joel 3:10). Perhaps you are recalling the popular song that uses these words, "Give Thanks," by Henry Smith and made popular by Don Moen.

**Check the Heart**

The Bible says, *"For the mouth speaks what the heart is full of"* (Matthew 12:34b).

Mom, realize that a way to keep a check on your child's heart is by the overflow. Words begin in the heart. When you hear foul language, a bad attitude, poor condemnations, or viewpoints that are anti-biblical, then your "mom antenna" should begin to discern a heart problem. Prayerfully consider how to challenge it. Prayer is key, and in most cases, you are nipping a problem in the bud!

**Choice of Words**

Recently Grace, my eight-year-old granddaughter, had some anxiety over learning to drive an ATV we bought for fun on the farm. Her lack of confidence was drained more after running it into a fence. We wanted her to overcome the fear and have fun. Of course, we walked her through the steps, had the ATV programmed for slow, and ran alongside her to give her confidence and make her feel safe. I asked Haynes, her brother, to remind her of Philippians 4:13: *"I can do all things through Christ who strengthens me"* (NKJV). We asked Grace to say it. We heard a weak, *"I can do all things through Christ who strengthens me."*

I said, "Okay, now say it like you believe it." After a few cheerleading-type encouragements, we heard a strong, "I CAN DO ALL THINGS THROUGH CHRIST WHO STRENGTHENS ME!"

I cheered Grace on and said, "I see your game face! The eye of the tiger! *You* have what it takes to make this happen."

Why did I include this story in the chapter on the power of our words? Our words involve using Scripture to build our faith. Our words involve using words that will instill confidence. Saying, "You have what it takes to make this happen" was a purposeful choice over "Good luck" or "You can do this." Do you see the difference?

With a couple more turns around the pastures by everyone, it was time to take the ATV back to the barn. Guess who shouted with confidence, "I want to drive it back! Let me do it!" This grandmamma beamed with satisfaction as we heard the sound of success in one overcoming fear and exercising confidence.

**Name It and Claim It? Oh No!**

Some people might practice the "name it and claim it" mentality in their prayer life, thinking they can ask the Lord for anything on their wish list and get it. Please do not mistake this teaching for this mentality. It goes without saying, that God is not a vending machine for our wish lists.

The difference is this: A believer can claim anything that is a promise from Scripture, Now, be careful that the condition is fulfilled. Salvation is a gift, but most other promises have a condition. For example, Isaiah 26:3 says, *"You will keep him in perfect peace, whose mind is stayed on You, because he trusts in You"* (NKJV). The condition for perfect peace is keeping one's mind on the Lord. Claim the promises — they are yours to claim — but be sure to do your part.

There can also be a misunderstanding if someone has heard from the Lord about what He is going to provide and he or she continues to pray and declare that outcome. If someone has spent time in prayer and has heard the voice of the Lord, then be cautious about accusing him or her to be part of the "name it and claim it" group. This person is only naming what they perceived to hear from the Lord. There is a difference. Again, practice discernment, not judgment, when observing prayer practices that are not familiar to you.

**Sometimes God Says "Wait" or "No"**

*"Now faith is confidence in what we hope for and assurance about what we do not see. This is what the ancients were commended for.... These were all commended for their faith, yet none of them received what had been promised, since God had planned something better for us so that only together with us would they be made perfect"* (Hebrews 11:1-2, 39-40).

There are times we know we have heard from God and waiting for the answer feels like an eternity! Abraham comes to mind. He waited 25 plus years for his promise of Isaac to be fulfilled. The Bible says that the testing of our faith produces perseverance. (See James 1:3) Abraham can testify to this firsthand!

Sometimes the Lord says "no" like when Mary and Martha asked for Lazarus to be healed. God had a better plan in mind. (See John 11)

Training our children to trust God through the process, while at the same time encouraging them to pray with conviction — the promises of God — is a faith walk. Paul encouraged us to *"Rejoice always, pray continually, give thanks in all circumstances; for this is God's will for you in Christ Jesus. Do not quench the Spirit. Do not treat prophecies with contempt but test them all"* (1 Thessalonians 5:16-21a). The reason we are able to *thank Him in all circumstances* is because we trust Him with the outcome.

Faith is increased when we spend time in the presence of God. Encourage your kids to focus on God and listen to His voice. Through this process, it makes it easier to handle the answers to prayer that don't go along with our first desires. Point out the benefits of waiting when God says "wait" and the importance of trust when His answer is "no."

## *Prayer Corner*

**Reality check:** Are your words filled with facts or with truth? What comes out of your mouth? It is a reflection of your faith, *"for the mouth speaks what the heart is full of"* (Luke 6:45b). Where is your faith level? None of these questions are posed to give condemnation but to give a reality check that helps force a paradigm shift in thinking and seeing a difference between facts and truth. Awareness is more than half the battle!

Do you already have a good understanding of the power of your words? Ask the Holy Spirit to increase your awareness and to tweak your vocabulary and conversation.

**Prayer:** Dear heavenly Father, I confess that I didn't realize the importance or the power of my own words. Please forgive me. I am willing to change and realize that I might need help, so I invite You to give me a check in my spirit when my words are not reflecting truth and/or Your Word.

Lord, increase my faith level so that it lines up with Your Word. Help me to base my viewpoint on Your Word rather than my experience. Activate my faith with my words.

(OR) Lord, I have already been working on this concept of the power of my words and the difference between facts and truth. Open my eyes to further understanding, and help me improve my perceptions to see things the way you see things.

In the process of me learning, I want to train my kids in the use of their words so they won't have to experience a difficult change in thinking. May my ceiling be their floor, meaning their starting point with this truth will be catapulted from a higher place for further growth in their faith. In Jesus' name. Amen.

# Chapter 19
# *Generosity and Blessing Enemies*

*"A generous person will prosper; whoever refreshes others will be refreshed."*
(Proverbs 11:25)

That's a strange section title! What do the two have to do with each other? Hopefully by the end of the chapter, you will understand this concept.

My youngest son, Mark, was planning a trip to China with Global Expeditions. The trip would be most of a summer, between college semesters. He would serve as the group photographer. The cost would be a few thousand dollars, and I wondered how he would raise the money. Being shy, he was not one who enjoyed speaking in front of groups and raising support. He was planning to work as a photographer for family portraits to help fund his mission trip.

My mouth dropped as I saw the money come in faster than expected and before any of the usual deadlines. I was praising the Lord for His blessing and giving Mark such quick success. The Lord told me, "Tell Mark the money and Christmas gifts that he anonymously donated to a single mom and her children did not go unnoticed by me." I remembered! Let me share with you.

While in high school, Mark worked as a cashier at Target. One time he came home excited about something he had observed. Someone had gone through the line with a variety of toys for all ages. The customer told Mark he was buying the gifts to give to families in need, in hopes that each child would have a great

Christmas. This man's generosity touched Mark's heart, and he wanted to do the same thing. I witnessed Mark find out from our church who he could help. He received some specific information on ages and gender and set out to bless a family. He shopped for toys and clothes for the kids and purchased a gift card for the mother. The church was preparing food baskets for families and so he arranged to have his gifts be connected with the food basket, to keep his offering anonymous.

As a mom, I was so full of gratitude to the Lord for witnessing Mark give with such generosity. You see, the Bible says that we reap what we sow (Galatians 6:7). The Lord was graciously allowing Mark to reap far more than he had sown.

Mark is very generous and receives much pleasure in giving to needy causes. When he was little, about 2 years old, I would give him two cookies and say, *"A generous man will prosper"* (Proverbs 11:25). I would then watch him give a cookie to his brother and to his sister. I would then cheer him on and call him back to me and exclaim, "Oh Mark, you are so generous, and the Bible says that a generous man will prosper. Here are two cookies for you." I gave him the immediate gratification for demonstrating the verse, because I was teaching and training.

Never did I see Mark or my other kids give with the idea that they would get something back. I realize that can be a concern, but it never seemed to be a problem. Instead, I saw all three of my kids develop a generous heart.

**Generosity and Sacrifice**

Another way to look at being generous is being sacrificial. Someone with the gift of generosity does not feel like they are giving sacrificially. They tend to look for ways to give. However, many others feel like there is a sacrifice involved when they give generously.

When considering Jewish tradition and history, "sacrifice" was a prominent part of their lifestyle. They sacrificed animals for the forgiveness of sin and a part of their worship. The purpose of the sacrifice was to help the worshiper feel closer to God. Rabbi Lapin says, "Giving a gift to a person has a similar result. It causes us to be a little closer to that person; making a sacrifice for someone causes us to love that person a whole lot more."[6]

**It All Belongs to the Lord**

Psalm 24:1 says, *"The earth is the LORD's, and everything in it, the world, and all who live in it."*

As you teach Psalm 24:1 to your kids, help them recognize that everything belongs to the Lord. If you develop this mentality, then you are trusting God to supply. When your children see a need or even have a desire to bless someone, they can learn to ask the Lord, "What do I have that would meet this need? Or, what do I have that would bless this person?" The Lord often gives a creative answer.

**Money Management**

Some quick tips for teaching money management:

1. Look for teachable moments to train on finances as you go about your day. For example, involve them in the grocery store experience, showing them how to compare prices.
2. Teach earning, tithing, spending, and saving through allowances. The process will also teach them a difference between wants and needs.
3. When age appropriate, help them organize a lemonade stand or some other business of interest. They will learn math skills, expense and profit, and how to set goals.

4. Teaching kids to tithe is essential. In the process, they can learn some math skills. Include in your teaching that to not tithe is robbing God (Malachi 3:8). However, giving the tithe is an act of trusting Him to supply and knowing that it all belongs to Him.

For more details on money management, I recommend these resources:
1. *Raising Money-Smart Kids* by Ron and Judy Blue
2. *Smart Money Smart Kids* by Dave Ramsey and Rachel Cruze
3. *Junior's Adventures: Storytime Book Set* by Dave Ramsey

**Blessing Our Enemies**

The Bible says in Romans 12:14, *"Bless those who persecute you; bless and do not curse."* Matthew 5:44 says, *"But I tell you, love your enemies and pray for those who persecute you."*

It does seem odd to talk about blessing our enemies and generosity together. But let's think about it. This is the next step in generosity. We are asked to be generous with those who have offended us. This sure doesn't make sense to our emotions, but nonetheless, Jesus told us to do it.

Let me give a couple of illustrations on how we did this. One time a neighbor child invited Ann and Mark to a birthday party, but did not invite Pete. They were 7, 6, and 5 at the time. We could not explain it away that they only wanted boys or only wanted girls or by age since Pete was the middle child. So I figured it was a mistake. When I called to RSVP, I said, "Yes, the kids can come. Pete's name wasn't on the invitation; I figure that was a mistake."

The mom told me it wasn't a mistake, that the child didn't want Pete (can we say awkward moment?).

Obviously, a child is not an "enemy" in the way we think of the meaning of enemy, but she *was* someone who had offended Pete. So this is what we did. I explained to all three kids the situation and that this was our opportunity to bless. Normally I would give a gift from the family, but this time we choose to get three gifts — one from each child. We prayed for our neighbor. We showed our generosity and blessing by all three kids sending a gift and giving her our time in prayer.

Party day came. The other two went on to the party, carrying Pete's gift with them. Pete and I did something special together. That very day, Pete was invited to two other birthday parties. One was a horseback riding party, and the other one was a dinosaur hunt in the park. The Lord blessed Pete for doing his part and "blessing his enemy" (by enemy we mean one who has offended).

Let me give another illustration. When Ann was in the first grade, another little girl was poking fun at her and calling her names. We tried to work it out, but the child continued. What to do? This child was being offensive. We again read the verses on blessing our enemy. We prayed for the child and then decided to make her some brownies. We put two servings of brownies in Ann's lunch box, one for Ann and one for her to share with her "enemy." I notified the teacher ahead of time and told her what was going on and how we were responding to it.

The child accepted the brownies, and her bad behavior stopped.

More than likely, most of us are not dealing with "enemies." But probably all of us, whether adults or kids, do at times need to deal with people who offend us. It's important that we get past our emotions and help our kids learn how to deal with offenses. Jesus wants us to be generous with those who offend us because we are told to bless and love our enemies.

Let's look again at some Jewish wisdom to help us understand how this works. We just discussed that generosity helps us grow closer to a person we are giving to. We could look at it as an investment we are making in the other person. When the person is one who has offended, then there is all the more reason to give an investment. Paul reminds us in Acts 20:35, *"And remember the words of the Lord Jesus, that He said, 'It is more blessed to give than to receive'"* (NKJV).

How can it be that it is more blessed to give than to receive? Rabbi Lapin explains it this way: "The root for the Hebrew word for giving is NaTaN…. It reads the same forward and backward: No matter from which end you view this word, the effect is identical. This indicates that in giving, we also receive."[7] When we sacrifice and give, we are giving of ourselves, so it becomes an investment from something we like. We may not feel like giving or blessing one who has offended us, but when we do it, our feelings follow our actions.

Giving or blessing our enemies or those who have offended us may not always change them, but it will eventually change the way we feel toward them. We need to walk the process out and teach our kids to do so in order not to harbor a bitter root (see Hebrews 12:15).

**Steps to Bless**

The first thing to do is offer a prayer of forgiveness. Forgiveness does not mean lay over and play dead and let someone walk all over you. What forgiveness does is help release your emotional tie to the person and the situation. Whether you or your child feels like it or not, pray this prayer: "Lord, _____ has offended me through his unkind or unloving actions or words. I do not feel like forgiving, but I am willing to do so through faith. I release forgiveness toward him and ask you to bless him. If he doesn't know you, make yourself known to him. If he does know you, enrich his walk with you. Where he needs finances, provide; where he needs protection, give it; where he needs health, heal him. Give me wisdom in my responses. In Jesus' name."

Ask the Lord to give you a strategy. We often made brownies or did some other nice gesture, without expectations. Sometimes we purposefully prayed, in detail, for the person, asking the Lord to bless his or her health, finances, and family.

Harboring an offense will keep you or your child from a blessing. Moses was an amazing intercessor for the Israelites, but he did get angry and was not able to go into the Promised Land (Numbers 20:7-12, Deuteronomy 32:48-52). Keep offenses in check, and be generous with your prayers toward those who have offended.

**Speak to Your Unforgiving Emotions**

When Jesus taught us about offenses, He said there was no doubt we would be offended in life. He told the disciples, *"It is impossible that no offenses should come"* (Luke 17a). He continued to explain that with faith as small as a mustard seed, we could cast the offense out by the root.

Jesus then explained how to get rid of offenses. To get rid of the evil forces of unforgiveness and bitterness, the technique is to use the authority of your voice to speak to these attitudes. Jesus taught, *"If you have faith as small as a mustard seed, you can say to this mulberry tree. 'Be pulled up by the roots and be planted in the sea' and it will obey you"* (Luke 17:6). Develop the discipline of speaking to these attitudes, using your God-given authority represented through your voice. Let's face it, if you don't speak to the offenses, then they will continue to speak to you through your thoughts and emotions.

Training your kids to do the same will save them years of heartache, where they are bound by the evil forces of unforgiveness and bitterness. Just think of all the time and money saved from going to a therapist if only this one technique is practiced faithfully!

For further insight, consider why Jesus compared unforgiveness to the mulberry tree. It has deep and large roots. The wood was used for building caskets. The fruit from the mulberry tree is a fig that is very bitter to eat. Imagine such a tree of unforgiveness in your life or the lives of your children.

## *Prayer Corner*

**Reality check:** Does your child enjoy giving? Have you taught him how to be a good steward of what he has? How is sharing displayed in the household and with others? Have you taught how to bless those who offend your little ones? Have you spent time practicing the prayer of forgiveness?

**Prayer:** Dear heavenly Father, please help me build generosity into _____. Teach us the value of sowing generously. May my children be cheerful in their giving so that it brings them pleasure to watch others enjoy their spirit of giving (see 2 Corinthians 9:6-8).

May _____ learn to acknowledge that You own everything and that he will always look to You to meet all of his needs according to Your glorious riches in Christ Jesus (see Philippians 4:19). Lord, please help _____ be content with what You have given and not to develop a love of money.

Lord, help _____ to bless his enemies and be generous to them with his prayers and, when led, by giving of himself. Sometimes we don't feel like blessing or giving, but help us to be willing to put our feelings aside and learn from You. In Jesus' name, Amen.

# Chapter 20
# *Friends and Fools*

*"Walk with the wise and become wise, for a companion of fools suffers harm."*
*(Proverbs 13:20)*

As a child grows older, next to parents, often friends have the most influence over our kids. From the very beginning, teach your kids how to be a good friend and how to look for good friends. I used to tell Ann to "shoot for the stars" with her friends. I would often give her little gifts with stars as a reminder of our friend discussions. I gave her a star frame with a picture of her and one of her best friends with a note saying, "Thanks for choosing 'stars' for friends. Y'all have fun together." When she married, I told her she found a "star" to be "her man." Having your own lingo or inside jokes not only helps create fun reminders; it also gives a sense of belonging and bonding.

Our communications and activities depend upon the different levels of friendship. Help guide them to what is appropriate for an acquaintance as opposed to a close friend. What are some the character qualities that one would look for in choosing friends? Point out that we often become like our friends.

**Choose Your Friends Wisely**

When children come over to our farm and I am showing them around, I like to point out our duck that thinks she is a chicken! She has learned to run like a chicken, eat like a

chicken, and scratch like a chicken. I often wonder, if her momma had been able to raise her duckling, how different her lifestyle might be. She would take flight and explore all the nearby ponds, looking for her food. I conclude our tour at the chicken coop by telling the kids, "Be careful who you choose to be your friends, because you will start to act and think like them."

Furthermore, the friends we choose affect our relationship with God: *"Anyone who chooses to be a friend of the world becomes an enemy of God"* (James 4:4b). Wow. When you think about it that way, wouldn't anyone be more careful about the friends he or she hangs out with?

I hear someone saying, *"But Jesus hung out with the sinners"* (Matthew 9:9-13). This is true. Why was Jesus having dinner with the sinners? He was in the process of evangelizing! This is a good opportunity to discuss motive and purpose. There is a call for some to evangelize in places and with people whom we would not call "close friends." Help your young evangelist know that there is a call and a strategy that comes from the Lord.

Sometimes when warning older children or teens about the character of others, they might quote a verse and say, "The Bible says that we are not to judge." That is true, but we are to have discernment, and we are to learn to examine the fruit. Train them on the difference between discerning and judging.

Discernment is investigating the truth and asking questions until all of the important factors are understood. Judgment is giving a verdict, usually accepting other opinions without knowing all the facts. When one is discerning, they are usually willing to be involved in the restoration process. Judgment is usually a rejection of both the sin and the sinner.

**Answered Prayer for Friends**

I have a great "Praise the Lord!" type of story that I can't wait to share with you. God is so good, and He is so interested in the details of our lives. I have discovered that He is the "Master Networker" and will bring friends to your kids. Go get a cup of coffee, and sit down with me while I share this fun and exciting story!

When Ann and Pete were both in Florida for school, they came home to California for the summer. Usually when someone goes "home for the summer," it is to the same location they had spent in high school and would have had plenty of friends. Due to a move across the country, that was not the case. I knew that the summer would be more fun for them if they had friends. I just simply asked the Lord to send my kids some friends quickly so they could have a great summer.

On the first Sunday they were home, I sent them to a good church that I knew had a great reputation and a large college group. They came home all excited, telling me all about it. "Mom, you are not going to believe who we met! We sat down next to another brother and sister who also just came into town for the summer. You are not going to believe this: They are missionary kids from Panama and know our aunt and uncle. They have spent a lot of time at their camps!"

Wow! As the story continued to unfold, I found out that there was another mom in Panama also praying that her kids would find friends for their summer stay in California.

Later that evening, I called my aunt and said, "You are *not* going to believe who is sitting in our Jacuzzi with my kids!"

Needless to say, the summer fun was a gift from God, and this mom had a knowing smile pasted on her heart as she constantly reflected on God's goodness and His desire to meet all of our needs and yes, even our desires.

*"Delight yourself also in the LORD, and He shall give you the desires of your heart"* (Psalm 37:4 NKJV).

**Don't Get a Fool for a Friend**

Little Johnny and Little Susie need to learn how to recognize a fool and what their correct response should be. Proverbs is full of information about fools. A good devotional with the kids would be to do a search through Proverbs contrasting the wise man and the fool.

I once heard the types and characteristics of a "fool" explained like this: "In the Old Testament, the word 'fool' is actually a translation of five different Hebrew words that reflect subtle differences in 'types' of fools. Unfortunately, the English translation makes it more difficult to identify the characteristics of five types of fools, but with a careful search of Scripture, these differences can be distinguished.

Wise counselors — parents, pastors, friends, spouses — need to understand the progression of rebellion that is reflected in the Bible's description of fools. If you learn to perceive the characteristics of a simple fool, silly fool, sensual fool, scorning fool, and steadfast fool, you will be equipped to identify and respond to such fools with wisdom and discernment."[8] This same source, *The Institute of Basic Life Principles*, has identified several different types of fools. Here is an example of five of them:

**The simple fool:** The simple fool simply doesn't know any better; he is very gullible. He is without knowledge and can be easily tricked with flattery, false teachers, and deception. Proverbs 14:15 says, *"The simple believe anything, but the prudent give thought to their steps."* And Proverbs 22:3 says, *"The prudent see danger and take refuge, but the simple keep going and pay the penalty"* (see also Proverbs 1:22).

**Response:** It is okay to try and help guide him. He needs instruction.

**The silly fool:** This fool is only interested in having a good time and believes he is justified in the way he thinks. He does not take instruction well and reacts in anger when things don't go his way or when his thinking is contradicted. One way to identify this fool is to notice someone who talks a lot without thinking (see Proverbs 17:28). *"The way of fools seems right to them, but the wise listen to advice"* (Proverbs 12:15).

**Response:** Teach your children to say, "This is not right. I am going to leave now," and then let them know that it is okay to come tell Mom or another authority figure. This is an opportunity to teach your kids how to stand alone. Also look at Psalm 92:6-7, Proverbs 1:7, and Proverbs 14:3, 17:28 and 20:3.

**The scornful fool:** He has rejected truth and delights in mocking Christians and their standards. His body language and facial expressions reflect his scorn toward authorities, including parents. (See Proverbs 13:1 and Proverbs 14:6). *"Blessed is the one who does not walk in step with the wicked or stand in the way that sinners take or sit in the company of mockers"* (Psalm 1:1). Characteristics of this fool include stubbornness, rejection of authority, and arrogance. Proverbs 14:16 says, *"A wise man is cautious and turns away from evil, but a fool is arrogant and careless"* (see also Proverbs 18:2).

**Response:** Train your children to discern the attitude of the scornful fool. When discerned, teach them not to pay attention to the person or behavior and to walk away quietly. The Bible says, *"Do not answer a fool according to his folly, or you yourself will be just like him"* (Proverbs 26:4) and *"Leave the presence of a fool, or you will not discern words of knowledge"* (Proverbs 14:7).

**The committed fool:** This is the most dangerous type of fool, often translated as "wicked" or "vile." He totally rejects God. *"The *fool says in his heart, 'There is no God.' They are corrupt; their deeds are vile; there is no one who does good"* (Psalm 14:1, see also Proverbs 17:21). This person can even give lip service to God and teach about God, yet deny Him in his lifestyle. (see Ezekiel 13:3, Job 2:10, 2 Timothy 3:5).

**Response:** Train your children to have no association with him. Walk away quietly, and tell a parent or someone in authority.

**The reactionary fool:** A hot-tempered person who simply wants his own way. *"Do not make friends with a hot-tempered person, do not associate with one easily angered"* (Proverbs 22:24). Chapter seven's bonus box suggests the slippery slope begins when the mind starts rejecting the truth. This fool is an illustration of the downward slide described in Romans 1. Proverbs 13:1 says, *"A wise son accepts his father's discipline, but a scoffer does not listen to rebuke."* This fool will mock Christians and their standards (see also Proverbs 1:22, Proverbs 9:7-8).

**Response:** Have no association with him. "See then that you walk circumspectly, not as fools but as wise" (Ephesians 5:15 NKJV). If this person is in a group and leaves, then usually the group will behave better. *"Drive out the scoffer, and contention will go out, even strife and dishonor will cease"* (Proverbs 22:10).

**Tattling**

This teaching on friends and fools has inadvertently brought up tattling, because in some of the responses children are encouraged to let an authority figure know what they are discerning. As we all know, tattling can be a wearisome battle, and we don't want our kids tattling over every little thing. In general, a rule of thumb I used to explain when tattling was a good idea was if 1) a person was getting hurt or 2) property was being damaged.

In the above scenarios with a "fool," the committed fool or the reactionary fool could be dangerous and fits into these guidelines.

However, discussions are not tattling. Many interactions a child has with friends and acquaintances can be topics of conversation. Discern the difference.

> ## *Prayer Corner*
>
> **Reality check:** Have you spent time training your kids on how to be a friend? On how to find friends? What character qualities have you taught them to look for? Have you taught your kids the characteristics of fools and how to respond to them?
>
> **Prayer:** Dear heavenly Father, thank you for the wisdom on how to choose friends and how to discern who is a fool. I pray for godly friends for my children. Please put them in our path; bring them into our lives. Lord, I would even like to pray for family friends so that our whole family can enjoy spending time with other families. Father, we pray for friends who love you and that our kids will have good discernment in choosing friends that they hang out with at school (see 2 Timothy 2:16).
>
> May our kids be like a tree planted by streams of water, yielding good fruit and delighting in Your ways and plans concerning their friendships. May their advice and counsel be from kids who reflect Psalm 1:1-3 and not the fool of Psalm 1:4-5.
>
> May they "walk in the ways of *the* good and keep to the paths of *the* righteous" (Proverbs 2:20). In the name of Jesus. Amen.

# Chapter 21
# *Eternal Thoughts*

*"He has made everything beautiful in its time.*
*He has also set eternity in the human heart;*
*yet no one can fathom what God has done*
*from beginning to end."*
*(Ecclesiastes 3:11)*

At the time of this writing, my Sunday school class is studying Revelation, and we have just looked at the last few chapters. One cannot help but grasp with awe how our lives are eternal. We will live long past this life and forever and ever into the next. Decisions we make in this life will effect where we will live in the next. More than that, in eternal Heaven or eternal Hell, there seems to be different rewards given at the judgment seat of Christ or different levels of judgment given at the great white throne. After freshly studying some of these passages, I am compelled to look at my own life and consider the eternal impact.

What does all this have to do with raising kids in the here and now? I know, I can see the young mom with a toddler on her hip and a baby in her arms and an endless load of laundry and dishes wondering why I am talking about the bye and bye.

The reason this is important is that if your child, teenager, or young adult has a sense of eternity in her heart, it will impact her decisions. When it came time to send our kids off to college, I wanted to be sure they each had a sense of eternity. Yes, praise God they were saved and knew Jesus. Of course, their first 18 years had given us plenty of opportunities to instill in them our belief of Heaven and Hell. Nonetheless, I felt compelled to pray for this specifically and consider some purposeful teaching on the subject.

**Be There**

Often, I would retell the story I heard from James Dobson soon after Pistol Pete's death. Pete Maravich was a great NBA player. They were good friends, and Dobson was there when Maravich died an early and unexpected death while playing basketball.

> *On resurrection morning, be there. I will be looking for you then. Nothing else matters. Be there.*

Soon after Maravich's death, Dobson had a discussion with his son about dying and Heaven. He said something like, "If life goes as it normally should, one day, I will go before you." He continued with what seems like a living will. The discussion impacted me. He continued (and I quote), "Pete Maravich didn't have an opportunity to speak with his family one last time. But I want to tell you, *be there*."

I chose to have a similar discussion with my kids, telling this story and letting them know how important it was to me to let them know that I will be waiting for them, so *"Be there."*

Lately, there seems to be a lot of books about people having pre-death experiences and coming back to tell stories of Heaven. Some are good and validate our belief that Jesus is the only way to Heaven. Others could be deceitful. There is a book I found years ago about a lady who remembered a dream or vision that she experienced while in a coma. In reading the book, I didn't find anything that went against my Christian faith. At the time, it helped me mourn the loss of my dad as I could visualize how the next life is a continuation of this life as personality and experience follow us. I asked each of my kids to read *Within Heaven's Gates* by Rebecca Springer. Use this book at your own discretion. Regardless, give your kids a sense of eternity.

## *Prayer Corner*

**Reality check:** Have you taught your kids that their spirit lives forever? This life, this moment, is but a speck in all of eternity. Do they understand that decisions and actions done in this life affect their future?

**Prayer:** Dear heavenly Father, You have promised to pour out Your spirit on all flesh and that they would have visions and dreams (see Joel 2:28, 1 Peter 1:5). Don't let anything keep our kids from what You have called them to, not only in this life but in the life to come. Help keep their eyes focused on You. Help them to make decisions with their destiny and all of eternity in mind. Give them a sense of eternity in their souls and spirits. In Jesus' name. Amen.

## Chapter 22
# *Purity*

*"Flee from sexual immorality. All other sins a person commits are outside the body, but whoever sins sexually, sins against their own body. Do you not know that your bodies are temples of the Holy Spirit, who is in you, whom you have received from God? You are not your own; you were bought at a price. Therefore, honor God with your bodies."*
(1 Corinthians 6:18-20)

This started out as a difficult section to write, not because of the sensitive topic but because our society has become so accustomed to the worldly view of purity that it seems people in the church have turned a blind eye to any kind of standard.

In the 60s, we had the hippies, with communal living and celebrating love and peace. I remember the slogan "Anything goes. If it feels good, do it." Sitcoms on TV were not yet showing what was done in the bedroom. Fast-forward to today, and most TV shows are casual about sexual relationships and include transgender and homosexual implications. It seems to be the norm on even the first date. The media really does influence society, and now there seems to be an unspoken admission that if sex is consensual, then it is okay. Seldom does one ever hear the biblical standards for sex and marriage.

I remember being concerned about high school prom and what seemed to be expected on those nights. One year, many of the prom dates and parents from our youth group all gathered at our house for a fun pre-party. We celebrated the night taking countless pictures and eating appetizers. As parents, we had so much fun sending the kids off, and it felt great that as a group there was an unspoken accountability. When prom was over, the plan was for the group to go to another parent's house for an after party.

There was another year where I felt confident in Ann's standards but not in her date. I am not shy. A few days before prom, Ann was taking a little too long to get ready for her date, and he was sitting in our family room. I decided to take advantage of the opportunity and have a talk with him. I explained to him that we used to live in Louisiana, and during the New Orleans Mardi Gras parades, people did shocking things they would never do at any other time. It was like there was a blanket of permission granted in an atmosphere of "anything goes."

I then reflected, "It seems that the same thing has happened with prom night. It seems there is a spirit of permissiveness over the atmosphere of prom night, causing all guards to go down." I looked him in the eye and firmly said, "Jess (name changed to protect the innocent), permission is *not* granted. All of our kids have signed a contract of purity, and I would like for you to read it." I then gave him the contract to read. He gave it back and said, "I agree with all of this."

Part of the point of doing this was so that others realize that when they are dating my daughter or sons, there is a family and a standard behind the date. It seems to add a little more unspoken accountability to the process. They know they will have to answer to someone if anything goes wrong or anything happens.

Young mom and dad, before we go further with this part of the training, you need to decide, where is your heart? I have seen the relaxed, permissive attitude of the world infiltrate the Church. No, I have not seen it taught from church pulpits, but I have seen the individuals in the church not practice the biblical standards or care if their children do or not. It might seem like an impossibility to train, knowing that all of the modern-day media shouts permission to have an intimate relationship even on the first date. Sadly, our society today is also very accepting of same-sex marriage. The biblical standard is totally undermined.

In your opinion:

- Is sex before marriage okay as long as the couple is consenting?
- Do you view your role as only giving the proper safety precautions?
- Is your attitude one of, "It's going to happen anyway, so let's just prepare"?
- Where is your heart on this issue?

The reason I am asking is that I want you to come face-to-face with what your expectations and goals are. If you think this is totally old fashioned, and there is a spirit of permission over pre-marital sex, then this chapter is not for you. You cannot train what you do not believe.

I am not saying what you have "experienced"; I am saying "what you believe." There is a difference. If you were caught in the blanket of permissiveness, that doesn't mean you can't train your kids to follow biblical standards. Just confess it — it's under the blood — and purpose your heart and goals toward godly standards.

I recognize that because of our permissive society, you as a parent are going against the flow. This is not an easy journey. Let's remember that *"with God nothing will be impossible"* (Luke 1:37 NKJV).

Do you uphold the biblical principals of sex and marriage? If so, then let's roll up our sleeves and get busy. Let's approach this as a great opportunity to be able to train our kids in the very best values. We serve an amazing God, and He had the best for us in mind when He created the biblical standard for us to follow for our protection and happiness.

**The Beautiful Wedding Gift from God**

One of the first questions that a young teen might ask is, "Why? What's the big deal? Why did the Lord put all of these restrictions?" There are some very deep and powerful answers to this question, but I will just address the one I used, which seems good enough for a young mind. Carol Kohl, my mentor, told me this illustration, and I used it effectively. I will relate it my way and in the context of our family.

"Ann, remember the day that you snuck around and found out what your Christmas gifts were? Christmas morning came, and we would give you a package, and you would say, 'Oh is this the sweater?' We would give another one, and you would say, 'Oh yes, the game. Thank you.' There was no excitement with the gifts you already knew about. So it is with your honeymoon night. God has a beautiful and wonderful wedding gift for you — something so special that He created, and He wants you to value and enjoy. If you open His gift early, the specialness will be gone. Also, saving this gift for the man of your dreams, the one you are committing to spend your whole life with, is your wedding gift to him."

She understood. Every now and then we would be out shopping, and she would point someone out to me and say, "Her package has been opened."

Occasionally, a classmate or a teenager we knew would be pregnant. We would talk about how there was still so much life to live that could have been before these responsibilities came about. We rejoiced that the young single mom had chosen life, but we were sad that she could no longer be a cheerleader, and that finishing school would be more challenging.

The day came, and my little girl became a beautiful bride. I don't know how this happened, but her best friend's mom and I found ourselves in the room that would be the honeymoon room. We left some typical fun things, but there was also a beautiful wedding gift package with some special things from Gene's and my heart to theirs. I also included the purity contract, so that she could give it to John as promised. We knew that John was the young man that we had prayed for, and we wanted to leave them with our blessings.

**The Contract and Purity Ring**

Let's get real. Life is full of temptations and, as I have already said, our society does not make it easy to make a strong commitment. In the 90s, many churches were promoting purity rings and contracts. The church we were part of was not doing this, so we decided to do it as a family. I wrote a simple contract, and we went shopping for a ring that would represent a promise that would be between God, our child, and us. We felt the time was right for this was different for each one of our kids.

We renewed the contract every year around New Year's Day. Sometimes, if the kids were in a relationship with someone, we invited them to be part of our contract signing. I remember one young man was willing to sign it, too. I told him I really appreciated it but declined his offer. I wanted the contract only to have our family names on it when it was presented to the groom.

The reason that we renewed it every year is because as they grew older, life and hormones changed. Each year, they were facing life in a different way, and we wanted them to freshly process the commitment and the contract each year. This gave us an opportunity to talk about it and address anything that was important.

This contract was kept framed in their bedrooms.

Here is the wording of our contract with Ann. Pete and Mark had a very similar one with small differences to fit them. You can use it or create your own. You can see the date of the first signatures. After this, when we renewed yearly, we signed down the back of this page.

> Because:
>
> My body is the temple of the Holy Spirit,
>
> A pure body is the greatest gift I can give my husband on our wedding night,
>
> I love my future husband and want to have a healthy and beautiful relationship with him,
>
> I love my future children and want them to grow up in a home with a mother and father,
>
> And many other reasons,
>
> I, therefore, commit to staying free from any sexual activity, including petting as well as intercourse until the day I get married. Thank you, Jesus, for the power to stay pure and holy every day!
>
> My special covenant ring will always remind me of this covenant that I have made with my parents and before God.
>
> Signed  _Ann Hensley_                January 4, 1997
>
> Signed  _Gene Hensley (Dad)_         January 4, 1997
>
> Signed  _Lori Jane Hensley (Mom)_    January 4, 1997
>
> Signed  _The Heavenly Father_        January 4, 1997
>
> *"No temptation has overtaken you except what is common to mankind. And God is faithful; He will not let you be tempted beyond what you can bear. But when you are tempted, He will also provide a way out so that you can endure it"* (1 Corinthians 10:13).

**A side note**: Our family is pro-life, and our kids were well versed on abortion not being an option because we see abortion as taking a life. When the kids were as young as early elementary, we lived in Baton Rouge and were involved in protests at the Louisiana Capitol for pro-life legislation. We didn't talk about sexual relations at this time, because they were very young, but they did grow up with the idea of pro-life. Eventually, as they grew older, they knew abortion would not be an option for them. They also would lovingly nudge people they knew toward having a baby, with adoption as a choice.

## *Prayer Corner*

**Reality check:** What is your heart for your child? What is your attitude? Is any media allowed in the house that promotes wicked standards? (see Proverbs 12:26)?

**Prayer:** Dear heavenly Father, I pray for purity of soul, spirit, and body for _____. This is challenging for the day we live in, so I give this to You and ask for divine wisdom and accountability for our family (Philippians 2:15). Give my children a check in the spirit to protect them from the impurity of social media, computers, and all media (Proverbs 4:23). Lord, give _____ a sense that their bodies are the temples of the Holy Spirit so that they will walk in the reality of this truth (1 Corinthians 3:16-17).

I pray for the future spouses of all our kids, that they will be people who love you with all their heart, mind, and soul. Help them all to remember that they are clothed in the righteousness of Christ Jesus and are not to be unequally yoked. Let them be attracted to those who pursue righteousness, faith, and purity of heart (2 Corinthians 6:14, 2 Timothy 2:22).

May they all be an *"example for the believers in speech, in conduct, in love, in faith and in purity"* (1 Timothy 4:12). In Jesus' name. Amen.

# Chapter 23
# *Holidays and Summers*

*"The LORD said to Moses, 'Speak to the Israelites and say to them: "These are my appointed festivals, the appointed festivals of the LORD, which you are to proclaim as sacred assemblies."'"*
*(Leviticus 23:1-2)*

**We Serve a Party God**

Did you know we serve a "Party God"? Leviticus 23 gives specific directions for seven of the feasts and how to observe the Sabbath. God's purpose in encouraging the Jewish people — no, on second thought, *commanding* the Jewish people — to celebrate is to remind them of what He has done for them and to look forward to how the Messiah would bring fulfillment. It is a time for families to get together and share their love and thanksgiving for how the Lord provides. Out of the seven feasts, only one is somber. The rest are full of food, fun, and festivities.

As American Christians, we don't typically observe these seven feasts, but we do have traditional holidays and times when we celebrate. There is value in the family tradition and heritage. Traditions give our families and us a sense of identity and link one generation to another as we pass down rituals that are familiar to that particular family and shared by many others. For example, most Americans traditionally hang Christmas stockings on a fireplace mantle, but how each family does it and what they fill the stockings with is unique to each family.

**Traditions**

Not all traditions are faith-related, but still serve other family purposes. It is fun to keep the old and introduce the new. For example, in 2005, a book came out called, *The Elf on the Shelf*. It seems that in record speed, the mischief of a little elf during the Christmas season went viral and was practiced in homes all across America. Regardless of what your family practices, it is important to instill traditions and make memories.

Traditions tell a family story, and they play a part in the identity of a child. It gives a sense of belonging to something bigger than self and plays a part in building the confidence of a child. Traditions and celebrations develop family unity and create a time of bonding.

Most importantly, celebrations are a time of teaching and training values. The values of faith can be instilled while celebrating Easter, Christmas, baptisms, and many other times of celebration. The value of each individual is celebrated with birthdays. As Americans, the values of our American heritage are celebrated on the Fourth of July. I know some families who traditionally vacation together every year at the same time and place so that extended family members can purposefully get together. You get the idea. The list can go on and on as we think through our own memories of family traditions.

**Easter**

Easter is one of the most important holidays for families to embrace traditions that help each member grasp the reality of Christ's Resurrection. Inwardly, we rejoice with the women who went to the tomb to prepare a body but left with great joy, exclaiming, "He is risen! He is no longer in the tomb" (see Matthew 28:1-8). It is this fact that sets our faith apart from all other religions. We serve a Risen Savior, and this truth must be experienced by each of our kids. In fact, the Spirit gives witness to our spirit so that we can walk in the power of it (see John 15:26, 2 Corinthians 1:12, Romans 8:16).

The following verse should make us all jump up and shout "Hallelujah" and be sure that all know the advantage a true believer has: *"But if the Spirit of Him who raised Jesus from the dead dwells in you, He who raised Christ from the dead will also give life to your mortal bodies through His Spirit who dwells in you"* (Romans 8:11 NKJV). Can you even fathom the reality that the same power that raised Jesus from the dead is indwelt in the believer? If we could all only grasp this powerful truth, the world would change!

An idea to incorporate truth with our typical American tradition of Easter egg hunts would be to have the kids hunt for the one empty egg, representing the empty tomb. The child who finds the empty tomb receives a special prize.

And, when buying new clothes for Easter Sunday, talk about this verse: *"Therefore, if anyone is in Christ, he is a new creation; old things have passed away; behold, all things have become new"* (2 Corinthians 5:17 NKJV).

You can also serve lamb for the Easter family meal and talk about how Jesus was the Passover Lamb. It has already been mentioned that we do a Passover meal with others during the Easter season. This tradition powerfully highlights the story of Easter and helps all understand clearly the practice of communion. I have sadly discovered that many Christians don't realize that Jesus was observing the Passover during the "Last Supper," which instituted the Lord's Supper (Luke 22:14-23).

Explaining the foods used during Passover, tell the story of the Exodus and point the participants to the work that Jesus did on the cross and at the Resurrection. The Jewish tradition for a family celebrating Passover was planned and  directed by Moses. As he gave the instructions for the first Passover, he included what to say to the kids - then and now.

Three times before the tenth and last plague Moses anticipated and included instruction on teaching the kids:

*"When your children ask you, 'What does this ceremony mean to you?' then tell them..."* (Exodus 12:26-27).

*"On that day tell your son, 'I do this because of what the Lord did for me when I came out of Egypt'"* (Exodus 13:8).

*"In the days to come, when your son asks you, 'What does this mean?' say to him, 'With a mighty hand the Lord brought us out of Egypt, out of the land of slavery'"* (Exodus 13:14).

Moses wanted every generation to remember what God had done and for it to be passed down to each future generation. It is important to remember the past in order to protect the future. Jewish families weaved celebration and education together through family and faith traditions.

Recently, a Sunday School teacher in our community wanted to teach her kids how Passover and Easter were related. She asked me if I would bring one of our lambs to her class on Easter Sunday. I willingly did so, knowing that she wanted a cute little "Hallmark" type lamb. The kids loved taking turns holding the baby lamb and learned much in the process.

I also took pictures of what the size of a Passover lamb would have been. The Passover lamb is a year old and much larger. I don't think they wanted one of these bad boys in their Sunday School class. The lamb was to also be without blemish, to signify that Jesus was without fault (see Exodus 12:5, John 8:46).

You may not have access to a farm or a lamb – but there are so many creative ways that you can train and experience the deeper meaning of Easter.

## "Happy Birthday to Jesus" Party

I wanted to share one of our traditions that I didn't really think of as a tradition until a friend who I have known for more than 30 years, recently commented, "I see you are still doing birthday parties for Jesus!" As I wondered how she knew, I remembered Facebook. She has seen pictures.

Every year, we invite the neighborhood children and other friends to come to a birthday party for Jesus. It is the perfect way to share the true meaning of Christmas with fun and laughter. We do the traditional birthday party-type things like cake, games, and party favors. There are two other things that I include every year:

1) Read *Rudolph the Red-Nosed Reindeer*. I teach two principles as I tell the story:

a. I point out how sad Rudolph felt when others made fun of his red nose — so much so that he would hide. This is a good place to point out the value in using kind words and not being a bully.

b. When Santa uses Rudolph to lead the sleigh, Rudolph becomes a hero, and his perceived weakness is now viewed as a strength. Likewise, the Lord will use something we perceive to be a weakness in ourselves, and it will become a strength as we yield to Him. *"But he said to me, 'My grace is sufficient for you, for my power is made perfect in weakness.' Therefore, I will boast all the more gladly about my weaknesses, so that Christ's power may rest on me"* (2 Corinthians 12:9).

2) Tell or read the Christmas story from Luke 2. After the story, every child gets an opportunity to be part of the nativity scene. The costumes are provided in a variety of ways. Some are real from previous church plays, some are bathrobes, and some are pillowcases with a slit for the head. I gather up scarves from my wardrobe or old pieces of fabric to be the headdress. I have kept a couple of stuffed animals for this purpose and a few long sticks to be shepherd staffs. Sometimes we have a real baby, and sometimes we use a doll.

We pose for pictures, and each child goes home with a picture of himself or herself performing in the nativity scene. Of

course, every little girl wants to be Mary. No problem! We just change characters until all the children are able to receive the picture they want. In the old days, we used Polaroid cameras. Now, multiple digital pictures can be taken and printed in no time.

We have only had the fun of doing this activity on a farm for a few years. I had imagined that it would be great to have live sheep and goats in our nativity scene. But that didn't work so well. We ended up with angels chasing sheep (1), shepherds and Wise People playing with animals (2), and animals distracting the nativity scene (3). I wonder if the goats and sheep ate the hay out of Jesus' bed? (4)

Another activity we occasionally used for this party was sharing the meaning of each child's name and/or prophesying over the name of the child. This is fun, edifies the child, and ties in with the Christmas story. Matthew 1:23 says, *"'The virgin will conceive and give birth to a son, and they will call him Immanuel' (which means 'God with us')."*

If you know the families who you are inviting and feel comfortable; you can suggest bringing a Christmas gift for Jesus.

The gift can be a donation to a charity or gifts for a needy family.

Always start with some fun, active games. Most of the time, we have lived in the South, so one of our favorite activities was taking huge marshmallows and pretending they were snowballs. First, we would play "Snowball Toss." We divided up into teams, and the teams lined up. About 10 feet in front of each team is a person holding a bucket. Each team member gets about five turns to toss the "snowball" into the bucket. The team with the most snowballs in the bucket wins.

What is a bunch of snowballs without a snowball fight? Southern kids *loved* having a good ole fashioned snowball fight using the large marshmallows.

For other fun Christmas game ideas, refer to Google, Pinterest, and "Minute to Win it" websites.

The birthday party for Jesus has continued to be a tradition that my daughter does with her kids. It provides an opportunity to share Jesus with other families who may not know the true meaning of Christmas.

**Creating Family Traditions**

As a new family, how do you decide what traditions to keep and which ones to discard? You might desire to create new traditions for your family. First, think about the purpose. What are you hoping to get from it? Does it instill faith values or family unity? Consider how to make it personal. Is there a way to combine a tradition from each spouse that makes it uniquely personal to your family?

A new tradition that I recently began is my answer to the "The Elf on the Shelf". I wanted to do something just as fun with my grandchildren, but I wanted to do something that trained in the faith. My idea was to go on a "Wisdom Journey" using the Wise Men from our nativity set. In the process of developing this idea, my daughter told me about the Jewish "The Mensch on a Bench." He comes with instructions related to Hanukkah. I have instead created my own stories and activities that take the kids on a wisdom adventure, where they can both learn and have fun.

Here is a tease. Look for more about this idea in bookstores soon!

Some traditions merge with the times. For example, Gene and I grew up with lots of casseroles and pies as part of the Thanksgiving menu. Recently, we have realized that the society and the family trend is toward fresh veggies and "clean" eating. Sometimes we need to change our ways to accommodate the new. It's okay to create or eliminate traditions as times and seasons change.

**Summer**

Proverbs 10:5 says, *"He who gathers crops in summer is a prudent son, but he who sleeps during harvest is a disgraceful son."*

Summer gives us an opportunity to have more valuable free time with our kids — even when the time might sometimes feel like too much! It is also a great time to create new traditions, such as having a pool party on the first day the pool is open, planning getaways both near and far, catching fireflies, campfires, and eating s'mores.

When my kids were young, I found a book called *Sanity in the*

*Summertime* by Linda Dillow and Claudia Arp. It was filled with great ideas for activities and games for the family. Their ideas are very practical and planned to strengthen family relationships.

We often included hiking in our summer family activities. It became more and more valuable as the kids grew older. There was something about walking and talking that helped strengthen family values. And then, what a joy it was to reach the goal — the top of a mountain — and share the victory and the view together.

Then there is the traditional last day of summer. Leading up to this day are school shopping days, fresh haircuts, and "last" activities. On this last day of summer, create an atmosphere of sharing the memories and looking over photos from some of the summer adventures. Take time to write fresh visions and goals for the coming school year. In a way, the start of the new school year is much like the "New Year" that we celebrate on January 1.

## *Prayer Corner*

**Reality check:** What traditions do your family practice? Do they serve a purpose? Are they personal? Do you feel overwhelmed, or is it fun for you and the family to connect? Are there new traditions you want to start? Are there some you would like to eliminate? After prayerfully considering your traditions and understanding the value of purpose, does it add more value to the time and effort?

**Prayer:** Father, I am so happy to know that you love festivities as well. We want our festivities to serve the purpose of identity, fun, fellowship, and even training. We want to make the most of every opportunity, including how we spend our time enjoying festivities and recognizing You. In Jesus' name, Amen.

# Chapter 24
# *Times Are Changing: Raising Generals for the Kingdom of God*

*"And afterward, I will pour out my Spirit on all people. Your sons and daughters will prophesy, your old men will dream dreams, your young men will see visions."*
(Joel 2:28)

Lately, I've been thinking about how much things have changed in our society since I was growing up and since I raised my own kids and even since I started writing this book. I have pondered about what I should change or leave out. As I considered this, I went back to a principle already stated: "Principles do not change. Standards change." This book is written based on biblical principles that would be the desire of godly parents.

The challenge of the day is that the standards in our society have changed so much that the lines between worldly standards and biblical principles are clearly defined. This widening gap between the secular worldview and a biblical worldview changes the atmosphere of the society we were once privileged to live in. In fact, some would say that persecution of Christians has started in the U.S.

Paul predicted these things in his charge to Timothy: *"There will be terrible times in the last days. People will be lovers of themselves, lovers of money, boastful, proud, abusive, disobedient to their parents, ungrateful, unholy, without love, unforgiving, slanderous, without self-control, brutal, not lovers of the good, treacherous, rash, conceited, lovers of pleasure rather than lovers of God"* (2 Timothy 3:1-4).

We know God has a plan, and He wins! Notice the verses that opened this chapter. Your sons and daughters are going to see visions, have dreams, and prophesy! God is pouring out His Spirit on this generation. It has already been said that the kids are hungry for the supernatural. We know that one of the characteristics of the upcoming generation is that they want to make a difference.

**Four Young Men**

Parents, do not be discouraged by the times we live in. Let me tell you a true story of four young men who were taken captive in a country that did not know their God or His ways. They were chosen to be groomed in the king's palace because they were young, good-looking, gifted in all wisdom, possessing knowledge, and quick to understand. In other words, they were handsome and smart! Yes, you know them: Daniel, Shadrach, Meshach, and Abed-Nego. You have met them in the book of Daniel.

They were tempted by the king's delicacies but did not want to eat and defile their bodies and affect their relationship with God. We discussed in chapter 8 how they made an appeal and impressed the eunuch and the king. Let's dig a little deeper. Later, a government-sponsored law came about that whenever the music sounded; all must bow down and worship a golden image of King Nebuchadnezzar. Whoever didn't bow down and worship would be thrown into the fiery furnace. Shadrach, Meshach, and Abed-Nego did not bow down, and others in political circles accused them before the king.

When questioned by King Nebuchadnezzar, who gave them a second chance to bow, *"Shadrach, Meshach, and Abed-Nego answered and said to the king, 'O Nebuchadnezzar, we have no need to answer you in this matter. If that is the case, our God whom we serve is able to deliver us from the burning fiery furnace, and He will deliver us from your hand, O king. But if not, let it be known to you, O king, that we do not serve your gods, nor will we worship the gold image which you have set up'"* (Daniel 3:16-18).

King Nebuchadnezzar was so angry that he commanded the heat in the furnace to be turned up to seven times greater than normal. It was so hot that the fire even killed the men who threw them into the furnace. But it did not kill Daniel and his friends. And when King Nebuchadnezzar called them out of the fiery furnace, they did not even have a tinge of ash on their clothes, nor the smell of fire on them!

We can praise God for His protection. We can also praise Him that Nebuchadnezzar not only praised God, but he also promoted Shadrach, Meshach, and Abed-Nego (Daniel 3).

Remember the story of Daniel in the lion's den? Daniel was well favored by God and King Darius, but some in the political arena plotted his downfall by creating a law that would go against Daniel's faith. The law prohibited anyone from praying to anyone except the king. The consequence of violating this law was the offender would be thrown into the lion's den.

What did Daniel do? He went home, threw his window open, and prayed and gave thanks to the Living God three times a day. As a consequence, Daniel was thrown into the lion's den, and an angel of the Lord shut the lion's mouth. The next morning, Daniel walked away with no injuries whatsoever!

Most of us grew up with these wonderful stories, but have you thought about how they are there to encourage you in such a time as this? In our country, we have not been captured and taken away to a far away land, but we are seeing many of our freedoms and values challenged. So in a sense, this generation is raising kids in captivity. We are captive to the new interpretation of the laws that affects our freedom of practicing our religion. Some of our new laws that we are held captive to are an abomination to God and even go against His first covenant with man (Genesis 1:27-30).

We have gone from being able to freely share the Christmas and the Easter stories in the town squares and in schools to now being silenced with threats of lawsuits. Sadly, if we were to go to a city park and ask children about some of the Bible stories we just reviewed, most would not know the stories. How does all of this affect raising your child to honor and love the Living God just as Daniel and his three friends did?

**Role of the Parents**

At the time Daniel and his friends were taken into captivity, Jewish society was deep into the evils of idolatry. In other words, they were not raised in a society that practiced worshiping the one true God. More than likely, their parents were devout and were influenced by King Josiah, who restored true worship before the captivity.

Think about it: their strong, godly stance and influence at the time of captivity didn't "just happen." These young men were prepared with hearts for the one, true Living God! Since society was backslidden, I think it is safe to speculate that the training and preparation came from their parents, not the influence of society.

**Moses**

Moses was raised by Pharaoh's daughter, in Pharaoh's palace — hardly a godly atmosphere. Let's consider the back-story. In order to avoid a sure death sentence just for being a boy, his mother hid him and prayed over him for three months. She then sent him down the Nile River in a basket with a kiss and a prayer. Miriam was able to follow from afar and watched what happened. I'm sure you remember the rest of the story: Moses's mom not only got to nurse him, but she was paid to do so! In those days, they weaned much later than our culture does. What do you think she was feeding him while nursing? She was feeding his soul with the truth of the one, true God. Yes, he was later educated and saturated with the ways of Egyptian culture, but when the time was right, he knew who he was, and he knew who the great I AM was!

**Disciples**

Consider the disciples. Brothers Peter and Andrew, along with two other brothers, James and John, were career fishermen. When Jesus called them, they immediately left their nets and traded a life of economic security for a life of unpredictability. Speculate with me. Men in the first century were no different than men in the 21$^{st}$ century. They did not just carelessly drop their fishnets and livelihood to follow a man who said, "Come with me." Their hearts and minds were ready. How? What did they know at that moment? Could it be that their parents spoke to them often of the coming Messiah? They may have begun to sense Jesus' greatness and authority while with John the Baptist. He clearly knew that Jesus was the Messiah. Later, when many followers left, Jesus asked why they didn't leave. *"Peter answered him, 'Lord, to whom shall we go? You have the words of eternal life'"* (John 6:68, see also Matthew 4:18-22, John 1:35-55).

**Prepare**

Psalm 78:5-7 says, *"Which He commanded our fathers, that they should make them known to their children; that the generation to come might know them, the children who would be born, that they may arise and declare them to their children, that they may set their hope in God, and not forget the works of God, but keep His commandments"* (NKJV).

One generation prepares the next generation for their calling. Parents, we do live in challenging times, but we also live in the best of times! You have the opportunity to train and prepare the generals for the end time's army of God! You have the opportunity to prepare the hearts of your little ones for the Holy Spirit, who will be able to lead their generation into truth and flood our society with love and miracles. Is it easy? No. It sure wasn't easy for the three friends to be thrown into a blazing fire, but what an incredible miracle when they came out untouched. It wasn't easy for Daniel to be thrown in with some wild, hungry lions, but he walked out without a scratch.

**Pass the Baton**

Are you ready to pick up the baton and be sure that it is securely placed into the hands of the next generation? Are you ready to prepare them so that they will be so in tune with the Holy Spirit that they will hear *"a voice behind you, saying, 'This is the way; walk in it'"* (Isaiah 30:21)? If you have come this far in the book, then you have made your commitment and counted the cost. Don't let the times we live in discourage you. It is no accident that the Lord designed you to be the parent of your children. He knew you would have what it takes to face the challenge.

**Wisdom**

Culturally, we have begun to see the consequences of standing up for our faith. We need wisdom from above like never before. We don't need to live our lives with a chip on our shoulders. There is a time and a place to speak up. The key is training your children to be in tune with the guidance of the Holy Spirit. He will direct and give strategy for what battles to fight and when to fight them. *"But the wisdom that comes from heaven is first of all pure; then peace-loving, considerate, submissive, full of mercy and good fruit, impartial and sincere. Peacemakers who sow in peace reap a harvest of righteousness"* (James 3:17-18).

**Esther**

For example, let's look at the life of Esther. Her uncle, Mordecai, raised her. When the young virgins were gathered for the king to choose his new queen, Mordecai counseled her to not reveal her faith or family (Esther 2:10, 20). This was wise counsel as she continued the process of preparation to be chosen by the king.

Esther was chosen to be queen. Over time, Mordecai discovers a plot by Haman, the king's top aide. Haman conspired to kill the Jews throughout the kingdom. There came a time when it was right for Esther to reveal her faith. Mordecai told her, *"Yet who knows whether you have come to the kingdom for such a time as this?"* (Esther 4:14b NKJV)

Esther agreed, knowing that she was putting her own life on the line. She purposed in her heart to take the risk and trust God and said, *"So I will go the king, which is against the law; and if I perish, I perish!"* (Esther 4:16)

Esther sought wisdom and asked for the Jews to fast and pray for three days. The Lord gave her a strategy for when and how she would reveal her heritage and the plot against the Jewish people. She did not blindly or carelessly take a stand. Esther went against protocol with much prayer and guidance. She had a strategy. I would speculate that she heard from the Holy Spirit as she walked through her plan.

You know the rest of the story. The king was pleased with Esther, and he hung Haman on Haman's own gallows. Mordecai was promoted in the kingdom, and the Jews were saved.

May I point out one more time and ask who trained and prepared Esther for such a time as this? The answer is her uncle, who raised her as his own daughter. Again, parents, you are preparing the next generation for greatness in the Kingdom of God!

**Inquire of the Lord**

Before I close this chapter, I want to give you, mom, one more thought on obtaining wisdom. Reading through the Pentateuch and the Books of History, there is a phrase repeated over and over: "Inquire of the Lord" or "did not inquire of the Lord." What happened after that phrase was either success or failure. An example of this is when Joshua made a treaty with the Gibeonites. He leaned upon his own understanding and did not inquire of the Lord. As a result, the Israelites were deceived (Joshua 9, see also Proverbs 3:5-6).

> *It's never too late to inquire of the Lord. Seek His wisdom and His strategies.*

Continue to inquire of the Lord when you're stuck and faced with a major decision at each stage of your children's lives. It is so easy to go about our day and simply lean on our own understanding. *If* you do, do not beat yourself up. Simply repent and seek Him. It's never too late to seek the wisdom of the Lord and His strategies.

A personal project that I did was to keep track of this saying, "Inquire of the Lord." It would be a great project to do with your kids, so I created a work page in the appendix. Make a copy of it for yourself and your kids. Make it the size of your Bible, and tuck it in there to keep it handy. When you see this saying, record it on this worksheet.

**Ephod**

There were a couple of times in David's life that while he was inquiring of the Lord, he also asked for the Ephod. I scratched my head wondering why since this was part of the priestly breastplate. As far as I know, David was unique in asking the priest for the Ephod. It seemed to be reserved for the priest.

One such time was when David and his men had come to Ziklag and had discovered that the Amalekites had invaded and burnt their camp and taken everyone captive. In great distress, David strengthened himself in the Lord and then asked Abiathar the priest to bring him the Ephod. The Ephod had two stones in its inner pocket called the Urim and the Thummin. Somehow, these stones would answer to "yes or no" questions. *"So David inquired of the Lord, saying, 'Shall I pursue this troop? Shall I overtake them?' And He answered him, 'Pursue, for you shall surely overtake them and without fail recover all'"* (1 Samuel 30:8 NKJV).

The Ephod[9] had stones that represented each tribe of Israel — six on each shoulder and all twelve on the front of the breastplate. Speculate with me. I believe that when David prayed with the Ephod, he was not only using the two special stones but also praying with all of the tribes of Israel in mind. Remember, David's wives and children were taken captive, and he was in great distress. It would be easy to pray with all of the emotion of a husband and a father. He knew he needed the will and direction of God for the whole community. The Ephod put the weight of Israel on his shoulders and over his heart. He could pray with a pure motive.

**The Bigger Picture**

My takeaway from this is to encourage you to consider the bigger picture when you are praying for your family. Sometimes the prayers only need to be for the one child, sometimes with all of the family in mind, and sometimes with your child and school in mind — you get the idea. It gives perspective during the prayer.

**A Better Communication**

Let's get back to the Urim and Thummin. When you read what they were for, did you think, "Sign me up for one!" I know I did. After all, we are visual people, and that sure would be helpful — along with the cloud by day and the fire by night that the Israelites were able to see as they were led through the desert. Of course, the Holy Spirit reminded me, and I will remind you, that we have something better! We have the Holy Spirit residing in us and desiring to communicate! *"We have the mind of Christ"* (1 Corinthians 2:16b)!

We have a better means of communication and ability to hear God's voice. We also have the written Word of God, with the Holy Spirit helping us to understand it (see John 14:26).

> ### *Prayer Corner*
>
> **Reality check:** Have you grown fearful and lost hope after experiencing the changes in our society? Does it seem like your faith is being hidden with so much political correctness? Do you want more? Do you want to see God work through the circumstances?
>
> **Prayer:** Lord, I admit to being frustrated with our society. I desire to prepare my child to be able to hear Your voice and follow Your instructions during good and challenging times. I seek You for wisdom. I ask You to help myself and my kids to fine tune our hearing of Your instructions. Help us to set aside our own fears or desires and to see the bigger picture of what You would like for us to do. In Jesus' name. Amen.

# Now, go forth and pass the baton to the next generation. You have what it takes!

# PART 4:
*Bits and Pieces That Add Value to Your Training*

# Chapter 25
# *Prompts and Ideas for Family Talks*

*"She speaks with wisdom, and
faithful instruction is on her tongue."
(Proverbs 31:26)*

*"The teaching of the wise is a fountain of life,
turning a person from the snares of death."
(Proverbs 13:14)*

May the Lord give you creative ideas and strategies on how to use any of these ideas. They can be dinner table discussions or topics to talk about on drives or walks. Look for any opportunity. I give credit for these principles to Carol Kohl. They seemed to be part of the notes I jotted down more than 30 years ago, sitting in her living room and craving the ability to raise godly kids!

**Train to:**
- Obey: Genesis 22:18, Ephesians 6:1, 6.
- Show respect: Romans 13:7, Philippians 2:14-15, 1 Thessalonians 4:12, 1 Peter 2:17.
- Give thanks: Psalm 106:1, Philippians 4:6, 1 Thessalonians 5:18.
- Have a positive attitude that works miracles: Proverbs 15:2, 4, 7, 26, 16:23-24.
- Listen to wise counsel: Psalm 1, Proverbs 1, 11:14, 19:20.

- Take responsibility: Genesis 39:22-23, Matthew 25:21.
- Never give up: Proverbs 12:24-27, Philippians 3:14, 1 Timothy 4:15.
- Follow a schedule: Ecclesiastes 3:1, Ephesians 5:16.
- Please God: Hebrews 11:5-6.
- Do unpleasant things, like take out the garbage and eat your squash: Proverbs 1:3, 5:23, 6:23.
- Choose friends well, because evil company corrupts: Psalm 1:1-3, Proverbs 2:20, 13:20.
- Be an example: Proverbs 23:26, 31:26, Luke 6:40. Remember the old saying, "I can't hear what you say for watching what you do?" Actions speak louder than words.
- Commit works to the Lord: Proverbs 16:3.
- Learn from mistakes: Proverbs 24:16.
- Be impartial: Proverbs 28:21.
- Be a good worker: Proverbs 6:6, Matthew 5:16, 1 Timothy 4:12, 1 Peter 2:13-18.
- Have a vision: Proverbs 11:14, 29:18.
- Use money wisely: Luke 12:42, Philippians 4:19.
- Tithe: Nehemiah 10:37-38, Malachi 3:8-10.
- Be honest: Genesis 30:33, Psalm 25:21, Proverbs 10:9, 11:3.
- Appreciate the blessing of church life and preparing for Sunday (the Sabbath): Isaiah 58:13-14, Mark 15:42.
- Respect life: Genesis 1:27-28, Judges 13:1-7 (law applied to unborn child), Job 10:18, Jeremiah 1:5, Hosea 12:3.

- Teach how to fight temptation: 1 Corinthians 10:13, James 1:15, Ephesians 6:17.
- Teach absolutes: Psalm 11:7-8, 93:5, John 17:17.
  - There is a God: Malachi 3:6.
  - God loves you. However, what you sow you will reap: Lamentations 3:32, Galatians 6:7.
  - Secular standards will change. Every house has its own set of standards. Every generation has a standard, and they get worse. But God's principles are absolute and will never change: Matthew 24:35.

**List of Principles (this is just a start):**

1. What you sow, you reap: Numbers 32:23, Proverbs 22:8; 12:14; 28:13, Galatians 6:7.
2. When you are generous, you are blessed: Proverbs 22:9.
3. When you borrow, you are a slave: Proverbs 22:7. Be quick to return, and don't borrow.
4. A gift subdues anger: Proverbs 21:14. Gifts can be praise, love, and understanding.
5. When you confess and forsake, you will find compassion. When you hide, you don't prosper: Proverbs 28:13.
6. Work brings success: Proverbs 14:23.
7. Laziness casts a deep sleep: Proverbs 19:15-16. Need a project? Go to the ants (Proverbs 30:25).
8. Don't be enticed by or envious of sinners: Proverbs 1:10.
9. Don't argue, or you will get a bad report: Proverbs 25:8. Arguing is a sign of rebellion, and people don't like a person who argues.

10. Don't be friends with a gossip or a hot-tempered person: Proverbs 18:8, 22:24.

11. Don't rejoice when your enemy falls: Proverbs 24:17.

12. Teach them to be a friend of God and not a friend of the world: James 2:23.

13. Choose God's way. Proverbs 3:5-6, Proverbs 16:25, Matthew 7:13-14. Raise a Daniel or an Esther.

14. A good name is to be desired more than anything: Proverbs 22:1. Say, "You are making a name for yourself that will be remembered for eternity."

15. Kindness is very desirable: Proverbs 19:22.

16. He who is slow to anger is better than the mighty: Proverbs 16:32. Count to ten, and begin again.

17. If you want to be strong, then be wise: Proverbs 24:5.

18. The wise son is a true friend. He who has friends must show himself friendly (Proverbs 17:17). Think of the other person more than yourself.

19. You will be known by your deeds: Proverbs 20:11. Say: "Everyone is going to know what kind of child you are, and I am so proud. People are already talking about it."

20. Choose the right friends: Proverbs 13:20.

21. A quiet answer stops anger: Proverbs 15:1.

22. Your sins will be exposed. It is like gravity; it is God's law (Numbers 32:23).

23. Don't dabble in evil. Be wise about what is good (Romans 16:19).

24. Don't cheat or steal: Proverbs 20:17.

25. Be content: Proverbs 15:16-17.

26. Pay your debts: Proverbs 3:27.
27. Don't fight: Proverbs 20:3.
28. Don't believe everything you hear: Proverbs 14:15. Think about the right thing; don't just rush right into things.
29. Get even by doing good; good overcomes (Proverbs 20:22, Mark 5:4).
30. Show respect: respond positively and it will go well for you. Respond to your teacher correctly. (Proverbs 12:15, Titus 3:1, 1 Timothy 2:1-2).
31. Have a servant's spirit: Proverbs 14:35.
32. There are right and wrong reasons to tattle: Proverbs 11:13.
33. Control your temper: Proverbs 14:17.

**Challenge:** Throughout this book, there are many examples of how to teach godly principles with application. Along with this, I would like to pass along a challenge that Carol Kohl gave me that I took her up on.

*Take the time to categorize Proverbs.* Write it out, or type it. Don't just read it. A list of categories will be in the appendix. Yes, I know there are books out there that have done this already, but you are not doing it for a book. You are doing it to strengthen your own character in biblical principles so that you can train them in your children. Let the Holy Spirit amaze you as He did me when I took the challenge. As you write or type Proverbs topically, the Word of God will be written upon your heart.

**Practical tip:** You will rise to "supermom" status if you not only take up the challenge but also get creative! Record your verses on 3x5 cards. Get a 3x5 card holder, and label it "Recipes for Living." Make a card divider for each category. As you read through Proverbs, start creating your cards for your new box of godly principles and character qualities. Keep the box in a convenient spot in the kitchen. Use it for devotions with the children. Or, when you are talking to your child about a certain topic, you can use your personally created tool by saying to little  Johnny or Susie, "Let's see what Scripture tells us about choosing friends or fools." Pull out your "Recipes for Living" box and — presto! There it is — your own personal commentary.

The fun thing about this project is that it grows. When you finish Proverbs, you can add verses from all over the Bible and just keep adding to your file system as you would a recipe book.

**The Telephone Box**

How many times, as soon as the phone rings and it's a friend you would enjoy chatting with, does your toddler suddenly demand your attention or get into some mischief? Carol Kohl gave me an idea that worked wonderfully, if done correctly.

(I have to admit and laugh at the changes in our society. This may not be as big of an issue as it was in my day. We used phones that were tethered to the wall, limiting our mobility while talking. Nonetheless, perhaps this idea will be applicable for other reasons.)

Find a box, like a large shoebox, wrap it to make it look attractive, and top it off with some pictures of phones. Fill it with some age-appropriate things to keep your little one busy. Change these items occasionally to keep interest. The items could include old cards with fun pictures, safe scissors, crayons, paper, a new

Lego set, or a slinky toy. Use your imagination while walking around the dollar stores.

**Rules of the Telephone Box** (They *must* be followed, or it won't work.)

1. Keep it out of reach.
2. It can *only* be used when that special chat-time phone call comes. If you abuse this rule, the anticipation and specialness of the box will lose its appeal.
3. Be sure that the babysitter, dad, grandparents, and all who might care for your child know the rules. Remember, this is for you, not them. You have my permission to be selfish and not let them use your telephone box for their needs. It will lose its desirability if it is overused.
4. When that special friend calls and you need a quiet five to ten minutes, give your child the box, and let him or her explore. Obviously, stay in the same room so you can watch how the fun items are used.
5. When the call is done, or the child is done, put the box up, not to be touched again until the next special chat call.

## *Prayer Corner*

**Reality check:** Do you look for those "God moments" or teachable moments? Are you ready in season and out of season to train when opportunity presents itself (see 2 Timothy 4:2)?

**Prayer:** Dear heavenly Father, Thank you for these extra tips and prompts for a continual supply of ideas for training. Keep my ears and eyes tuned to You, Lord, for these moments. Give me the energy to keep on keeping on. In Jesus' name. Amen.

# Chapter 26
# *Choices: The Bottom Line*

*"Keep his decrees and commands,
which I am giving you today,
so that it may go well with you and your children
after you and that you may live long in the land the
LORD your God gives you for all time."
(Deuteronomy 4:40)*

If you don't get anything else from this book, this would be it: Kids need to learn that life is about personal responsibility and the choices they make. One of the first choices that they need to learn is:

**Obedience brings blessings, and disobedience brings discipline or consequences (judgment) (see Leviticus 26, Deuteronomy 28).**

It is a choice of the individual. Kids have to learn that they are continually making choices — choices for blessings or choices for discipline. The ball is in their court. We need to stop making excuses for their bad behavior. The sooner they experience the consequences of bad choices, the sooner they will choose to make healthy choices. Yes, we were all given a free will. Let's help them use their will to the best of their advantage.

Every time I hear of a school shooting or some other devastating event that is brought on by a teenager, I am motivated to communicate this one point. I really believe that imparting this one truth

> *Kids need to learn that life is about personal responsibility.*

will make a big difference in the choices a child will make and the direction he or she will go.

Our modern culture has taught parents to excuse the behavior of their children and not teach them to take responsibility for their choices. Kids need to learn that there is a consequence to sin, and this training begins while they are still infants. Children can comprehend things much earlier than they can articulate their thoughts.

This is the biggest lesson that I learned from my mentor, Carol Kohl, and it stayed with me throughout all the years of my kids growing up. No matter what age, this can be applied. Since then, I have taught it to countless other parents, and they have seen quick changes in their kids' behavior when using these principles.

All through Scripture, we see *that "obedience brings blessings, and disobedience brings judgment."* There is a whole chapter dedicated to this concept in Deuteronomy 28. It begins off by saying, *"If you fully obey the L*ORD *your God and carefully follow all his commands I give you today, the L*ORD *your God will set you high above all the nations on earth. All these blessings will come on you and accompany you if you obey the L*ORD *your God"* (verses 1-2), and then it goes on to describe bountiful blessings.

Mid-chapter, we see the other side of the coin: *"However, if you do not obey the L*ORD *your God and do not carefully follow all his commands and decrees I am giving you today, all these curses will come upon you and overtake you"* (verse 15), and then the rest of the chapter spells out the judgments. A more modern word for judgment would be "discipline."

Do you need more proof? Read Leviticus 26:2-13. If that is not enough to convince you that this principle is throughout Scripture, be on the look out for it with every story.

**How and When Do You Teach It?**

I hear Julie Andrews singing, ♪♪ "Let's start at the very beginning — a very good place to start." ♪♪ This concept of obedience is second to teaching the love of God! However, we usually do a good job teaching "God loves you" while overlooking this principle.

What happens? A typical scenario goes something like this: "Johnny, pick up your toys." Johnny ignores that command and keeps on playing. Again, a little firmer, "Johnny, pick up your toys." Johnny looks your way — but keeps on playing. "Johnny, I am going to count to three. Pick up your toys — or else!" Then, slowly (giving him more time and chances) "One ... two ... okay, don't make me say three!" And then maybe little Johnny will reluctantly start picking up toys. This little scene could be better or worse depending on how strong-willed the child is and his experience with your level of frustration.

You see, a child knows where your breaking point is and where you will get serious and follow through. Why not save yourself a lot of aggravation and follow through after making your request the first time?

I recently saw this cartoon on Facebook and thought it captured the point I am trying make.

Try this approach instead: "Johnny pick up your toys." Johnny ignores the command and keeps on playing. "Johnny, what are you choosing (using your hands as you speak)? Are you choosing blessings or discipline?" Johnny will make his choice; giving you the opportunity to either give a blessing or a discipline. Blessings can be simply a praise.

This little technique, taught from the beginning and followed through with consistency, will make a *huge* difference in the peace in your home and your child's ability to make choices.

I think a lot of kids don't realize they are making choices. As parents, we tend to excuse their behavior or compensate for them.

Say this phrase often: "Obedience brings blessing, and disobedience brings discipline." At the same time, illustrate with your hands, like this:

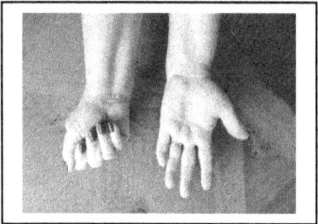

The open hand represents blessings, and the closed hand represents withholding blessings or discipline (not a fist). Soon, you will be able to be out in public and without a word - communicate with your eyes and hands, "What are you choosing? Blessings or discipline?" You will not have to say a word.

*When necessary say, "What do you choose?"*

Every choice they make will either bring them blessings with obedience or discipline with rebellion. Next time you want the toys picked up, try this:

"Johnny, pick up your toys." He ignores you. "Johnny, it is your choice. Do you choose blessings or discipline?" Immediately respond to his response. If he ignores you, then give the discipline (this would have already been pre-determined, and Johnny would clearly know what the expectation and discipline would be). "Okay, Johnny, it's time-out

> *Catch them doing it right so you can bless them.*

time." But it is more likely that, since Johnny is well trained and knows what to expect, he will start picking up toys. Now, it is very important that you bless him. Say, "Johnny, I am so proud of you for choosing blessings." The verbal blessing is often enough. During a training process, you may want to use other things such as a star on a chart or something special from the treasure chest.

A mistake we often make is not noticing the times of obedience, so we don't bless our kids' good behavior enough. Make it a point to observe their obedience to your instructions, and give them at least a verbal blessing. It will go a *long* way. Kids want to please their parents.

When given the opportunity, purposefully and so they can hear, brag about them to others. This helps build their self-esteem and also reinforces the good behavior.

Another mistake I often see is the parent "stringing the process along." Now the parent understands the concept of the child making choices and reminding them to make the correct choice. They give chance after chance to respond. This is very similar to the scenario I used at the beginning of this segment. Let me clue you in on a little secret: Your child knows you! She knows your frustration level, and she will continue in disobedience until she almost reaches it. Keep this simple. Instruction is given. A choice is made. The result of the choice is given. Over time, things will become automatic, and you won't have to "work hard" at catching the good behavior and giving the blessings. Consider when you are potty training; you might offer M&M's for every successful attempt. But they don't continue for years getting M&M's every time they go to the bathroom successfully. There comes a time when the training is done, and you move on to another area of training, with a whole new set of opportunities to give blessings or discipline.

## *Prayer Corner*

**Reality check:** Does your child realize that that his behavior, good or bad, is a choice he is making, and that choices have consequences? When it comes time for discipline, have you put and kept the ball in his court, meaning he is making a choice? Do you string the process along with "one more chance," counting numerous times, or endless discussions?

**Prayer:** Dear heavenly Father, I pray for my child to eagerly want to obey with a happy heart. Please help me to see more often when he is responding correctly with a good attitude so I can bless him. I admit that sometimes I take his good behavior for granted. When necessary, Lord, help me to be consistent and quick to help him make a choice between blessings or judgment. Give me wisdom to handle and respond fairly. In Jesus' name, Amen.

## Chapter 27

# *Weaving the Gospel into Discipline*

*"My son, do not make light of the Lord's discipline, and do not lose heart when he rebukes you, because the Lord disciplines the one he loves, and he chastens everyone he accepts as his son."*
*(Hebrews 12:5b-6)*

*"Honor your father and your mother, so that you may live long in the land the LORD your God is giving you."*
*(Exodus 20:12)*

Training in obedience is so important. Children's attitude should be one of doing what they are told with a happy and submissive spirit. Discipline yields holiness (Hebrews 12:7-11).

Discipline is not fun, but it is fruitful. *"No discipline seems pleasant at the time, but painful. Later on, however, it produces a harvest of righteousness and peace for those who have been trained by it"* (Hebrews 12:11).

**Teach them why they need to obey.**
1) It is protection from the enemy. Obedience will guard their soul from the god of this world (remember the umbrella illustration in chapter 3).
2) It is protection in difficult circumstances. Study Matthew 7:24-27 and notice the circumstance for each person. Is it the same or different? What makes the difference in the outcome?

3) It pleases God. Say often, "When you obey Mommy, God is so pleased" (Proverbs 3:8, 10:27).

4) It preserves their life (Exodus 20:12).

5) They need to learn the consequences of sin and personal responsibility.

Ask the Lord to give you creative ideas to motivate your child to choose blessing (obedience). Obedience and the desire to obey needs to come from within the child. This is the fruit of all the times you have spent training him to please the Lord, looking beyond his own desires.

Uh oh. Your sweet little fellow has crossed a line and defiantly looked you in the eye and did what you had clearly told him not to do. Reality check: Our kids have a God-given free will. They can choose to obey or not obey. Sooner or later, they will push the envelope to see how far they can go.

It's time for discipline. At this point, you have already made your rules and desires clear, and your child has clearly disobeyed. The fear of the Lord and consequences of sin have to be taught. You can't be in the trust phase of training if this has not been learned.

Remember during the process of disciplining that you are a channel of His love to your child. We are all familiar with the love chapter, 1 Corinthians 13. All of it applies to the process of discipline. To help articulate the process better, consider the difference between reacting to a situation and responding to a situation. You may be frustrated and even angry, but you want to be guided by the Spirit and logic rather than by your flesh and emotions.

An example of someone who responded rather than reacted to a difficult situation is Joseph, Mary's fiancé. Scripture says that he was a righteous man, meaning he was in right standing with God and man. When he heard the news that Mary was pregnant, he could have stoned her according to the Old Testament laws. Matthew 1:20 says that he took the time to think it through. During that time, an angel appeared with further direction. Joseph responded instead of reacting. And, as they say, you know the rest of the story.

When disciplining, always keep in mind the difference between childish misbehavior and rebellious misbehavior. James Dobson covers this concept well in his book *Dare to Discipline*. Rebelliousness is sin, whereas childish misbehavior is a matter of age. Your choice of how you bring the correction will depend on your discernment.

Remember from a previous chapter the importance of consistency. Your children will test you, and if they think they can get away with something, then they will. They are smart enough to know when you are tired or don't feel well, so you must be consistent during this time or they will take advantage of your state of mind.

Be understanding but lovingly firm. Use your eyes as you communicate. Your eyes tell the message (Matthew 6:22-23).

Now for the part that I don't want to talk about because it is so politically incorrect, but someone has to…so here goes. Sometimes we do have to spank. Okay. I said it. Notice I said "spank" and not "hit." Recently there was a news story about a celebrity who disciplined his child with spanking, and the press called it "hitting." Hitting is something done in anger. Spanking is something done under control and with love.

This is what you need to keep in mind. Only spank with rebellious or defiant misbehavior, not childish misbehavior. Use a spanking spoon, never your hand. You won't have to do this often if all the training and discipline is taking place. A strong willed child might require a spanking more often.

Have the child lay across you lap so that you are spanking the fatty part of their bottom. You will not abuse them over the fat.

After spanking, have a fellowship time. Sometimes you have to work at it or wait for the fellowship time, but be sure it happens. Ask the Lord to do the work. Remember, He will build the house (Psalm 127).

Weave the Gospel into your discipline. This is a perfect opportunity to present the Gospel. You can say, "You chose to sin, and you chose judgment." They are aware of the sin and know their need for a Savior. Weaving in the truth with how much God loves them will prepare their little hearts for knowing they need a Redeemer. When they are ready, they will ask more questions, so expect the discussion and be ready.

**Steps to Correction**

The Lord will give you the best strategy for your steps. This is a guideline. Remember, never discipline out of anger. Call a "time out" — even for you, until your spirit is ready.

> *Weaving in the truth with how much God loves them will prepare their hearts for knowing they need a Redeemer.*

For the first offense: Train them to be attentive; they are responsible for their thoughts, words, and actions. For the second offense: Give a warning, clarifying your instruction and expectation. Have them look you in the eye, and communicate your grief over their choice. Give only one warning. As part of the warning, appeal to their conscience and ask, "What do you choose?" Hopefully, they will make the correct choice, and then you can give them praise. Do *not* string them along by counting to three or trying to reason with them.

Remember, at this point they know the rules and they know their choice.

For the third offense: Follow these ten steps of discipline:

1. **Establish personal responsibility**. Be lovingly firm and say: "Johnny/Susie, you know what the rule is. What have you done?" When a child is guilty, he usually won't look you in the eyes. Ask for him to look into your eyes. Rule with your eyes. The eyes are the most important part of the body: *"The lamp of the body is the eye. If therefore your eye is good, your whole body will be full of light"* (Matthew 6:22 NKJV). Proverbs 20:8 says, *"When a king sits on his throne to judge, he winnows out all evil with his eyes."* Shakespeare said that the eyes are the window to the soul.

2. **Find a private room.** If you are not home, go to a bathroom or back to the car. Privacy is important to protect his spirit. You do not want to break the spirit, only the will.

3. **Reflect your grief.** Show that you are very disappointed. "I love you so much, but I am very disappointed in what you did." Wait for repentance.

4. **Associate correction with love and your responsibility to bring correction**. The Bible says, *"Foolishness is bound up in the heart of a child; the rod of correction will drive it far from him"* (Proverbs 22:15 NKJV).

5. **Win his will without breaking his spirit**. The spirit of a child is broken when discipline is given in anger or with irritation, unfairness, and misunderstanding. If you are so upset that you

can't deal with the situation without anger, then send your child to his room until you get right.

6. **The purpose of crying is to clear the conscience**. Signs of a strong will are temper tantrums, no crying, bitterness, retaliation, and threats.

7. **For more difficult cases, demonstrate more grief**. Let him see that sin makes you sad: "I'm disappointed, but there is tomorrow." Examine yourself for rebelliousness. In case you missed it, you can read more about this in chapter 3. While you are re-reading this part, take note of the "umbrella of protection" principle. *"But if we would examine ourselves, we would not be judged by God in this way. Yet when we are judged by the Lord, we are being disciplined so that we will not be condemned along with the world"* (1 Corinthians 11:31-32 NLT, second edition).

8. **Give comfort, affection, words, and understanding**. Josh McDowell said, "Rules without relationship leads to rebellion." I would call rules without relationship "legalism," and that does lead to rebellion.

9. **Prompt a desire for proper restitution**. Visualize how he hurt God and others.

10. **Evaluate results**. If the spirit was broken, then ask for forgiveness. Remember, keep a positive attitude. Desire the best. *"His compassions never fail, they are new every morning"* (Lamentations 3:22b-23a).

11. **Unity.** You and your husband must be in one accord in the area of discipline. You do not want to create an atmosphere where the child pits one parent against the other.

---

## *Prayer Corner*

**Reality check:** Do you string discipline along endlessly? Do you get frustrated with your child's lack of response and then finally get angry before he responds? Have you taught him that he is responsible for his choices and either the consequence or blessing from them?

**Prayer:** Dear heavenly Father, it never even occurred to me to put the ball back in my child's court. He has a free will and is responsible for his actions. I need help making this shift happen in our house. Father, open up my eyes of awareness, and give me strategy to know appropriate blessings and discipline. Nudge me when I am not consistent, and help me get back on track with loving discipline. In Jesus' name. Amen.

# Chapter 28

## *Prodigal, Come Home!*

*"When he came to his senses, he said, 'How many of my father's hired servants have food to spare, and here I am starving to death! I will set out and go back to my father and say to him: Father, I have sinned against heaven and against you. I am no longer worthy to be called your son; make me like one of your hired servants.'"*
(Luke 15:17-19)

What if the unthinkable happens and your child chooses a prodigal lifestyle?

First of all, if you are reading this book, then you have a heart for raising a temple for the Holy Spirit, and the Lord will continue to give you wisdom and direction — every step of the way. I believe the promise in the Word of God that says, *"Delight yourself also in the LORD, and He shall give you the desires of your heart"* (Psalm 37:4 NKJV).

Second, your heart must be aching. I pray right now as you read this that the Lord of Comfort will console you this very minute. I pray that in the depth of your grief, you will experience His presence. May He light an expectant hope that comes from knowing His promises are for you (2 Corinthians 1:3-4; Psalm 139:7).

Third, think back to a time when you know that the Lord began His good work in your child. It could have been when you were praying over your nursing baby or perhaps it was a time when he or she came home from VBS excited about Jesus. Take a moment and remember. Now, rest in the assurance that God's promise of completing the work in your child is real. You can be *"confident of this very thing, that He who has begun a good work in you will complete it until the day of Jesus Christ"* (Philippians 1:6 NKJV). In prayer, remind the Lord of that time and of His promise. You can be sure that His promises are true.

Most of all, you must not harbor a feeling of condemnation or hopelessness. Romans 8:1 says, *"There is now no condemnation for those who are in Christ Jesus."* Think of it this way: God is the perfect parent, yet Adam and Eve rebelled. The hope is in His redemption and that He provides a way back. He is busy, through your prayer and His power, devising the process of redemption. *"God does not take away a life; but He devises means, so that His banished ones are not expelled from Him"* (2 Samuel 14:14b NKJV).

> *God is the perfect parent, yet Adam and Eve rebelled. The hope is in His redemption and that He provides a way back.*

Some people come to the Lord late in their child rearing time and feel like they have missed valuable opportunities. Our God is so awesome; He provides encouragement for the lost time. The Bible says, *"So I will restore to you the years that the swarming locust has eaten"* (Joel 2:25a NKJV). My prayer for you is this: "May the Lord restore to you all the times and missed opportunities."

An effective prayer that I often prayed for my kids and for many teenagers is: "Lord, shower them with Your love, because You said in Your Word that Your loving-kindness brings us to repentance (Romans 2:4). Father, cause them to seek first Your Kingdom and Your righteousness, because You said that as we seek first Your kingdom and Your righteousness that all these things will be added to us (Matthew 6:33). Father, I take that to mean that not only food and clothing but also all the things we moms worry about will be taken care of as they seek You." I trust the Lord, so I would also pray, "Lord, my daughter (or my son) isn't listening to me anymore, so will You please tell them _____." Sure enough, within a few days I would hear, "Mom, guess what ..." And I would listen to an answer to prayer, nodding my head with a smiling heart.

Mom, if you are seeking godly wisdom on how to manage a child who has chosen a rebellious lifestyle, then you need to look with me at how the father of the prodigal handled his son.

Most of us are very familiar with this story that demonstrates the father's love for his son. It helps us realize the love that God the Father has for us. In spite of our background or lifestyle, we know that our heavenly Father is 100 percent accepting of us. Proverbs promises that if you "cry out for discernment, and lift up your voice for understanding… then you will understand the fear of the LORD, and find the knowledge of God" (Proverbs 2:3, 5 NKJV). We can gain more discernment from the story of the prodigal son if we approach it in the full context of Luke 15 and analyze the three scenarios involving lost things and how each was found differently.

1. **Lost sheep:** This is a picture of a sinner who has gone astray. Sheep are known for their ignorance, and thus some wander away, unaware of the traps they are walking into. The shepherd left the ninety-nine to go look for the one that was lost. Keep in mind; the shepherd knew the ninety-nine were safe and would remain safe during the search.

2. **Lost coin:** This is a picture of a sinner that is lost because of carelessness. The woman searches the house and puts all her energy into finding the lost coin.

3. **Lost son:** This is a picture of a sinner who is lost because of willful disobedience. The father did not leave the house to search or bail him out after he had spent his money. He allowed the son to learn the hard way. At the same time, the father was ready, willing, and waiting to *love* him back into the home when he returned. I hear you — you are thinking that the father might not have known that the young man was living a prodigal lifestyle and had squandered all of his money. I beg to differ. First of all, the father "knew" the son and his characteristics. His rebellious attitude didn't just come overnight. I have been in third world countries where cell phones and The Internet were not available, yet communication traveled quickly. The father probably had a stream of reports coming in as he waited and prayed.

**Discern the Root Cause**

What do we learn from this chapter of three lost things? The Lord is showing us how to handle a problem based on what we discern is the motivating root cause. Is the child reckless and has wandered away out of ignorance? If so, *go get him*! Or is the child lost because of carelessness and just flat wasn't thinking and was fooled into wrong choices? If so, *hunt him down*! Or did the child, knowing right from wrong, make a willful decision? If so, wait and pray. This is *tough love* and so hard to do. If the father had continued to bail him out, the son would have never ended up in the pigsty, which caused him to come to his senses.

I admit that tough love is easy to talk about and hard to do. But without proper discipline, many people will continue accepting handouts with no concern for change. In these tough situations, I suggest getting before the Lord and seeking His counsel.

*"Foolishness is bound up in the heart of a child; the rod of correction will drive it far from him"* (Proverbs 22:15 NKJV).

## *Prayer Corner*

**Reality check:** Are you in the difficult time of having a prodigal son or daughter? Has your child demonstrated defiant misbehavior, making choices that do not reflect the training you have given? This prayer is for you. Do not lose hope. Keep your eyes on our Redeemer.

**Prayer:** Lord, I need help knowing what category my child fits in. Has he/she made wrong choices out of ignorance or out of carelessness? Has he/she made his/her choices out of willful defiance to You? Regardless, hear my heart cry for my child to return to You! Baptize him/her with Your loving kindness, for this brings repentance (Romans 2:4). Bring _____ to a place where he/she will seek You with all his/her heart. Hear my heart's cry, just as you heard the cry of Hannah. I know I am praying in Your will because You are a family/generational God and because it is not Your will that any should perish, but all should come to the saving knowledge of who You are (2 Peter 3:9). In Jesus name. Amen.

# Chapter 29
# *Grown Kids*

*"However, I consider my life worth nothing to me; my only aim is to finish the race and complete the task the Lord Jesus has given me — the task of testifying to the good news of God's grace."*
*(Acts 20:24)*

*"Now I commend you to God and to the word of His grace, which is able to build you up and give you an inheritance among all those who are sanctified."*
*(Acts 20:32 NKJV)*

I have talked a lot about my kids throughout the book, and I thought you might want to know where we are today.

When it was time for Ann to go to college, we prayed she would be admitted to one that was about two hours from home. I wanted those occasional weekend trips home and was even willing to take on laundry duty to bribe her and her friends home for a visit. Our prayers were answered, and she was admitted to the college of her choice.

However, a couple of months before high school graduation, we took a career change opportunity across the country. Yikes — that was not in my plan! Ann comforted me by giving me a picture frame with her as a baby and as a graduate and said, "It's okay, Mom. You have done your job!" That may be true, but my heart suddenly knew how far "the East is from the West."

During college, Ann met a godly young man named John who became her husband. He is the one we prayed for all these years. We are so blessed to have him as a member of our family. John has often sent us a letter on Ann's birthday expressing how blessed he is to have her and thanking us. They are raising three children who are so precious! Ann remains strong in the faith, purposefully training her children in the Lord. As suspected, she does have a degree in education and has been the director of her homeschool community, Classical Conversations. She and John are very active in church and have a heart for serving the Lord in whatever capacity or assignment He gives to them. They have a heart for supporting missions and missionaries in several capacities, including participating in mission trips.

We have already seen their kids make commitments to Christ. We see them faithful with their walk. They have a heart for evangelism and are always eager to pray for the sick, faithfully expecting God to answer their prayers.

When we made our cross-country trip for a career change, Pete was entering his senior year of high school. We all know how difficult it is to move a senior, so we gave him a choice. He chose to come with us. He loved our new area and was accepted on the high school baseball team. However, there came a time when I "knew" Pete would be happier finishing high school with his old alma mater. He agreed.

We quickly gave him his graduation gift, a car, a year early. We set him up with a family who graciously allowed him to live with them. I signed him off at the high school as an adult, meaning I could no longer call the school for any information about him. He was on his own for attendance, discipline, and grades. As we hugged goodbye, a year before the usual time of empty nesting, I said, "Pete, these are tears mixed with joy and sadness. I am joyful that you are already the man I raised you to be. My job with you is done, and now the Lord will continue doing His work through a fresh experience and with new people. I am sad because I will miss you. I will miss watching you play high school baseball. I will miss taking prom pictures and doing a send-off." I turned and walked away to begin a long flight home, leaving two of my kids across the country.

The Lord is good and, in spite of the distance, we were able to have visits during holidays. Over Spring Break, I made the visit, and my time was filled with so many things that I initially thought I would be missing. There was a baseball tournament, and there is nothing better than a baseball game when your own kid is in it! I was there for the senior prom and was able to take the "mom pictures" and be part of this memorable event.

Something else happened that was beyond anything I would have expected. Pete chose to be baptized. He had accepted Christ at the age of 4, but with all of our moves and the churches we belonged to, the opportunity for baptism did not happen. The baptism took place at a beach. Before he went into the water, he was given the microphone to give his testimony. In it, he said, "John 3:16 has become more real to me over the past year. God had sent His only Son to Earth for us, because it was the best thing for all of humanity. He loved enough to sacrifice His Son. Through the past year, I also experienced the great love through my mom and dad, when they sacrificed to allow me to live in a different location, before the usual time of empty nesting. The pain of 'letting go' and understanding the sacrifice is more real at this time." He continued his testimony, but frankly I don't remember it. My heart was weeping with joy, gratitude, and amazement!

Fast-forward many years, and Pete is happily married to Andrea. Together they are serving the Lord in their careers. Pete is very intuitive and uses his gifts in business and being the "salt of the earth" in the secular world. He is a great motivational speaker and writer. He knows how to help others achieve their goals.

Our youngest, Mark, loves the Lord and married June, whom he met in Africa while both were serving with Youth with a Mission. He was there as a journalistic photographer, telling the stories of missionaries and mission opportunities for others "back home" to increase their awareness and prayerful support. His wife is also an artist, and together they share the joy of expressing God's faithfulness through their creations.

They are currently establishing a family life. Mark is working in business and occasionally uses his photography. The Lord is so good. It just so happens that his wife is from the town where our family was located. So when it was time for him to come home from the mission field, his future was already waiting for him. Like I have already said, God is the greatest networker of them all!

Mark and June have just welcomed their first child, and there is much joy in the household as we watch our baby, now a mature young man, have a baby! Their son is our fourth grandchild. Proverbs says that grandchildren are a crown to the grandparents (Proverbs 17:6). It is so true. I declare that I literally *feel* the crowns.

*"The steps of a good man are ordered by the* LORD, *and He delights in his way"* (Psalm 37:23 NKJV).

# Chapter 30
# *Loving Final Thoughts for You, Mom*

*"Can a mother forget the baby at her breast and have no compassion on the child she has borne? Though she may forget [and you know a mom never forgets!], I will not forget you! See, I have engraved you on the palms of my hands; your walls are ever before me."*
*(Isaiah 49:15-16)*

As I conclude this book, after years of putting it together and dreaming about it, I can finally see the finish line and you, young mom, reading it and being encouraged. My heart is just bursting with love and honor for our Lord. My prayer is that my ceiling has become your floor. May you be able to have tools to give you a head start in raising godly kids. This book doesn't have all the answers, and you might not have agreed with all. I do pray that the Lord will use this to trigger fresh ideas for you and become your springboard.

Thirty-some years ago, when I met Carol Kohl and had a desire to raise godly kids, I had no idea what it even meant. I had not seen it modeled. All I knew was Jesus and wanting to raise my kids in a way that would honor Him. After recalling and reviewing and teaching all of this material, I have felt amazed at how much my short time with Carol had so much impact on my life. There were times on the journey when I missed it. I know now much more than I knew while raising my kids. I jokingly say I could do even better now if given the chance to have a second round.

Remember, it is never too late to sow good seed in our kids and the next four generations! This is but a springboard for many more creative ideas and tools.

It is my heart's desire that God will take the truths in this book and plant them deep into your heart, giving you the desire, vision, and creativity to lovingly raise temples for the Holy Spirit. Looking back and after watching Olympic sports, I want to encourage all of you to "go for the gold!" You and Jesus can do it! You can raise a *golden temple* for the Holy Spirit to dwell in. Moms, you are the golden coaches that your kids need! I want to hug each of you and encourage you to keep your eye on the prize (Philippians 3:14)!

Consider, the love that Jesus has for you, dear mom: "Can a mother forget the baby at her breast and have no compassion on the child she has borne? Though she may forget [and you know a mom never forgets!], I will not forget you! See, I have engraved you on the palms of my hands; your walls are ever before me" (Isaiah 49:15-16).

Have you imagined the love that God has for your baby? My husband pointed this verse out to me and what is true of Moses, applies to your little one, because "God does not show favoritism" (Romans 2:1, Acts 10:34). Listen to this: "At this time Moses was born, and was well pleasing to God;" (Acts 7:20a NKJV). Take a moment and meditate on how well pleasing your little one is to God! Does that not warm your heart?

Moms, I believe that we are living in the end times. More than ever, we need to raise champions for Christ — kids who know their God and can hear His voice. The Lord has given you this assignment for training and preparing — don't doubt it. You may not even know where to begin and may even feel overwhelmed. Let me encourage you to just start. When I have felt overwhelmed, I have considered Joshua and the promise God gave him that he would be given every place that he set his foot. He was promised great success if he meditated on the Word of God. Think about it: What part of the Word did he have? Only the first five books (see Joshua 1)! He had not read the rest of Joshua or the encouraging words of praise and victory in Psalms. You have so much more than that!

Just start — one step at a time. You, too, can claim Joshua 1:3: *"I will give you every place where you set your foot, as I promised Moses."* Where can you put your foot down? Your family, your home, your work, your ministry — claim it! If God gave you the responsibility, then it is your territory. Go for it! You are equipped, and you have within you what it takes to get the job done!

***Now, go forth, and be a world changer!***

# Appendix A: Yearly Goals
## (three-month segments)

**January-March**

| Child's Name | Spirit | Soul | Body |
|---|---|---|---|
|  |  |  |  |
|  |  |  |  |
|  |  |  |  |
|  |  |  |  |

**April-June**

| Child's Name | Spirit | Soul | Body |
|---|---|---|---|
|  |  |  |  |
|  |  |  |  |
|  |  |  |  |
|  |  |  |  |

**July-September**

| Child's Name | Spirit | Soul | Body |
|---|---|---|---|
|  |  |  |  |
|  |  |  |  |
|  |  |  |  |
|  |  |  |  |

**October-December**

| Child's Name | Spirit | Soul | Body |
|---|---|---|---|
|  |  |  |  |
|  |  |  |  |
|  |  |  |  |
|  |  |  |  |

# Appendix B: Proverbs Categories

This challenge is suggested in chapter 24.

| | |
|---|---|
| Anger | Proverbs 29:22 |
| Animals | Proverbs 12:10 |
| Appetite | Proverbs 13:25 |
| | Proverbs 16:26 |
| | Proverbs 18:20 |
| | Proverbs 23:1-3 |
| | Proverbs 27:7 |
| Arguing | Proverbs 25:8-10 |
| Arrogance | Proverbs 8:13 |
| | Proverbs 28:25 |
| Attitude, positive | Proverbs 15:2, 4, 7a, 26b |
| | Proverbs 16:23-24 |
| Beauty | Proverbs 31:30 |
| | 1 Peter 3:3-4 |
| Bickering | Ephesians 4:31 |
| Boldness | Proverbs 28:1 |
| Borrowing | Proverbs 22:7 |
| Bragging or Boasting | Proverbs 27:1-2 |
| Bribing | Proverbs 17:8 |
| | Proverbs 18:16 |
| Carelessness | Proverbs 19:16 |

| | |
|---|---|
| Cautiousness | Proverbs 14:16 |
| | Proverbs 19:2 |
| Cheating | Proverbs 10:2 |
| | Proverbs 11:1 |
| | Proverbs 16:11 |
| | Proverbs 20:10 |
| | Proverbs 20:17 |
| | Proverbs 20:23 |
| Cheerfulness | Proverbs 15:13 |
| Compassion | Proverbs 28:13 |
| | 1 John 3:17 |
| Complaining | Proverbs 15:10, 15 |
| Conceit | Proverbs 3:7 |
| Conduct | Proverbs 20:11 |
| Confidence | Proverbs 14:26 |
| | Philippians 4:13 |
| Contentment | Proverbs 15:16-17 |
| | 1 Timothy 6:6-8 |
| Correction | Proverbs 15:31 |
| | Proverbs 29:17 |
| Creativity | Psalm 104:24 |
| | Proverbs 31:13b |
| Creator | Proverbs 20:12 |
| | Proverbs 22:2 |
| Curiosity | Romans 16:19b |
| Debts | Proverbs 3:27 |
| | Proverbs 13:13 |

| | |
|---|---|
| Deceitfulness | Proverbs 20:17 |
| Decision | Proverbs 16:33 |
| | Proverbs 18:18 |
| | Proverbs 21:1 |
| Dieting | Proverbs 13:25 |
| | Proverbs 27:7 |
| Diligence | Proverbs 6:6 |
| | Proverbs 12:24 |
| | Proverbs 12:27 |
| | Proverbs 13:4 |
| | Proverbs 21:5 |
| Discernment | 1 Samuel 16:7 |
| Discipline | Proverbs 12:1 |
| | Proverbs 13:1 |
| | Proverbs 19:18 |
| | Proverbs 19:20 |
| | Proverbs 22:15 |
| | Hebrews 12:4-11 |
| Endurance | Proverbs 24:16 |
| | Galatians 6:9 |
| Enemies | Proverbs 16:7 |
| | Proverbs 24:17 |
| | Proverbs 27:6 |
| Elderly | Proverbs 16:31 |
| | Proverbs 17:6 |

| | |
|---|---|
| Evil | Proverbs 8:13 |
| | Proverbs 16:6 |
| | Proverbs 16:17 |
| | Proverbs 19:23 |
| Evildoer | Proverbs 16:30 |
| | Proverbs 17:4 |
| | Proverbs 24:8-9 |
| | Proverbs 28:10 |
| | Proverbs 29:6 |
| Evil words | Proverbs 8:13 |
| | Proverbs 17:20 |
| | Proverbs 19:1 |
| Eyes | Proverbs 4:25 |
| | Proverbs 15:30 |
| | Proverbs 17:24 |
| | Proverbs 20:8 |
| | Proverbs 21:4 |
| | Proverbs 27:20 |
| | Proverbs 28:22 |
| | Proverbs 30:17 |
| Fear | Psalm 56:3 |
| | Proverbs 3:25-26 |
| | Proverbs 12:21 |
| | Hebrews 13:5 |
| | 2 Timothy 1:7 |
| Fighting | Proverbs 20:3 |
| | Proverbs 29:22 |

| | |
|---|---|
| Forgiveness | Ephesians 4:32 |
| Fraud | Proverbs 13:11 |
| Friends | Proverbs 17:17 |
| | Proverbs 27:6, 10 |
| Friends, choosing | Proverbs 13:20 |
| | Proverbs 18:24 |
| Friends, wrong | Proverbs 16:29 |
| | Proverbs 19:4, 6 |
| | Proverbs 27:14 |
| Generosity | Proverbs 11:25 |
| Golden Rule | Matthew 7:12 |
| Gossip | Proverbs 10:18 |
| | Proverbs 16:28 |
| | Proverbs 17:9 |
| | Proverbs 18:8 |
| | Proverbs 20:19 |
| | Proverbs 25:9-10 |
| | Proverbs 26:20 |
| | Proverbs 26:22 |
| Grace | Proverbs 3:34 |
| Grumbling | Philippians 2:14 |
| Guidance | Proverbs 10:8 |
| | Proverbs 11:14 |
| | Proverbs 13:10 |
| | Proverbs 15:22 |
| | Proverbs 27:17 |
| Hatred | Proverbs 10:12 |

| | |
|---|---|
| Hiding sin | Numbers 32:23 |
| | Proverbs 28:13 |
| Honesty | Proverbs 11:3 |
| Honor | Proverbs 3:35 |
| | Proverbs 3:9 |
| Humility | Proverbs 15:33 |
| | Proverbs 16:19 |
| | Proverbs 18:12 |
| | Proverbs 22:4 |
| | Proverbs 29:23 |
| | James 4:6b |
| Hunger | Proverbs 10:3 |
| Idleness | Proverbs 19:15 |
| Inner healing | Proverbs 20:27, 30 |
| Instruction | Proverbs 9:9 |
| Instruction for wisdom | Proverbs 15:33 |
| Jealousy | Proverbs 27:4 |
| Justice | Proverbs 28:5 |
| | Proverbs 29:4, 26 |
| Kindness | Proverbs 3:3 |
| | Proverbs 14:22 |
| | Proverbs 19:22 |
| | Ephesians 4:32 |

| | |
|---|---|
| Laziness | Proverbs 6:6-11 |
| | Proverbs 10:26 |
| | Proverbs 12:24 |
| | Proverbs 15:19 |
| | Proverbs 18:9 |
| | Proverbs 19:15 |
| Listening | Proverbs 12:15 |
| | Proverbs 15:31-32 |
| | Proverbs 18:13, 15 |
| | Proverbs 19:20, 27 |
| | Proverbs 20:5 |
| | Proverbs 28:9 |
| Love | Proverbs 10:12 |
| | Proverbs 17:17 |
| | Proverbs 27:5 |
| | 1 Corinthians 13:3 |
| Loyalty | Proverbs 20:6, 28 |
| | Proverbs 21:21 |
| | Proverbs 24:6 |
| | John 15:13 |
| Lying | Proverbs 12:22 |
| | Proverbs 14:5, 25 |
| | Proverbs 17:4, 7 |
| | Proverbs 19:5, 9, 22 |
| Meddling | Proverbs 26:17 |
| Memorization: It will keep the mind clean. | Proverbs 22:17-21 |
| Mouth | Proverbs 13:3 |

| | |
|---|---|
| Naïveté | Proverbs 14:15 |
| | Proverbs 22:3 |
| Name | Proverbs 10:7 |
| | Proverbs 22:1 |
| Neatness | 1 Corinthians 14:40 |
| Neighbor | Proverbs 11:12 |
| Obedience | Proverbs 19:16 |
| | 2 Corinthians 10:5 |
| | Ephesians 6:1 |
| Offended | Proverbs 18:19 |
| | 2 Timothy 2:3 |
| Offense | Proverbs 19:11 |
| | Proverbs 20:22 |
| | 1 Corinthians 13:5 |
| Orphans | Proverbs 23:10, 11 |
| Partiality | Proverbs 28:21 |
| Path of the righteous | Proverbs 4:18 |
| Path of the wicked | Proverbs 4:14-17 |
| Patience | Proverbs 15:23 |
| | Ecclesiastes 7:8b |
| Peacemaker | Proverbs 12:16, 20, 23 |
| | Proverbs 15:18 |
| | Proverbs 29:8 |
| Persuade | Proverbs 16:21, 23 |

| | |
|---|---|
| Poverty | Proverbs 10:4 |
| | Proverbs 17:5 |
| | Proverbs 18:16 |
| | Proverbs 20:13 |
| | Proverbs 21:13 |
| | Proverbs 22:16, 22, 23 |
| | Proverbs 28:3, 6 |
| Praise | Proverbs 27:2, 21 |
| | Proverbs 31:30 |
| Pride | Proverbs 11:2 |
| | Proverbs 13:10 |
| | Proverbs 15:25 |
| | Proverbs 16:5, 18 |
| | Proverbs 18:12 |
| | Proverbs 21:4 |
| | Proverbs 22:8 |
| Promises | Psalm 4:3 |
| | Hebrews 13:5 |
| Quarreling | Proverbs 17:14 |
| | Proverbs 20:3 |
| | 2 Timothy 2:24 |
| Quiet | Proverbs 11:12 |
| | Isaiah 30:15 |
| Rebelliousness | Proverbs 13:1 |
| | Proverbs 21:29 |
| | Proverbs 29:1 |
| Reproof | Proverbs 29:15 |

| | |
|---|---|
| Revenge | Proverbs 20:22 |
| | Proverbs 24:29 |
| Reward | Proverbs 13:13 |
| | Proverbs 17:8 |
| | Proverbs 22:29 |
| Riches | Proverbs 11:4, 28 |
| Righteousness | Proverbs 10:6-7 |
| | Proverbs 20:6, 7 |
| | Proverbs 21:3, 21 |
| | Proverbs 24:16 |
| Seeking good | Proverbs 11:27 |
| Servant's spirit | Proverbs 14:35 |
| | Matthew 20:26-27 |
| | John 3:30 |
| Self-control | Proverbs 16:32 |
| | Proverbs 19:11 |
| | Proverbs 25:28 |
| | Galatians 5:24-25 |
| Selfishness | Proverbs 11:24 |
| | Proverbs 23:6-7 |
| Self-righteousness | Proverbs 25:6-7 |
| | Proverbs 27:2 |
| | Proverbs 28:11 |
| | Proverbs 30:12 |
| Sharing | 2 Corinthians 9:7 |
| Sinning | Proverbs 20:9 |
| | Proverbs 28:13 |

| | |
|---|---|
| Slothful man | Proverbs 12:27 |
| | Proverbs 18:9 |
| | Proverbs 19:24 |
| | Proverbs 20:4, 13 |
| | Proverbs 21:25 |
| | Proverbs 22:13 |
| | Proverbs 24:30-34 |
| Spirit of man | Proverbs 20:27 |
| | Proverbs 27:19 |
| Stealing | Proverbs 10:2 |
| | Proverbs 29:24 |
| Strength | Proverbs 24:5 |
| Strife | Proverbs 10:12 |
| | Proverbs 17:1, 19 |
| | Proverbs 18:6 |
| | Proverbs 20:3 |
| Stubbornness | Proverbs 12:15 |
| | Proverbs 14:12 |
| | Proverbs 16:25 |
| | Proverbs 21:2 |
| | Proverbs 26:12 |
| | Proverbs 28:14 |
| | Proverbs 29:1 |
| Tattling | Proverbs 11:13 |

| | |
|---|---|
| Talking | Proverbs 10:13, 19 |
| | Proverbs 12:13, 18 |
| | Proverbs 13:3 |
| | Proverbs 14:23 |
| | Proverbs 15:1 |
| Teaching | Proverbs 13:14 |
| | Proverbs 15:2 |
| Temper | Proverbs 14:17, 29 |
| | Proverbs 15:18 |
| | Proverbs 16:32 |
| | Proverbs 19:19 |
| | Proverbs 29:11, 22 |
| Testimony | Proverbs 20:11 |
| Thankfulness | Psalms 118:1 |
| Tithing | Proverbs 3:9-10 |
| Tongue | Proverbs 15:2, 4, 7 |
| | Proverbs 16:1 |
| | Proverbs 17:28 |
| | Proverbs 18:21 |
| | Proverbs 21:23 |
| | Proverbs 26:28 |
| | Proverbs 29:20 |
| | Proverbs 31:26 |
| Training | Proverbs 22:6 |

| | |
|---|---|
| Troublemaker | Proverbs 3:30 |
| | Proverbs 11:29 |
| | Proverbs 22:10 |
| | Proverbs 26:17 |
| | Matthew 5:9 |
| | 1 Thessalonians 5:13b |
| Trusting | Proverbs 3:5-6 |
| | Proverbs 18:10 |
| | Proverbs 29:25 |
| | Proverbs 30:5 |
| | Proverbs 31:11 |
| Truthfulness | Proverbs 12:17, 19 |
| | Proverbs 14:5, 22, 25 |
| | Proverbs 16:6NKJV |
| | Proverbs 16:13 |
| | Proverbs 20:28NKJV |
| | Proverbs 29:14 |
| | Ephesians 4:25 |
| Understanding | Proverbs 13:15 |
| | Proverbs 15:32 |
| | Proverbs 17:27 |
| | Proverbs 19:8 |
| | Proverbs 28:2 |
| Unkind words | Psalm 34:13 |
| Victory | Proverbs 21:31 |
| Vision | Proverbs 29:18 |

| | |
|---|---|
| Wealth | Proverbs 10:22 |
| | Proverbs 13:11 |
| | Proverbs 23:4-5 |
| Wickedness | Proverbs 4:19 |
| | Proverbs 21:10 |
| | Proverbs 24:15-16 |
| Widows | Proverbs 15:25 |
| Wisdom | Proverbs 9:10 |
| Witnessing | Proverbs 11:30 |
| | Proverbs 24:11-12 |
| Words rightly spoken | Proverbs 15:23, 26 |
| | Proverbs 16:24 |
| | Proverbs 25:11 |
| Words to ponder | Proverbs 30:5-6 |
| Worry | Proverbs 12:25 |
| Work | Proverbs 6:6-8 |
| | Proverbs 12:11 |
| | Proverbs 14:4, 23 |
| | Proverbs 27:18 |
| | Proverbs 28:19 |

# Appendix C: Inquire of the Lord

The teaching for this chart is in chapter 23.

| Inquired of the Lord | Results | Didn't Inquire of the Lord | Results |
|---|---|---|---|
| Genesis 25:22<br><br>Rebekah wondered why her twins struggled within. | The Lord gave her an answer and insight.<br><br>Communication | Joshua 9:14<br><br>Joshua and the elders sampled provisions from Gibeonites and leaned on their own understanding. | They were tricked and had to honor their word with the treaty. The Gibeonites were a thorn in their side. |
|  |  |  |  |
|  |  |  |  |

| Inquired of the Lord | Results | | Didn't Inquire of the Lord | Results |
|---|---|---|---|---|
| | | | | |
| | | | | |
| | | | | |
| | | | | |

| Inquired of the Lord | Results | Didn't Inquire of the Lord | Results |
|---|---|---|---|
| | | | |
| | | | |
| | | | |
| | | | |

| Inquired of the Lord | Results | | Didn't Inquire of the Lord | Results |
|---|---|---|---|---|
|  |  |  |  |  |
|  |  |  |  |  |
|  |  |  |  |  |
|  |  |  |  |  |

# Appendix D:
# Lessons from Shadowland

*I went to church with Craig von Buseck, and when I read this on CBN.com, I asked him if I could share it in my book. Enjoy!*

**Lessons from Shadowland**

By Craig von Buseck

I love my dog. His name is Shadow, and he's a beautiful Golden Retriever/Collie mix. My kids named him after the gentle Golden Retriever from the *Homeward Bound* movies from a few years back — and for good reason. He is just like him. He has the perfect temperament for children. He's playful when they're playful, and he becomes totally mellow when it's time to settle down.

I always let Shadow out first thing in the morning into a section of our yard that I built just for him. We lovingly refer to this area as "Shadowland." He usually runs right out the door and into the yard. But on one particular morning, just as he was about to dart out into the yard, he stiffened like a board and, for a split second, the hair on his back raised straight up. I was puzzled by his actions, and I looked out to see what was going on, just in time to observe a family of ducks waddling through the yard.

Shadow is a Retriever, so his nature is to pursue these hapless creatures and bring them home for dinner. I looked down at Shadow and noticed that he had relaxed slightly. He looked back at me with those sad Golden Retriever eyes, as if to say, "Everything in me wants to go after those ducks, Dad. But I know that would displease you, so I'm not going to do it."

I was filled with so much love for Shadow at that moment. I got down on one knee, hugged his neck, and said, "Shadow, you are the best dog in the world."

Once the ducks were safely out of the yard, I let Shadow out into the yard and began getting ready for my day. But throughout the next hours that moment kept playing again and again in my mind.

You see, Shadow wasn't always so obedient. We live on a busy street, and I won't allow the dog to go out in front of the house. When I work on the front yard, I often leave the garage door open and Shadow wanders out to watch. He knows he is not allowed in the front yard, and so he sits at the edge of the garage with his paws right on the line where the concrete driveway meets the house. He knows what his boundaries are, and he usually obeys — that is, until that one fateful day.

I was out working in the front garden, and Shadow was at his perch in the garage. Suddenly a rabbit dashed out from between the houses and ran into the busy street. Instinct took over, and Shadow was after him like a flash. Out of the corner of my eye I watched Shadow cross the line of safety, running headlong into the path of danger. In a split second I sprang up, spun around, and yelled at the top of my lungs, "Shadow, no, no, no!"

Shadow knows his father's voice, and before he could reach the street he stopped cold and crouched down in a humble position, looking back at me. I was relieved, but I still rushed over to grab him by the collar — I knew that his hunting instincts might yet overcome his obedience to me. Once he was firmly in hand I chastised him again, leading him back into the house. After a stern warning I leaned over and hugged my dog, thanking God for protecting him from himself.

As a child I had lost two dogs that were dear to me. One had run away, and the other had been hit by a car. I remember the pain I felt then, and I was glad that my kids would not experience that same anguish on that day.

After that day Shadow never darted out into the front yard again. But when those ducks waddled past our door, I know that it took every fiber of love and respect that Shadow had for me to keep him from enjoying the hunt and the kill.

We humans are a lot like Shadow in that way, aren't we? In our fallen nature we have desires that seem almost overwhelming. These passions may be different from one person to another, but we all have them. Some people have the urge for wealth and power, others are motivated by the desire to be accepted and loved, others just want security and peace. If we're not watchful, these desperate urges can manifest themselves in destructive behavior that the Bible describes as sin — sexual sin, drug and alcohol addiction, gambling, verbal or physical abuse, greed, violence, murder, rape, envy, lying, stealing, cheating — the list goes on and on.

Over the years I have lovingly cared for Shadow. I have taught him to obey the rules that I set for him — rules that I establish for his protection, because I love him, not to keep him from having fun.

Now if Shadow grew up in the wild, he would never have had the input of a loving father, and he would be subject to the dangers of this world. He would be ruled by his instincts, and those instincts would have mastery over him. Had he been a wild dog chasing that rabbit, he very well may have followed it out into that busy street, and the very urge that drove him could have brought about his destruction.

Does any of this sound familiar?

The Bible tells us that we humans are fallen beings who are ruled by our sinful nature. In the book of Romans the Apostle Paul details our wretched condition apart from God's mercy:

"I have discovered this principle of life — that when I want to do what is right, I inevitably do what is wrong. I love God's law with all my heart. But there is another power within me that is at war with my mind. This power makes me a slave to the sin that is still within me. Oh, what a miserable person I am! Who will free me from this life that is dominated by sin and death?" (Romans 7:21-24 NLT, second edition)

Sounds a bit like Shadow, doesn't it? In our sinful condition this is our tragic lot. But as Paul writes, "The answer is in Jesus Christ our Lord." The first couple of verses of the next chapter in Romans gives us the key to freedom from this slavery to sin.

"Now there is no condemnation for those who belong to Christ Jesus .... [For] the power of the life-giving Spirit has freed you through Christ Jesus from the power of sin that leads to death" (Romans 8:1-2).

When you yield to the Lordship of Jesus Christ in your life — when you recognize that Jesus is the Son of God and that He died on the cross to pay for the sins of every person who ever lived — when you accept Him as your Savior, the grace and power of His shed blood brings freedom to your life like you can't even imagine.

Those worldly things that seemed so fun and important suddenly lose their luster. The sinful things that once brought such pleasure seem empty and meaningless. The habits that held you in bondage are weakened and in time completely broken by God's grace.

And most wonderful of all, you learn that you are a child of your Heavenly Father. You discover that He speaks to you, He guides you, He instructs you by His Holy Spirit — and like a good earthly father, He disciplines you because He loves you.

When I disciplined Shadow that day it was because I love him and I could see what he could not — that obeying his instincts could lead to death, but obeying my instructions would lead to life. Over time Shadow has learned to trust me. He has learned that I am a loving father who is interested in his good. That day when the ducks waddled by he demonstrated his trust and love for me by resisting his instincts and looking instead to his loving father.

The Bible says that God sets the choice before us. Will we obey our sinful instincts, or will we submit to the direction of our loving Heavenly Father? We can choose life or death. The reality is that no matter what we choose, we are a slave to something or someone — either a slave to sin or a slave to God.

The Bible tells us that the wages of sin is death, but the free gift of God is eternal life through Christ Jesus our Lord (Romans 6:23). If you submit to the Lordship of Jesus Christ, you are a slave who is given complete Liberty. If you stay in your sin, however, your slavery will ultimately lead to your death — physically here on earth, and spiritually in eternity.

You can trust God to free you from your sin and to give you a victorious life in Him. You don't have to be ruled by your instincts. When temptation arises you can look to your Heavenly Father and know that His way is the best way.

It's not always easy, and sometime our instincts get the best of us — just like Shadow's. But it is also comforting to know that when we blow it our Father is always there to forgive us, to instruct us, and to bring us back to a place of love and safety.

*Used with permission. This article first appeared on CBN.com.*

# Footnotes

**Dedication**

**1.** My definition of "knower": I use the term "knower" to describe a "knowing feeling" I have in my gut that this is communicating to me. It is the Holy Spirit speaking to me. Let me explain: We hear with our natural ears, and we hear with our spiritual ears. Our spiritual ears are heard by what most people call a gut feeling, so we usually hear and see spiritually in our guts. Some people call it "women's intuition" or "conscience." My friendly term or slang term for it is "knower."

**Introduction**

1. barna.org/teens-next-gen-articles/528-six-reasons-young-christians-leave-church

2. Genesis 32:22-32. This concept of wrestling in prayer comes from the story of Jacob wrestling with the Angel of the Lord. Jacob would not let go until the Lord blessed him.

**Part 1**

1. My definition of "knower": I use the term "knower" to describe a "knowing feeling" I have in my gut that this is communicating to me. It is the Holy Spirit speaking to me. Let me explain: We hear with our natural ears, and we hear with our spiritual ears. Our spiritual ears are heard in what most people call a gut feeling, so we usually hear and see spiritually in our guts. Some people call it "women's intuition" or "conscience." My friendly term or slang term for it is "knower."

2. The term "corporate prayer" refers to people getting together to pray, usually at a set time and place. I am clarifying this because someone not familiar with the term thought it meant having prayer at a place of business. Corporate prayer is a familiar term used among intercessors.

3. Now called Moms in Prayer. Go to momsinprayer.org to find a group near you, or call 855-769-7729 or 858-486-7729.

4. The phrase "under the blood of Jesus" is a term meaning the sinner has identified the sin and has prayed to Jesus, asking for forgiveness. Once forgiven, our Savior, Jesus, forgets the transgression, and therefore the sinner needs to forget and move on as well. Some additional verses for understanding this are 1 John 1:9 and Psalm 103:12.

5. *Wiersbe's Expository Outlines on the New Testament* by Warren W. Wiersbe (Victor Books, 1992, 109)

6. Image credit:

bing.com/images/search?q=Girl+Lion+Roaring+at+Male+Lion&view=detailv2&&id=EC2FF

6E8690B19D8E3895D2CC06689CEC51EAA05&selectedIndex=1&ccid=fJS1cPPN&simid=608021018776767347&thid=JN.X%2f7RmXxVSkFLBNQN4%2b5fUQ&ajaxhist=0

## Part 2
1. Adapted from *Gideon* by Priscilla Shirer (Lifeway Press, 2013, 34)

2. Image credit:

telegraph.co.uk/news/graphics/2004/07/18/wmid118.jpg

3. *Hearing God's Voice* by Becky Fischer (Kids in Ministry International, Inc., 2013, 18)

kidsinministry.org/childrens-ministry-curriculum/more-stuff/hearing-gods-voice/ (Get a 10 percent discount by using code KIMITN13.)

4. *Our Amazing God* by Becky Fischer (Kids in Ministry International, Inc., 2002, 176-77)

kidsinministry.org/childrens-ministry-curriculum/more-stuff/1-our-amazing-god/ (Get a 10 percent discount by using code KIMITN13.)

5. religionfacts.com/judaism/practices.htm

6. Lesson on Object Lessons (The Practical, Course #3): sscmkimi.org/welcome-to-sscm/titles/ (Get a 10 percent discount by using code KIMITN13.)

7. Image credit: chicagocarless.com/wp-content/uploads/Tefillin-diagrams.jpg

8. kidsinministry.org/childrens-ministry-curriculum/more-stuff/3-the-blood-of-jesus/ (Get a 10 percent discount by using code KIMITN13.)

9. *You and Your Child* by Charles R. Swindoll (Thomas Nelson Publishers, 1977, 18)

10. *Research in Principles of Life, Advanced Seminar Textbook* (Institute of Basic Youth Conflicts 1989, 5th printing, 80, 82)

11. Image credit: media.photobucket.com/user/SimViper66/media/funny-cat-picture-cute-kitty picki.jpg.html?filters[term]=cat%20sees%20a%20lion%20in%20mirror&filters[primary]=images&filters[secondary]=videos&sort=1&o=1

12. *You and Your Child* by Charles R. Swindoll (Thomas Nelson Publishers, 1977, 80)

**Part 3**

1. kidsinministry.org/resources/more-stuff/understanding-children-and-worship-sscm-36/ (Get a 10 percent discount by using code KIMITN13.)

2. *Breaking Free* by Beth Moore (LifeWay Press, 1999, 76)

3. kidsinministry.org/childrens-ministry-curriculum/more-stuff/hearing-gods-voice/
(Get a 10 percent discount by using code KIMITN13.)

4. kidsinministry.org/childrens-ministry-curriculum/more-stuff/adventures-ivy-god/
(Get a 10 percent discount by using code KIMITN13.)

5. For more information or clarity about the difference between facts and truth, this website has a good article on the subject: bibletruthsonline.org/#!truth-vs-fact/c1ud.

6. *Buried Treasure: Secrets for Living from the Lord's Language* by Rabbi Daniel Lapin and Susan Lapin (Lifecodes Publishing, LLC, 2012, 43)

7. *Buried Treasure: Hidden Wisdom from the Hebrew Language* by Rabbi Daniel Lapin (Multnomah, 2001, 46)

8. "Five Types of Fools" by Bill Gothard, iblp.org/questions/what-are-five-types-fools

9. Image credit: guidedbiblestudies.com/topics/priest7.jpg

**Recommended Books**

**General**

*You and Your Child* by Charles R. Swindoll

*Have a New Kid by Friday* by Dr. Kevin Leman

*Shepherding a Child's Heart* by Tedd Tripp

*Redefining Children's Ministry in the 21$^{st}$ Century* by Becky Fischer

kidsinministry.org/childrens-ministry-curriculum/more-stuff/redefining-childrens-ministry/

(Get a 10 percent discount by using code KIMITN13.)

**Worship**

*Worship the King* by Malene Anderson (This is a *Kids in Ministry* curriculum. It can be used as a devotional for family use. Use "KIMITENN13" at checkout for a 10 percent discount. Go to kidsinministry.org/childrens-ministry-curriculum/more-stuff/worship-the-king/.)

*Presence – Driven Family Worship* by Alicia White, Ohio Director for Kids in Ministry

### Warfare and Breaking Curses

*Monsters in My Closet* by Becky Fischer (This is a book for children, teaching them the authority they have over "monsters." Order it at kidsinministry.org/childrens-ministry-curriculum/more-stuff/monsters-in-my-closet/#reviews. Use the code:

"KIMITENN13" at checkout for a 10 percent discount.)

*Breaking Generational Curses* by Marilyn Hickey

*Breaking Free* by Beth Moore

*Spiritual Warfare for Women: Winning the Battle for Your Home, Family and Friends* by Leighann McCoy

*Spiritual Warfare for Your Family: What You Need to Know to Protect Your Children* by Leighann McCoy

*Spiritual Housecleaning: Protect Your Home and Family from Spiritual Pollution* by Eddie and Alice Smith

### Hearing God's Voice

*Hearing God's Voice* by Becky Fischer (This is a Kids in Ministry curriculum but can be broken down to smaller segments and used as a family devotional. Go to kidsinministry.org/childrens-ministry-curriculum/more-stuff/hearing-gods-voice/. Use the code "KIMITENN13" at checkout for a 10 percent discount.)

*Seven Keys to Hearing God's Voice* by Craig Von Buseck

*The Adventures of Ivy and God* by Becky Fischer (A children's book. Use the code "KIMITENN13" at checkout for a 10 percent discount.)

*A Woman's Guide to Hearing God's Voice* by Leighann McCoy

### Power of Words

*The Power of Your Words* by Don Gossett and E.W. Kenyon

*God's Creative Power* by Charles Capps

### Purity

*Passport2Purity* by Dennis and Barbara Rainey

*Passion and Purity: Learning to Bring Your Love Life Under Christ's Control* by Elisabeth Elliot

*Preparing for Adolescence: How to Survive the Coming Years of Change* by Dr. James Dobson

### Traditions or Festivities

*Let's Make a Memory* by Gloria Gaither and Shirley Dobson

*Creating Family Traditions: Making Memories in Festive Seasons* by Gloria Gaither and Shirley Dobson

*Sanity in the Summertime* by Linda Dillow and Claudia Arp

*A Christian Seder Meal for Kids and Their Families* by Becky Fischer (Available at kidsinministry.org/childrens-ministry-curriculum/more-stuff/christian-seder-meal-for-kids-family/. Use the code "KIMITN13" for a 10 percent discount.)

As a young mother, Lori Hensley observed that many young adults who were raised in God-fearing homes were choosing a different standard of living, leaving the church and embracing worldly lifestyles. As she meditated on the word "train" from Proverbs 22:6, she realized that as a culture we were missing what it really meant. This began a lifelong journey of understanding and implementing godly training with her own kids, other parents, children's church, and missions.

Today, Lori continues to pour into children's lives as the Tennessee Kids in Ministry director. She conducts *Schools of Supernatural Children's Ministry Training* and *Power Club* training events. She is available to speak in churches as a *Kids in Ministry* representative and is also available for parenting classes. You can email Lori at: kimilori@yahoo.com   http://kimitenn.org

*"I have no greater joy than to hear that my children walk in truth"* (3 John 4).

www.ingramcontent.com/pod-product-compliance
Lightning Source LLC
Chambersburg PA
CBHW071855290426

44110CB00013B/1160